RHETORICAL THEORY AND PRAXIS IN THE BUSINESS COMMUNICATION CLASSROOM

Rhetorical Theory and Praxis in the Business Communication Classroom responds to a significant need in the emerging field of business communication as the first collection of its type to establish a connection between rhetorical theory and practice in the business communication classroom. The volume includes topics such as rhetorical grammar, genre awareness in business communication theory, the role of Big Data in message strategy, social media and memory, and the connection between rhetorical theory and entrepreneurship. These essays provide the business communication scholar, practitioner, and program administrator insight into the rhetorical considerations of the business communication landscape.

Dr. Kristen M. Getchell is director of rhetoric and a visiting associate professor of Rhetoric at Babson College in Wellesley, MA. She has developed and taught undergraduate first-year writing and business communication courses as well as MBA professional writing courses. Her work has appeared in scholarly publications such as *Business and Professional Communication Quarterly*, *Journal of Writing Assessment*, *Teaching in the Two-Year College*, *Crosspol*, and *E-Source for College Transitions*.

Dr. Paula J. Lentz is associate professor and academic program director for the Department of Business Communication at the University of Wisconsin-Eau Claire. She has developed and taught undergraduate and MBA business communication courses. She is co-author of *Lesikar's Business Communication: Connecting in a Digital World* (2013), *M: Business Communication* (2014), and *Business Communication: A Problem-Solving Approach* (2017). Her research has appeared in *Business and Professional Communication Quarterly*, *Qualitative Research in Organizations and Management*, and the *Journal of Health Education*.

RHETORICAL THEORY AND PRAXIS IN THE BUSINESS COMMUNICATION CLASSROOM

Edited by Kristen M. Getchell and Paula J. Lentz

Routledge
Taylor & Francis Group

NEW YORK AND LONDON

First published 2019
by Routledge
711 Third Avenue, New York, NY 10017

and by Routledge
2 Park Square, Milton Park, Abingdon, Oxon, OX14 4RN

Routledge is an imprint of the Taylor & Francis Group, an informa business

Library of Congress Cataloging-in-Publication Data
Names: Getchell, Kristen M., editor. | Lentz, Paula, editor.
Title: Rhetorical theory and praxis in the business communication
    classroom / [edited by] Kristen M. Getchell and Paula Lentz.
Description: New York, NY : Routledge, 2019.
Identifiers: LCCN 2018019314 | ISBN 9780815354413 (hardback) |
    ISBN 9780815354420 (pbk.) | ISBN 9781351132879 (ebk.)
Subjects: LCSH: Business communication—Study and teaching. |
    Rhetoric—Study and teaching.
Classification: LCC HF5718 .R52 2019 | DDC 658.4/5071—dc23
LC record available at https://lccn.loc.gov/2018019314

ISBN: 978-0-8153-5441-3 (hbk)
ISBN: 978-0-8153-5442-0 (pbk)
ISBN: 978-1-351-13287-9 (ebk)

Typeset in Bembo
by Apex CoVantage, LLC

CONTENTS

FOREWORD

The essays in this volume offer valuable perspectives on the critical, fundamental roles that rhetoric plays in shaping both the discipline of business communication and the pedagogy of business communication instructors. While rhetoric's influences have been examined and explained over the years, no one volume has attempted to collect them. Therefore, this collection serves much like a DNA test, demonstrating that what some scholars have seen as a tangential relationship between business communication and rhetoric (or have ignored altogether) is actually a familial one. After reading these essays, I expect many scholars and teachers will want to begin deeper genealogical investigations.

The breadth of the scholarship here is noteworthy, beginning with a historical framework and ending with articles that offer "an invaluable opportunity for growth and development" for both instructors and the discipline as a whole (Intro, p. 8). The essays offer strong evidence in support of the editors' definitions of (1) business communication as "respond[ing] to the rhetorical exigence of workplace communication" and (2) business communicators as those who "use" "communication to solve business problems or achieve business goals" (Intro, p. 2). This connection to the workplace is essential, providing a link to foundational work by our discipline's scholars and leaders such as Kitty Locker (1998), who explained, quite simply and forcefully, "our [Business Communication's] object is communication in the workplace" (p. 15).

To place the value of this collection in context, I will share stories from my and our discipline's histories. I hope to demonstrate that the central premises of this collection are not radical departures or on the fringe. Rather, the essays here can be seen as living in history and being in line with it. Even more important, the pedagogical strategies, not to mention the pedagogical foundation outlined in these essays, can be read as an informed response to business communication scholars who have attempted, in the last 30 years, to imagine our future. In so doing, I hope to demonstrate not only the value offered here but also to offer some additional directions for further and needed research.

My History: Teacher, Writing Program Administrator, and Disciplinary Servant-Leader

As the editors have done, I begin with a story. Story is gaining traction as both "a lifelong and life-sustaining habit of mind, as well as an organizational inheritance, [and] a management tool that helps businesses develop and even thrive" (Forman, 2013, p. 1). In my story, which establishes what my colleague Bruce Pencek would call my "bona fides," I use my initial connection to the discipline as a teacher and writing program administrator to lay the foundation for my current perspective as someone who has served the discipline as an elected and appointed member of the Association for Business Communication (ABC), its professional organization, for over a decade. In these roles, which involve tactical and strategic perspectives, I have had to grapple with many of the questions the authors in this volume seek to address, particularly those addressing our discipline's academic identity.

In 1998, I was hired in a tenure-track position in an English department at a research-focused university. Beyond my research requirements, my mission was two-fold: (1) to build a program in professional writing for English majors and (2) to "fix" (the exact word the dean used in my welcome interview) the two service courses in business and technical writing to make them more responsive to the needs of students across the university.

At the time, our department was a traditional English department focusing on the periods of literature. One reason I was hired had to do with my "pedigree." I began my PhD in a program in rhetoric and composition, but I ended with a degree in rhetoric and professional communication after working with two other students to create a devised field in that area and then spending the last two of our four years as teaching assistants working in the Farmer School of Business.

In addition, I had spent 15 years on active duty in the US Army, and I was still in the US Army Reserves. In the US Army (I served one tour of duty at the US Military Academy in its Department of English) and during my PhD years, I had taught literature, composition, technical writing, and military writing courses. I, therefore, was not a traditional hire for a department such as mine (in fact, at the time, there were only a few tenure-track faculty whose primary focus was not literature: the director of first-year composition, a linguist, and several creative writers). However, my diverse background made it possible for me to work inter-disciplinarily and provided common ground that enabled me to build bridges and make connections with my colleagues. Still, I had what my great-uncle, a farmer all his life, always called a "tough row to hoe." The field was virtually fallow, and the climate was not entirely conducive to new plantings.

In 1998, my department was offering just two sections of business writing a semester; two years earlier, the College of Business had dropped the requirement altogether. The problem was not quite as dire from the College of Engineering's perspective, but the curriculum committees of both colleges, when surveyed, believed some improvement was essential to prepare their students for the workplace and to help them meet the more formal accreditation requirements. Thus, before I could begin course design/re-design, I had to more fully understand what those students needed and what differences existed between the courses as taught and the courses that were to be reimagined.

In addition, I had a challenge with the primary task of creating a professional writing program. When I arrived, while earning their degree in English, students could add a professional writing "cluster" by taking Business Writing (BW), Technical Writing (TW), and Advanced Composition. I was asked to frame a curriculum in professional writing (PW) that did not rely on these courses at all. So, I had to more fully understand and articulate skills and strategies English majors might need that students taking the two service courses did not. Thus, from the very beginning of my academic career, I was placed in a position that required me to examine questions that underpin this volume concerning the relationships among three fields: composition, technical communication, and business communication.

Early in my tenure, I, too, sought to understand those relationships and articulate definitional differences. I studied what scholars in these fields had written. I learned that business communication scholars had a long, distinguished history of examining this question (e.g., Du-Babcock, 2006; Reinsch, 1996; Forman, 1993; Locker, 1993; Shaw, 1993; Campbell, 1991; Hagge, 1989; Hildebrandt, 1988; Douglas & Hildebrandt, 1985; Weeks, 1985; Yates, 1982; Smith, 1969; Menning, 1951).

Another method I used was to pose this question of identity/definition to the Association of Teachers of Technical Writing (ATTW) listserv. That question, posed on 24 February 1999, brought in 12 distinct responses, which in turn generated additional replies and clarifications. I offer three responses that captured the diverse responses:

> [Our business writing course] focuses on business correspondence, case studies, and common types of business reports that involve both clear and persuasive writing done in organizations. [She went on to say that] business writing [is] relevant to everyone who writes/works, but . . . the scope of "technical writing" is broader—going beyond what is "routine" and what is mostly produced within organizational boundaries.
>
> *(Rachel Spilka, University of Wisconsin-Milwaukee,*
> *personal communication, 24 February 1999)*

> The differences . . . aren't so much in the professional discourse surrounding the two [courses], but in the types of students that are required to take each course—for the most part, management, and supervision students in business writing, and technical and engineering students in technical writing.

> Although there are certainly topics and processes that are more traditionally in one camp or another—computer documentation . . ., the areas overlap so much that we think students are better prepared if they understand workplace communication in broadly rhetorical terms, and then apply their skills to particular situations.
>
> *(Johndan Johnson-Eilola, Clarkson University, personal communication, 24 February 1999)*

> The line between business and technical writing is somewhat artificially drawn by educational institutions for pedagogical purposes and that line is far more blurred in the workplace.
>
> *(Roxanne Kent-Drury, University of Northern Kentucky, personal communication, 24 February 1999)*

In many cases, the preferred term that described connections between the two courses was "workplace writing," and, much like the editors of this volume, the programs' administrators argued that rhetoric should serve as a foundation, and the pedagogy of each course should be both transactional and situational.

In the end, after surveying the faculty members on the curriculum committees of both the College of Business and the College of Engineering, reading what others had learned by conducting similar surveys (e.g., Campbell, 1991; Rivers, 1985; Storms, 1983; Rader & Wunsch, 1980), and examining best practices at a wide range of peer institutions, the team of instructors who were interested in this subject and I moved forward with a curriculum that established commonalities and defined distinctions. I have written about that process and the curriculum we designed (Dubinsky, 2010), but in that piece, while my focus on rhetoric and its centrality is clear, I did not fully address these critical questions of identity and definition.

While we were not fully satisfied with the distinctions we drew, based on what we had learned about the needs of the students once they graduated, we re-designed the "service" courses in business and technical writing on a rhetorical foundation and, relying on the emphases of "particular situations" and "organizational boundaries" outlined by Johnson-Eilola and Spilka, we delineated distinctions in our application of rhetorical principles. In essence, we did our best to understand the workplaces students would find themselves in upon graduation and used that knowledge to choose appropriate genres and exercises to emphasize when creating assignments to prepare them for those workplaces. We also relied heavily on experiential or service-learning (Dubinsky, 2004).

In this way, my colleagues and I heeded the advice of members of the business communication community such as Janis Forman (1993), who advocated that business communication scholars and teachers should draw on "a shared affiliation with rhetoric" (p. 334), and Robert Gieselman (1989), who believed in "writing processes and products in specific organizational and cultural contexts" (p. 24).

That initial challenge as a teacher and program designer and administrator led me to see, even if I couldn't quite articulate it fully then, that the current editors' definition of the "key characteristics of business communication" as "transactional," "problem-solving," and "work-related," which they've drawn from other scholars (Bell & Muir, 2014; Rentz & Lentz, 2014), as well as their conviction that business communication has a distinct rhetorical exigence (Intro, p. 2), are absolutely and fundamentally in line with a critical line of thought that can be traced back decades to some of our discipline's finest and scholars and leaders.

Business Communication's Disciplinary History and Rhetorical/Pedagogical Roots

Much of the scholarship about our disciplinary identity has framed it in terms of questions about its "hybrid nature" (Shaw, 1993) or legitimacy (Krappels & Arnold, 1996). Shaw, Krappels, and Arnold, and other scholars, particularly those who have served as a past president or executive director of ABC (Locker, 1998; Gieselman, 1989), have documented a long history of introspection without resolution. This lack of resolution also surfaced over and over again in the interviews, focus groups, and surveys of ABC's members that resulted in our current strategic plan.

Thus, I applaud the contributors of this volume for their work to resolve these "blurred lines" (Drury-Kent, 1999). They make a case for more research into our disciplinary roots and for linking those roots to both rhetoric and pedagogy. In the opening chapter, Orwig makes a strong case for the importance of "understanding how our field has developed . . . as the field moves forward" (p. 23). Orwig's chapter, which also provides some intriguing data about the history and importance of genre, segues nicely with the editors' larger call for business communication to move away from what they describe as "friendly subversion," which involves "adapt[ing] and adjust[ing] to existing pedagogical maps of other disciplines" (Intro, p. 3), and instead create its "own pedagogical map" (Intro, p. 3). Our editors believe we can and should clear those blurred lines and refocus on the essential nature of our work.

In the earlier section, I explained how, as a teacher, scholar, and program administrator, I relied heavily upon business communication's disciplinary history, and I've indicated that it has played a critical role in the creation of the 2008 strategic plan, which was revised in 2014. That work on strategic plans led me to share my initial thoughts about the value of ABC's disciplinary history (Dubinsky, 2015). I relied upon the work of scholars who were also leaders in ABC, such as Fran Weeks (1985), Herb Hildebrandt (1988), Robert Gieselman (1985, 1989), and, of course, Kitty Locker (1998, 2003). Weeks and Gieselman, both of whom served as executive directors for ABC, published articles on the critical connection of pedagogy with disciplinary identity. Gieselman, in particular, stated, "the teaching of writing is our profession's principal strength" (1996, p. 28). Such an argument is clearly furthered here by offering a wide range of pedagogical perspectives on key topics such as the use of Big Data, the importance of visual rhetoric, the advantages of civic engagement, and the critical importance of teaching students the value of understanding rhetorical concepts and strategies linked to *ethos* and *kairos*.

These current articles are in line with earlier attempts at mapping the connections to rhetoric (e.g., Du-Babcock, 2006; Gieselman, 1989; Reinsch, 1996). As this volume's contributors have done, these scholars were explicit about the connections between our discipline and rhetoric. Gieselman (1989) stated, "business writing and technical writing historically are related . . . with similar rhetorical roots" (p. 24). Reinsch (1996) explained,

> a contemporary business communication course draws on the rhetorical tradition, modern scientific findings, and contemporary practice to produce a course tailored to improve the writing skills of undergraduate business students and builds on rather than duplicates a course in English composition.
>
> *(p. 40)*

Reinsch's definition is linked to the historical frame of commerce: "scholarly study of the use, adaptation, and creation of languages, symbols, and signs to conduct activities that satisfy human needs and wants by providing goods and services for private profit" (qtd. on p. 28). His focus on the historical connections to commerce aligned with the research Weeks (1985) had done previously. When looking to the future, Reinsch argues for connecting business communication "to larger issues (the life of the community) and . . . adapting to the increasingly international character of business activity" (p. 41). In this regard, he focuses on "multiple spoken and written English*es*," "adapting persuasion theory to business communication," and focusing on "communication genres" (p. 43).

Reinsch was prescient. In 2006, Du-Babcock contributed a piece to *The Journal of Business Communication* that also looked at the "past, present, and future." She, too, initially focused on how "in the early years" the focus was "to teach American students how to communicate effectively and efficiently in American business and commercial environments" (p. 254). That emphasis echoed Weeks's and Reinsch's focus on commerce (the workplace) and might be useful as we seek to draw a clear(er) line between technical and business communication on our pedagogical map.

Du-Babcock also acknowledged the field "was rooted in the study of rhetoric" with "an emphasis on proper forms and correct use of English" (p. 254). She indicated that the emphasis on "communication genres" that Reinsch predicted would gain in importance, indeed had done so. In her estimation, the discipline had expanded to address "communication barriers [that] are created as . . . professionals interact with professionals from other disciplines and with nonspecialists" (p. 255). She also highlighted the significance of communication technologies, particularly in the role of "global competitive pressure" (p. 256).

Du-Babcock outlines three foci for the future: language, culture, and context (p. 257). As I examine her foci and compare it with the chapters in this volume,

I see deep connections to language and context. However, I still see quite a bit of work for future volumes, particularly in the area of culture.

Du-Babcock's article was one of many attempts to reflect on the future. In 2006, the year her article was published, the ABC board of directors began a discussion on the future of ABC. That 20-minute agenda item at the annual meeting led to a three-hour brainstorming session that resulted, ultimately, in my being tasked to lead a task force designed to create a strategic plan. After 18 months of work and over 400 members having the opportunity to provide their ideas/input, ABC's board of directors approved its strategic plan in 2008, its first in nearly 20 years. That plan outlined four major goals. Two of those had to do specifically with the association as a vehicle for providing needed support to members of the discipline, but two were and remain relevant to the issues that frame the need for this volume:

1. Strengthen the discipline of business communication.
2. Ensure a deep level of internationalization throughout the organization.

These two goals were again emphasized in the revision of the strategic plan that was approved in February 2015, but the focus on internationalization was integrated into the three primary goals, the first of which, again, was strengthening the discipline.

The primary emphasis on strengthening the discipline is complex, but at its core lie concerns about identity, many of which are rooted in disciplinarity—who teaches our courses and where they find themselves located in the academic and business worlds.

Du-Babcock, in 2006, and the leaders of ABC, in 2008 and then again in 2015, recognized the growing importance of connecting the organization to the workplace and of linking the organization to the membership, which by 2008 was truly international: nearly 24% of ABC's members work and reside outside of the United States. To strengthen our discipline, we need to understand who we are, what we do, and the kinds of research that are relevant to the many workplaces in which our students find themselves upon graduation and the many English*es our students use*. We need to research how language works in a range of workplaces, which means adopting a socio-cognitive perspective on discourse along with rhetorical methods to understand the processes of organizational change.

Thus, we need to do more research and surveys that address the culture(s) and workplaces associated with our international members. Sharp and Brumberger's (2013) survey provides an updated window as to where programs lie in US colleges and universities. Their data demonstrate that, despite any theorizing to the contrary, we remain a hybrid discipline in terms of what and where we teach. Their responses from 50 programs placed the majority of business communication faculty in schools or colleges of business, but the other homes included departments of rhetoric/writing, communication, media studies, and English.

Within business schools, the homes included departments of economics, marketing, management, accounting, and business communication.

Having such a range of home departments creates problems, particularly regarding the central focus of the courses and the types of outcomes sought. Russ (2009) and then Laster and Russ (2010) discuss these issues associated with the breadth of disciplines that our teachers call "home." These two articles highlight issues associated with the editors' goal of mapping that still need to be addressed. In short, business communication courses, even within schools of business, are not necessarily equivalent; the disciplinary "sponsor of the introductory course greatly influences the type of topics taught and the levels of coverage afforded to those topics" (Laster & Russ, 2010, p. 257). This finding makes sense: faculty come from a range of disciplinary backgrounds, and their courses would naturally take into account the contexts in which they are taught.

These problems are further complicated because no one has yet surveyed the programs that house individuals teaching business communication in Europe or Asia, let alone South America or Africa. Until we have a more complete picture of the disciplinary homes for those who teach business communication and the impact of the disciplinary environments on how those courses are taught, we will not be able to fully or accurately map our discipline.

This fact is all the more evident when we consider that one of ABC's partner organizations, the Korean Association for Business Communication (KABC), has just published its first journal: *BCRP: Business Communication Research and Practice*. Du-Babcock (2018), one of ABC's past presidents, published the lead article, which again is a review of the work on business communication in Asia, past, present, and to come. In it, she modifies her projection from the 2006 article by adding "international business" (p. 5) as the third key area of interest. The wonderful point about this addition is its direct focus on the "transactional" nature of our work. The challenge is that it adds a modifier "international" that is all but left out of much of our theory. Despite the fact that ABC removed the modifier "American" from its name in 1985 (before that it was the American Business Communication Association or ABCA), and despite the fact that we now hold conferences across the globe yearly and have regional vice presidents representing all continents but the Antarctic, we still tend to be primary US-centric when we seek to understand our discipline and its needs.

As Kitty Locker (1998) said, "The skills we teach are informed by theory and cognitive material" (p. 39). These skills are further informed by the work in this volume, with its linkages to our rhetorical foundation and its view to the future by considering the importance of topics such as Big Data and visual rhetoric. Still, while we have looked into the future and addressed many of the concerns outlined by scholars such as Reinsch and Du-Babcock, we still have plenty of work that needs to be done.

James M. Dubinsky, Virginia Tech

Executive Director, Association for Business Communication

References

Bell, R. L., & Muir, C. (2014). A review of business communication under the leading function. In *6th annual general business conference proceedings* (pp. 80–105). Huntsville, TX: Sam Houston State University.

Campbell, P. G. (1991, June). Business communication or technical writing? *The ABWA Bulletin*, pp. 6–10.

Douglas, G. H., & Hildebrandt, H. W. (Eds.). (1985). *Studies in the history of business writing*. Urbana, IL: Association for Business Communication.

Drury-Kent, R. (1999, February 24). Email to attw-l@ttacs6.ttu.edu. Retrieved from http://s50.n238.n6.n64.static.myhostcenter.com/communities/listserv.

Du-Babcock, B. (2006). Teaching business communication: Past, present, and future. *The Journal of Business Communication, 43*(3), 253–264.

Du-Babcock, B. (2018). Business communication research and theory development in Asia: Past, present, and future prospects. *Business Communication Research and Practice, 1*(1), 4–17.

Dubinsky, J. (2004). The status of service in learning. In T. Bridgeford, K. Kitalong, & D. Selfe (Eds.), *Innovative approaches to the teaching of technical communication* (pp. 15–30). Logan, UT: Utah State University Press.

Dubinsky, J. (2008). *The future of ABC: A strategic proposal*. Retrieved March 10, 2018 from www.businesscommunication.org/page/strategic-plan

Dubinsky, J. 2010). A techne for citizens. In D. Franke, A. Reid, & A. Di Renzo (Eds.), *Design discourse: Composing and revising programs in professional and technical writing* (pp. 277–296). West Lafayette, IN: Parlor Press.

Dubinsky, J. (2015). Musing on historical scholarship: Can it light our field? Association for business communication's 79th west region convention, association for business communication, Los Angeles, CA.

Forman, J. (1993). Business communication and composition: The writing connection and beyond. *The Journal of Business Communication, 30*(3), 333–353.

Forman, J. (2013). *Storytelling in business*. Stanford, CA: Stanford Business Press.

Gielselman, R. (1985). Megatrends: The future of business writing, technical writing, and composition. *ABCA Bulletin, 48*(4), 2–6.

Gieselman, R. (1989). Business communication as an academic discipline. *Issues in Writing, 2*(1), 20–35.

Hagge, J. (1989). The spurious paternity of business communication principles. *The Journal of Business Communication, 26*(1), 33–55.

Hildebrandt, H. W. (1988). Some influences of Greek and Roman rhetoric on early letter writing. *The Journal of Business Communication, 25*(3), 7–27.

Johnson-Eilola, J. (1999, February 24). Email to attw-l@ttacs6.ttu.edu. http://s50.n238.n6.n64.static.myhostcenter.com/communities/listserv.

Krappels, R., & Arnold, V. D. (1996). The legitimacy of business communication. *The Journal of Business Communication, 33*(3), 331–352.

Laster, N., & Russ, T. (2010). Looking across the divide: Analyzing cross-disciplinary approaches for teaching business communication. *Business Communication Quarterly, 73*(3), 248–264.

Locker, K. (1993). The challenge of interdisciplinary research. *The Journal of Business Communication, 31*(2), 137–159.

Locker, K. (1998). The role of the association for business communication in shaping business communication as an academic discipline. *The Journal of Business Communication, 35*(1), 14–49.

Locker, K. (2003). Will professional communication be the death of business communication? *Business Communication Quarterly*, *66*(3), 118–132.

Menning, J. H. (1951, January). A half-century of progress in business writing. *The ABWA Bulletin*, *15*(4), 4–11.

Rader, M. H., & Wunsch, A. P. (1980). A survey of communication practices of business school graduates by job category and undergraduate major. *The Journal of Business Communication*, *17*(4), 33–41.

Reinsch, Jr., N. L. (1996). Business communication: Present, past, and future. *Management Communication Quarterly*, *10*(1), 27–49.

Rentz, K., & Lentz, P. J. (2014). *M: Business communication* (3rd ed.). New York: McGraw-Hill Irwin.

Rivers, W. E. (1985). The current status of business and technical writing courses in English departments. *ADE Bulletin*, *82*, 50–54.

Russ, T. L. (2009). The status of the business communication course at U.S. colleges and universities. *Business Communication Quarterly*, *72*, 395–413.

Sharp, M., & Brumberger, E. (2013). Business communication curricula today: Revisiting the top 50 undergraduate business schools. *Business Communication Quarterly*, *76*(1), 5–27.

Shaw, G. (1993). The shape of our field: Business communication as a hybrid discipline. *The Journal of Business Communication*, *30*(3), 297–313.

Smith, A. B. (1969). Historical development of concern for business English instruction. *The Journal of Business Communication*, *6*(3), 33–44.

Spilka, R. (1999, February 24). Email to attw-l@ttacs6.ttu.edu. Retrieved from http://s50.n238.n6.n64.static.myhostcenter.com/communities/listserv.

Storms, G. (1983, December). What business school graduates say about the writing they do at work: Implications for the business communication course. *The ABCA Bulletin*, pp. 13–18.

Weeks, F. W. (1985). The teaching of business writing at the collegiate level, 1900–1920. In G. H. Douglas & H. W. Hildebrandt (Eds.), *Studies in the history of business writing* (pp. 201–215). Urbana, IL: Association for Business Communication.

Yates, J. (1982). From press book and pigeonhole to vertical filing: Revolution in storage and access systems for correspondence. *The Journal of Business Communication*, *19*(3), 5–26.

CONTRIBUTORS

Valerie Creelman is an associate professor at the Sobey School of Business's Department of Marketing and Business Communication at Saint Mary's University in Halifax, Nova Scotia. Her research appears in such publications as *Business and Professional Communication Quarterly*, *Digital Business Discourse* (Palgrave-Macmillan, 2015), and *Advertising, Consumer Culture, and Canadian Society* (Oxford University Press, 2018). Her research interests include digital business discourse, language use in online customer care, crisis communication, and impression management.

Dale Cyphert, Ph.D., is an associate professor in business communication and director of the MBA program at the University of Northern Iowa. With a practitioner background in public relations, human resources, and operations management, Cyphert's research involves skill development as well as theoretical work in contrasting and evolving rhetorical norms. She has published her work in *Corporate Reputation Review*, *The Quarterly Journal of Speech*, *Business Communication Quarterly*, *The Western Journal of Communication*, *The American Communication Journal*, *Text and Performance Quarterly*, and *Exploration in Media Ecology*.

James M. Dubinsky is associate professor of rhetoric and writing in the Department of English at Virginia Tech (VT). From 1998 until 2007, Jim was the founding director of the department's professional writing program. He served the Association for Business Communication (ABC) as an elected officer (2006–2010), and since 2011 Jim has been serving as ABC's executive director. He has published a range of articles, book chapters, and a book on the teaching of writing.

Kristen M. Getchell is a visiting associate professor of rhetoric and director of rhetoric in the Arts and Humanities division at Babson College, in Wellesley, Massachusetts. In addition to teaching first-year writing, she has developed and taught undergraduate and graduate courses in business writing. Her current interests include business writing pedagogy, student feedback, and student engagement in face-to-face and computer-mediated peer review.

Holly Lawrence holds a Ph.D. in composition and rhetoric and is director of the business communication program in the University of Massachusetts Isenberg School of Management. She has taught business communication to undergraduate and graduate students for years. Her scholarly interests lie in career and professional development skills and communications.

Paula J. Lentz is an associate professor and academic program director for the Department of Business Communication in the College of Business at the University of Wisconsin-Eau Claire. She is also the director of the college's Business Writing and Presentations Studio. She has developed and taught undergraduate and MBA business communication courses. Along with Kathryn Rentz, she is co-author of *Business Communication: A Problem-Solving Approach*, *M: Business Communication*, and *Lesikar's Business Communication: Connecting in a Digital World*. Her research has appeared in *Business and Professional Communication Quarterly*, *Qualitative Research in Organizations and Management*, and the *Journal of Health Education*.

Marcy Leasum Orwig, Ph.D., is an assistant professor of business communication in the College of Business at the University of Wisconsin-Eau Claire. Her research interests include archival methodology, genre studies, and writing pedagogy. She has published on topics ranging from historical army report writing to hospital volunteer communication.

Ashley Patriarca is an assistant professor of English at West Chester University of Pennsylvania, where she serves as coordinator for the business and technical writing minor. Her previous work has appeared in *Connections*, *Journal of Business and Technical Communication*, and *College Composition and Communication*.

Jacob D. Rawlins is an assistant professor in the Linguistics Department at Brigham Young University, Provo, UT, where he teaches courses in editing, publishing, and grammar. He earned his Ph.D. in rhetoric and professional communication from Iowa State University. His research interests include professional communication pedagogy, workplace mythbuilding, and interactive data visualizations.

Danica L. Schieber is an assistant professor of business communication at Sam Houston State University, in Huntsville, TX. Her research interests include business communication pedagogy, transfer theory, the rhetoric of CEOs in financial documents, and visual rhetoric. She also serves as the ACE (Academic and Community Engagement) coordinator for the College of Business Administration at SHSU.

Matthew R. Sharp is an assistant professor of communication in the Humanities and Communication Department at Embry-Riddle Aeronautical University, Daytona Beach, FL, USA. With a background in professional writing, web development, fundraising, and enrollment management, his research analyzes organizational activity systems and their mediating genres from both cultural and rhetorical studies perspectives.

ACKNOWLEDGMENTS

The editors thank all the authors in this collection with a special thanks to James M. Dubinsky for his Foreword. The editors appreciate the work of Kristina Ryan, Felisa Salvano-Keyes, Nicole Solano, and the teams at Routledge and Apex, as well as the anonymous reviewers of this work for their valuable feedback. They also thank the Association for Business Communication's Rhetoric Special Interest Group members for the inspiration for this collection. Kristen acknowledges Keith Rollag, Julie Levinson, Nan Langowitz, Sharon Sinnott, and Bala Iyer for their support and her business writing students at Babson College for their continuous inspiration. She also extends thanks to Jacob Backon and her family. Paula extends a very special thank you to her family, friends, and colleagues who continually support her work.

INTRODUCTION

Business Communication at the Intersection of Rhetoric and Pedagogy

Paula J. Lentz and Kristen M. Getchell

At the 2016 Association of Business Communication Conference in Albuquerque, New Mexico, we, in conversation with others in the Rhetoric Special Interest Group (SIG), began to consider and explore the identity of the field of business communication and, by extension, the role of instructors in the business communication classroom with a specialty in rhetoric. SIG members agreed that audience, purpose, and context are foundational considerations in any communication—in business or any other field. The talk then turned to what considerations of audience, context, and purpose are unique to the field of business communication and subsequently to the question of our identity as business communication rhetors and teachers.

The discussion in Albuquerque is the impetus for this book—a collection of essays that illustrates, explores, and identifies the rhetoric and rhetorical practices that define the field of business communication and the pedagogy of business communication instructors. As evidenced by the Association for Business Communication's creation of a Rhetoric Special Interest Group and a rhetorical studies track at its annual convention, business communication instructors are eager to use a rhetoric *specific to business communication* to guide their teaching. This book provides them with such a guide.

Defining Business Communication

At the Albuquerque conference, members of the Association for Business Communication's Academic Environment Committee (Lentz, Nelson, Lucas, and Moshiri, 2016) presented its position paper entitled "The Ideal Academic Environment for Teaching Business Communication" (Lentz, Nelson, Lucas, & Cresap, 2016). Citing Bell and Muir (2014) and Rentz and Lentz (2014), the paper defines *business communication* as transactional, problem-solving communication that involves creating and disseminating work-related messages through appropriate channels, while being sensitive to the needs of the audience, the context, and culture in which the message is conveyed and the impression that the sender makes on the audience.

(p. 1)

These key characteristics of business communication—"transactional," "problem-solving," and "work-related"—highlight the distinct rhetorical exigence (Bitzer, 1968) of business communication compared to the related fields of composition and technical communication.

Business communication responds to the rhetorical exigence of workplace communication and the use of communication to solve business problems or achieve business goals; it moves the work of an organization and its employees forward. Other fields, such as composition, respond to the needs of the academy and students' needs to succeed academically in courses in a variety of disciplines. Technical communication, on the other hand, is communication about

technical or specialized topics, such as computer applications, medical procedures, or environmental regulations; communicating by using technology, such as web pages, help files, or social media sites; and providing instructions about how to do something, regardless of how technical the task is or even if technology is used to create or distribute that communication.

(Society for Technical Communication, par. 1)

Understanding the differences in rhetorical exigence in these fields that are closely related to business communication is important. These differences require that writers and speakers in these respective fields ask questions and deploy rhetorical strategies specific to accomplishing their academic or professional goals.

Likewise, in business communication, rhetorical exigence requires the business communicator to consider what the audience needs to think, feel, do, know, understand, or believe as a result of reading or hearing a message relative to the speaker's or writer's business goal (e.g., building relationships with customers, announcing a policy change, delivering bad news, giving a report to shareholders) (Rentz & Lentz, 2018). Consequently, business communication is highly rhetorical in that everything a speaker or writer does is ultimately a rhetorical choice based on business and communication goals. For example, a business communicator must consider the following:

- What does the audience know or need to know?
- What would be the best channel for delivering the message?
- What tone and style are appropriate?
- How should the writer/speaker organize material for the best effect, for instance, in a routine, negative-news, or persuasive message?

- Why does the organizational approach to a message differ depending on the type of rhetorical context?
- What are the features of various business genres (e.g., letters vs. emails vs. reports vs. social media genres), and why are these features important?
- What effect will the visual presentation have on a message?
- Why should a writer/presenter choose a bar chart over a line graph?

Apart from making sound rhetorical choices, no business person can be an effective communicator, and as such our book takes great effort to emphasize effective rhetorical choices as the source of all good business communication. Given its distinctive purpose, it is logical that business communication carve a space for its own rhetoric, particularly in the classroom as future business people learn to communicate in the workplace.

Making a Home for Business Communication Pedagogy

Currently, practitioners and theorists in the growing field of business communication find themselves lacking a disciplinary identity and home. While much of our work is defined by and co-created with practitioners of business communication in the workplace, we are informed by overlapping scholarship among business communication, composition, and technical communication. While this overlap is not necessarily bad, neither is it ideal for business communication, which struggles with disciplinary identity. That is, in both professional and academic communities, people will say, "Students need to learn to write; they must take more English classes" or "Technical communication? That's not what we do in business; that's for science majors and engineering students." What they are not understanding is that there *is* a place in the academy where students learn to write and speak for workplace purposes: the business communication course.

At the same time, we in business communication have historically found connections to the professional communication focus of the technical communication field. We also find significant overlap with the rhetorical foundation in the field of rhetoric and composition studies. As disciplines with writing and speaking foundations, composition and technical communication will always have a connection to business communication; and, while their work does not always squarely inform our own, for decades, edited collections of work in the fields of composition and technical communication have been the best we have had to draw from in developing our pedagogy and research. Sometimes, the overlap serves us well, but we also shoehorn and alter their theory and classroom practices into our own pedagogical models in the absence of anything more closely related to choose from.

In itself, borrowing theory or practice from other fields is not bad, nor is it uncommon; however, usually an academic discipline has defining and clearly articulated characteristics that distinguish it from other disciplines. The fields of technical communication and rhetoric and composition have carved out what rhetoric means to them and how it defines their disciplines; this text serves as the first step toward establishing our own perspective on rhetoric in business communication for a scholarly audience that has been long overlooked.

Breaking New Ground in Business Communication Pedagogy

A litany of popular sources tells us that employers value effective communication above other knowledge or skills, including vocational skills and knowledge acquired from course work in students' majors (NACE *Job Outlook*, 2017). Knowing the value of communication, schools have been creating curricula designed to train students to write and speak clearly, concisely, and effectively in the workplace. The Association for Business Communication's pedagogy journal *Business and Professional Communication Quarterly* and numerous textbooks offer great resources to guide pedagogy and curriculum development, much in the same way that journals and textbooks do in other fields.

What is missing from the picture are resources like those in composition and technical communication that shape the field and develop local, relevant pedagogical practice. In some ways, business communication rhetors and instructors provide an ideal example of de Certeau's (1984) argument that while language, tradition, and practices shape a culture, individuals within that culture (and thus consumers of it) will continually subvert these norms to suit the culture to their needs rather than adapting to the culture itself. His illustration of a government's use of a map to create a strategy for navigating a city compared to how citizens actually navigate a city is analogous to how business communication instructors currently function within the academic cultures of composition and technical communication frameworks. That is, the fields of technical communication and composition have spent well over a century mapping their pedagogy and disseminating that map not only in academic journals but also in collections such as the one in this book. To date, business communication rhetors and instructors have engaged in friendly subversion, as it were, to adapt and adjust to existing pedagogical maps of other disciplines even as they seek to map a space specific to business communication. However, as business communication develops as its own field, members of the discipline need their own pedagogical map. Friendly subversion, of course, will continue, but it will do so within a disciplinarily appropriate space and serve to develop the identity of the discipline itself.

Further, we are outgrowing the theories and practices addressed in the resources in composition and technical communication. No book-length manuscripts exist that focus on the intersection of rhetoric and pedagogy in business communication, and we are confident that this book is not just the first of its kind but that it will be a welcomed resource that defines and shapes the identity and practice in our field.

Why rhetoric? As we've discussed, the rhetoric of business communication as problem-solving, transactional, and goal-driven communication distinguishes it from its counterparts in composition and technical communication. Thus, a collection of essays on rhetoric and pedagogy seems a natural way to begin the conversation on the identity of business communication as a discipline and on the framing of business communication pedagogy within that identity.

Exploring the Intersection of Rhetoric and Pedagogy

Generally, we define rhetoric in traditional Aristotelian terms as "persuasion by all possible means." As editors of this volume, we hope to create a resource for instructors that reflects the variety of voices in the field of business communication and the various possible means by which business communicators accomplish their business goals. We aim to create a text that presents a compelling argument for the importance of rhetorical theory in the business communication classroom.

The essays in this collection focus on the way that rhetoric informs pedagogy in the classroom, but this text also provides perspective on the nature of undergraduate and graduate business education and its relationship to industry. Our authors advocate for shifting classroom practices that address important areas of business communication in corporations while being mindful to trends such as a changing job market, increasing participation in entrepreneurship, and a reliance on established and emerging technologies. As this text demonstrates, by adhering to practices that are predicated on a general understanding of the rhetorical situation, instructors and students are able to pivot and respond to the changing demands of context and audience.

We have invited a group of international teacher-scholars from a geographically and demographically diverse group of higher-education institutions. Their work in this collection addresses the question we posed to each author: How does rhetorical theory drive pedagogy in your business communication classroom? Their answers to this question provide a transformative pedagogical experience for new and seasoned business communication instructors. The essays in this collection can be read as a series of best practices in instruction or as an interrelated argument about the primacy of rhetorical theory in the development and design of business communication pedagogy.

As we explore the boundaries and overlap of other disciplines with the field of business communication, we need to focus on four areas to help us shape an identity: the history of the discipline, the scholarship of the field, the pedagogy of the field, and the artifacts of practitioners. The chapters in this text provide a place for instructors and scholars to enter the conversation on each of these categories. In doing so we offer, as James M. Dubinsky says in his foreword, "a DNA test, demonstrating that what some scholars have seen as a tangential relationship between business communication and rhetoric (or ignored altogether) is actually a familial one" (p. vii).

Section I: Reframing Business Communication

The first section of this text offers perspectives on the nature of business communication, questions the boundaries of the discipline, and problematizes the inherent power and privilege dynamics as well as the pedagogical assumptions that underlie our work as business communication instructors. These three chapters demonstrate that reframing roles as writers and speakers in relationship to the audience or in terms of professional *ethos* can reinforce a rhetorical situation wherein the writer or speaker has increased agency and motivation.

In Chapter One, Marcy Orwig illustrates how the history of business communication has been told largely from a pedagogical approach and encourages us to look instead at our history through a critical lens of genre. She argues that a critical approach to business communication history will help the field become more relevant and relatable as new genres arise in the workplace.

In Chapter Two, Jacob Rawlins presents a competency-focused pedagogy that privileges invention and helps students become more effective, versatile, and prepared business communicators. Business communication instructors continually face the challenge of teaching their students to communicate via current genres and emerging genres and to anticipate future genres. This competency-based approach is not rooted in any particular genre and thus provides students with the flexibility to adapt it to new or unfamiliar genres they encounter in the workplace.

In Chapter Three, Paula J. Lentz examines teaching English grammar in the business writing classroom. She challenges the master narrative in the composition field that grammar knowledge does not make students better writers and asserts that teaching grammar rhetorically can provide students with a sense of power, control, and choice in their business communication. Rather than learning a privileged rhetoric, students acquire a rhetorical understanding of grammar that provides them with the cultural capital essential to promoting their professional *ethos* and adapting to the many Englishes they will encounter in their business careers.

Section II: Rethinking Genre and Process

In this section, the authors demonstrate how reframing a rhetorical process can help us understand a communication act in new and different (and more effective) ways. Each of the authors applies rhetoric to specific business communication assignments on diverse topics, demonstrating the breadth and depth of the potential for applying rhetorical theory to course content.

In Chapter Four, Holly Lawrence asks instructors to develop pedagogy that is simultaneously writer- and reader-centered—a bold assertion in a discipline that has traditionally embraced the primacy of the audience in all communication. Specifically, she examines the commodification of the self and personal branding inherent in students' creation of employment-related materials. She advocates for prewriting and freewriting activities as ways that students can explore their career interests and think carefully about how they want to present themselves professionally.

In Chapter Five, Danica L. Schieber argues for greater focus on the rhetorical notion of *imitatio* in community-based writing projects. She contends that these types of real-world models help students transfer knowledge from a classroom context to authentic situations within their field of study. *Imitatio* and *inventio* give students a theoretical place and method for envisioning the modeling and development aspect of genre production.

In Chapter Six, Kristen M. Getchell presents a case for the versatility of the term *kairos*, a rhetorical notion of time. Closely related to opportunity, the term *kairos* refers to the landscape of moment in which an author or speaker chooses to communicate. This notion of exigence is not dissimilar to the considerations of entrepreneurs when launching a venture. In this chapter, she uses examples from a blog assignment in an MBA class to illustrate how discussing *kairos* can help students see a connection between timeliness and relevance of a writing occasion with entrepreneurial ventures.

In Chapter Seven, Matthew Sharp presents the traditional white paper as the ideal assignment for a dynamic entry to discussing rhetorical concepts, specifically the notion of delivery. He focuses on the ways that a white paper is an apt means of illustrating the interaction among genres and thus introduces students to the concept of genre ecologies. The white paper assignment can help students learn to successfully navigate the genre ecologies that inform or support their rhetorical goals.

Section III: Business Communication as Opportunity

In this section, the authors examine the application of visual rhetoric to business communication. Visual rhetoric is not always at the forefront of a business communication curriculum, but it should be. Today's visually driven, technology-dominated workplaces require students to be aware that the visual presentation of information, whether shared on a social media site, codified in a dress code, or communicated in charts and graphs, is itself a communicative act. The concept of the visual as complex and nuanced workplace rhetoric is a hallmark of the discipline of business communication. The following chapters unpack the complexity and the nuances and offer business communication instructors the opportunity to rethink how they teach visual communication.

In Chapter Eight, Valerie Creelman gives us a different perspective on the application of rhetorical theory as she applies it to the connection between impression management and organizational and individual *ethos*. Using the company dress code as her point of reference, she illustrates how workplace dress embodies an organization's values, beliefs, and norms. She encourages instructors to spend time in their classrooms teaching students to dress for the rhetorical situations they encounter in the workplace.

In Chapter Nine, Dale Cyphert asks us to rethink our understanding of the role of Big Data from that of Big Data as a tool in service to the message strategy to that of Big Data as a significant component of the development of the message strategy itself. Instead of isolating the presentation of data as a supplemental *logos* appeal, she argues that data visualization should be treated and valued holistically for its appeal to *ethos*, *logos*, and *pathos*. Such an approach requires a major paradigm shift in how we think about and teach data visualization, as these tools are not simply a means of delivering information but play a major role in the invention of a rhetor's argument itself.

In Chapter Ten, Ashley Patriarca concludes the collection by illustrating how the canon of memory can be applied to a company's social media presence. Using examples in today's news, Patriarca shows how social media frequently serves as the collective memory for an organization and those with whom it engages. She also provides ways instructors can use the rhetorical canon of memory to teach students to use social media for professional purposes.

We hope this volume will be a valuable resource for full-time and part-time faculty and graduate students teaching business communication courses. This collection of essays has the potential to serve as a heuristic for instructors of business communication to use as they consider how rhetorical theory informs their own teaching philosophy and practices. Like much of our work in the business communication classroom, reflection on practice provides an invaluable opportunity for growth and development in our individual classrooms and for developing our collective identity as an academic discipline.

References

Bell, R. L., & Muir, C. (2014). A review of business communication under the leading function. In *6th annual general business conference proceedings* (pp. 80–105). Huntsville, TX: Sam Houston State University.

Bitzer, Lloyd F. (1968). The Rhetorical Situation. *Philosophy and Rhetoric, 1*(1), 1–14.

de Certeau, M. (1984). Walking in the city. In S. Rendall (Trans.), *The practice of everyday life* (pp. 91–110). Berkeley, CA: University of California Press.

Lentz, P. L. Nelson, A., Lucas, K., & Cresap, L. (2016). *Position Paper: The Ideal Academic Environment for Teaching Business Communication.* Unpublished.

Lentz, P. L. Nelson, A., Lucas, K., & Moshiri, F. (2016). *Position Paper: The Ideal Academic Environment for Teaching Business Communication.* Paper presented at the 81st Annual International Conference of the Association for Business Communication, Albuquerque, NM.

Rentz, K., & Lentz, P. J. (2014). *M: Business communication* (3rd ed.). New York: McGraw-Hill Irwin.

Rentz, K., & Lentz, P. J. (2018). *Business communication: A problem-solving approach.* New York: McGraw-Hill Irwin.

Society for Technical. (n.d.). Defining technical communication. *Society for Technical Communication.* Retrieved April 4, 2017 from www.stc.org/about-stc/defining-technical-communication/.

1

EARLY PENMEN, SECRETARIES, AND GMAIL TEMPLATES

A Critical and Historical Approach to Business Communication Genres

Marcy Leasum Orwig

Examining Pedagogical Influences in Business Communication Scholarship

The field of business communication has a long and interesting history, but it has historically been told from a pedagogical approach. Locker, Miller, Richardson, Tebeaux, and Yates (1996) explain how the "business communication researcher used to teaching and thinking only about letters, memos, and reports would not be well prepared to think of very different kinds of documents—say, the logs written by ships' captains—as business documents" (p. 199). The focus, then, of researching our history only through the classroom lens limits the boundaries of published research on other topics such as genre that provide theoretical support for what we do in the classroom.

Cyphert's (2009) article in the *Journal of Business Communication* speaks to the source of disciplinary identity of our field. She presents survey results from members of the primary association for business communication instructors—the Association for Business Communication (ABC)—regarding disciplinary identity. In it, the members responded most favorably to pedagogical topics relevant to the classroom. The association's unique institutional history does generate "some resistance to abandoning the original business education mandate to teach practical workplace skills in favor of research" (p. 267). But, as Cyphert also notes, the association is attracting more research-active academics. While ABC began with a membership comprised of mostly a practitioner/consultant/instructor base, the number of such members has dropped by half in her cited survey.

Graham's (2006) article on the disciplinary practices used in business communication gives a good example of the tension between practical and research skills in the ABC membership. While the conference is usually a congenial space for all presenters, Graham explains how one of her colleagues spoke on Mikhail Bakhtin and was consequently accused by an audience member of using "high theory to distort practical work" (p. 271).

That preference for the "practical work" of teaching letters, memos, and reports is even evidenced in Du-Babcock's (2006) article on the past, present, and future of the field. Of the past she writes, "the teaching of business communication as a formal and distinct discipline originated in the United States. Business Communication has established itself as an important subject area and has become an integral component of business school curricular" (p. 254). Du-Babcock also notes how the general approach (e.g., form, structure, and process) is used in business writing courses to fit what the practitioner can apply. She writes:

> As a result, teachers of business communication could focus on teaching a general communication process and were not required to have specialized knowledge of professional disciplines and the communication approaches and styles of the professional genres of these disciplines.
>
> *(p. 254)*

For instance, a quick glimpse at the 1961 book titled *Informal Research by the Classroom Business Teacher* speaks to the types of research suggested to educators teaching communication, with topics relevant to courses taught such as "Shorthand and Transcription," "Typewriting," and "Office Practice."

Yet Du-Babcock offers that our past is rooted in rhetoric and the study and use of genres, which presents opportunities for our present and our future for research on the impact of technology, globalization, and culture on our discipline. As mentioned above, only researching, though, the history of business communication genres from a pedagogical approach limits us as an academic area. Cyphert notes how "if teaching is the thing that does bind this diverse band, we might do well to investigate better ways to leverage our common vocation toward the professional legitimacy we seem to feel we lack" (p. 270). Indeed, she notes that business schools are accepted in the academy not because of the professional training they provide but because of their "theoretical contributions" to their discipline (p. 271). A recent study by Moshiri and Cardon (2014) speaks to the lack of professional legitimacy that Cyphert highlights. In their article, Moshiri and Cardon explain that today not all courses are taught in business schools and that only 40% of the instructors have tenure or tenure-track positions (p. 316). If the research of our tradition took a more historical or theoretical, then, perhaps business communication would gain more legitimacy in the academy. However, according to Cyphert's survey, the "construction of theories and models was near the end of the [members' priority] list, with research on the 'historical evolution of business communication' rated dead last, a politely neutral 3.0 on a 0–7 scale" (p. 268).

One of the most well-known researchers in business communication, though, focused on that least popular topic of the "historical evolution of business communication." Locker published voraciously on topics ranging from early dunning letters (1985) to a history of business jargon (1987). In fact, the "Outstanding Research Award" that is presented each year at the ABC conference is named after her. The description for the award states, "The Outstanding Researcher Award recognizes and encourages excellence in business communication research. The recipient is an ABC member whose research has made an outstanding contribution to the business communication discipline." Interestingly, she herself noted:

> Understanding the historical, political, social, and material context in which earlier documents were created also helps us be more aware of the web of influences and constraints that affect business communication today and thus helps us be better able to assess and, if need be, work to change them.
>
> *(p. 123)*

Why does it seem, then, that we still want to tell our history from a pedagogical approach?

One answer lies in the fact that, as mentioned earlier, our disciplinary identity has the classroom as its one common denominator. But, as Cyphert notes, "If we see ourselves as drudges teaching remedial writing skills to students who should have paid more attention in high school, others will too" (p. 271). The second answer lies in that conducting historical research has its challenges. As Locker explained above, there are different approaches to such work. For example, will historical research focus on the *theory* of what experts in different eras said, or will it focus on the *practice* of what business communicators were actually doing in a specific time period? Further, basic understanding of the researched time period is important, and knowing what texts are available in which archive or library is similarly challenging to researchers. And many documents are a–contextual, so anyone who knew about their creation or use is probably no longer around to answer questions. But such research is necessary, since "if we focus instead on the research and theory that ground our instruction, we can earn the respect of our peers as well as the gratitude of our students' prospective employers" (p. 271).

A history-based approach to examining our discipline offers a way to understand, as Jim Dubinsky says in his foreword to this book, the DNA of the genetic map of our field. That map is based on how the discipline originated as different workplace genres developed. As with all history, there are uncomfortable truths to how certain types of writing done by certain people become privileged over others. The next section, then, traces the history of business communication through the lens of workplace practice. After that, the following section will compare the tracing of the history of business communication to that of the other, more well-defined tradition of technical communication that influences our work today. Finally, the end of the chapter discusses how a historical approach to understanding business communication allows us to look toward the future for ways to become more relevant and relatable as new communication challenges arise in the workplace. The point of this chapter is to consider one approach to historical research and inspire others to consider how they might contribute to the body of research in our field on topics such as historical studies and rhetoric.

Understanding the History of Business Communication

Jacob Rawlins shows us in Chapter 2 that good business communicators are flexible and adaptable across the genres they encounter. The history of our discipline throughout nearly the last three centuries establishes flexibility and adaptability as hallmarks of our discipline as we continually adapt to, adjust, and create genres. As the United States was formed, commercial education was not very different from that of the mother countries of Europe. The teachers were largely trained in Europe, and the textbooks were written and published there, too. The earliest mention of business education dates to the year 1635. This reference is made when a school was established in Plymouth, where a certain "Mr. Morton" taught students "to read, write, and cast accounts" (Knepper, 1941, p. 5). In the New World, businesses needed to keep track of the many goods, articles, and machines imported from the Old World. As a result, records needed to be kept in Europe as well as in the Colonies to maintain proper accounts of these transactions. In order to record these transactions in a legible manner, excellent penmanship was necessary. Knepper makes interesting comments about these early penmen:

> Many penmen were public scriveners, and the public scrivener was a very important individual. His services were in constant demand for drawing up wills, deeds, contracts, and for making "true copies" of documents for public record. He must be master of a large assortment of "conventional hands" and also of the "art of flourishing."
>
> *(p. 9)*

In other words, the penmen of this era, wittingly or not, were the keepers of the genre knowledge through which they applied their skills.

By the mid-nineteenth century, private business schools began to form and fill the need to educate people to work in growing industries. The development of business schools in the United States during this time period was no coincidence. The economics and demands of commercial enterprises were also changing from generally small family affairs to large organizations—which needed educated employees. Yates (1993) claims that this transformation began with the railroads and spread to manufacturing firms, such as DuPont, beginning around 1880. She explains, "During the years from 1850 to 1920, a new philosophy of management based on system and efficiency arose, and under its impetus internal communication came to serve as a mechanism for managerial coordination and control of organizations" (p. xix). Systematic management developed theories and techniques that transcended the individual by relying instead on the system. It had two primary principles: "a reliance on systems mandated by top management rather than on individuals, and the need for each level of management to monitor and evaluate performance at lower levels" (p. 10). Coupled with changes in management style were changes in how businesses were financed.

Porter (1973) explains that the typical American business establishment of the first part of the nineteenth century was financed by either a single person or by several people bound together in a partnership (p. 9). Since the business was comparatively small, it represented the personal wealth of just a few persons. Similarly, most manufacturing enterprises (with the exception of some textile mills and iron furnaces) were also relatively small, involving little in the way of physical plant or expensive machinery. It was relatively easy to enter business because the initial costs of going into trade or simple manufacturing were within the reach of many citizens. Corporations were rare, and business had a very personal tone. Since managers saw employees frequently and usually lived with them in the same town, they could at least be expected to know their names, the quality of their work, and perhaps even some things about their personal lives (p. 9).

As large business organizations of the late nineteenth century stitched regional networks together to create national markets, they altered both the form and meaning of local autonomy (Zunz, 1990, p. 12). Additionally, the nature of relationships between the labor force and the managers, as well as the highly individual identification of persons with their firms, underwent considerable change in the big businesses that had evolved by the turn of the century. The bureaucracy became more impersonalized as "complex administrative network[s] created a social and economic gap between men on various levels of hierarchy" (Porter, 1973, p. 21). As the operations of a single business grew larger, more involved, and more widely separated, individual employees often had no knowledge of the distant, almost invisible people who controlled and manipulated the business and, to some degree, their lives. Many workers had little or no understanding of their part in the overall operations of the giant organization, and work itself, as well as their relations with others in the organization, grew increasingly impersonal.

As a result of management's new way of interacting with employees, Yates explains how business communication changed from a system that was informal and primarily oral to one that was more formal, depending heavily on written documents. For example, old communication technologies such as quill pens and bound volumes gave way to typewriters, stencil duplicators, and vertical files that aided in creating and storing documents. New technologies also affected the function and form of communication within the firm. These new types of communication, such as orders, reports, and memoranda, developed to suit managerial goals and technological contexts. In doing so, "the management changes created new rhetors and buried them under layers of bureaucracy, created new interests that in turn produced new exigencies and constraints, and altered the means of persuasion" (Miller, 1998, p. 297). Who were those new rhetors, then, and how did they impact business communication genres?

As Yates (1993) asserts, while organizations used various genres in an attempt to control communication and their workforce, secretarial schools and business schools (and thus, by extension, the secretary) became both an influence on this control and simultaneously an agent through which genres were adapted, created, and maintained. A report from the 1876 US Commissioner of Education writes about business schools, noting that "to supply the increasing demand for stenographers, schools of shorthand and typewriting have been established in various parts of the country, and, with few exceptions, all business colleges now have a 'department of shorthand'" (Knepper, 1941, p. 90). The first shorthand writers were male, interestingly, because they would test the emerging techniques associated with the invention of typewriters. An 1893 circular from the Bureau of Education explains an increase in the use of shorthand.

As a result, between 1871 and 1890, there was a four-fold growth in the number of institutions that handled such courses.

As Knepper notes, for this new use of shorthand a new type of stenographer was needed—someone who was younger, had less experience, and had training to fill the enormous demand of growing businesses. So, of the enrollments in the emerging shorthand courses, the percentage of female students increased from 4 percent to 28 percent (p. 91). Knepper writes the following:

> The influence of the typewriter, and of shorthand with which it became almost inseparably joined, in relieving business executives of the tedium of communication and so making possible a higher type of business leadership, can hardly be overestimated.
>
> *(p. 77)*

The writing of new business communication genres, then, seems to shift to women during this time period. By 1890, it was common to not only have a stenography course, but also an English course, a commercial course, and a course of amanuensis—that is, an early version of secretarial work. Knepper writes:

> This invention [the typewriter] ... opened up to girls and women a profitable field of employment in business. Moreover, this employment of women did not displace other workers. The positions arose from the expansion of business and industry.
>
> *(p. 79)*

Interestingly, a review of Knepper's book drew some criticism about statements like the one above.

Fisk, of the Woman's College at the University of North Carolina, wrote in a review of the book in 1942 that "one does not always agree with the author in his interpretations of the evidence, for at times, he seems to include too much of personal opinion" (p. 58). Personal opinions—such as the one by Knepper above—are important to note, though. The narrative that women were helping to fill a needed position within a company was more favorable than one where she displaced a man. For instance, the prevalent prejudice against women in business was given voice by one male newspaper editor of the late 1800s. He happily declared that "in New York, Boston, and Chicago over 8,000 women had been relieved of their positions and their places filled by men" (*Today's Secretary*, 1959a, p. 19). However, by 1901, "the Remington company alone placed over 16,000 stenographers in seven of the biggest cities in the country. Only over 4,000 of them were men" (*Today's Secretary*, 1959a, p. 19). Further, another source wrote that women "would work for eight or ten dollars a week … and with a dollar raise every year or two you could keep them happy" (*Today's Secretary*, 1959a, p. 19).

Over the years, employers began to appreciate women stenographers more, and eventually many of the positions developed into secretarial work. According to one article,

> The stenographer may be a good speller, but the secretary knows words. She knows whether a new word or odd expression is correct and in good taste, etymologically and otherwise . . . The stenographer has studied to make a living, but the secretary has studied to make success. The difference comes after the training, for the stenographer's ability is the foundation upon which the secretary must build.
>
> *(Today's Secretary, 1959b, p. 41)*

In essence, as a knower of words, the secretary also knew how to control and adapt the language. As Paula Lentz argues in Chapter 3, controlling the language is one prominent way to control genres and their discourse.

Indeed, by 1984, Schindler provides advice for secretaries who want to "be prepared for upward mobility from the correspondence secretarial level into 'mahogany row'," where salaries increase by "$1,500 to $2,000 more" (p. 7). The main piece of advice by Schindler is for aspiring secretaries to continue to educate themselves, despite the declining opportunities to learn traditional skills in educational institutions. Further, she blames the short supply of qualified secretaries on "the women's movement, equal employment opportunities, low salaries, and declining population" (p. 3). She ends with:

> For many years and many reasons, there have been women struggling to escape the confines of their secretarial jobs. There are other women who have found secretarial work to be the stepping-stone to positions of higher responsibility. Any movement to attract men to enter secretarial preparation courses has had minimal impact on the supply problem.
>
> *(p. 3)*

Earlier, though, in 1980, a National Business Education Association (NBEA) publication titled *The Changing Office Environment* focused on the evolving nature of work within the business office and the development of the term "administration."

Today, business communication continues to adapt and respond to the needs of industry—which includes factors such as globalization, digital tools, and a reorganization of the labor force. Gordon (2016) explains how the digital revolution centered on the years 1970–2000 changed the way the office functioned. In 1970, the electronic calculator had just been introduced, but the computer terminal was still in the future.

> Office work required innumerable clerks to operate the keyboards of electric typewriters that had no ability to download content from the rest of the world and that, lacking a memory, required repetitive retyping of everything from legal briefs to academic research papers.
>
> *(p. 579)*

By the year 2000, though, every office was equipped with web-linked personal computers that could perform any word-processing task, and by the year 2005, flat screens had completed the transition to the modern office, with broadband service replacing dial-up service. Further, in the past decade, smartphones and tablets have become standard business equipment outside of the office. Gordon ends with:

> Paper has been replaced almost everywhere outside of the office. Airlines are well along in equipping pilots with smart tablets that contain all the information previously provided by large paper manuals. Maintenance crews at Exelon's six nuclear power stations in Illinois are the latest to be trading in their three ring binders for iPads. The switch to tablets boosts productivity by eliminating not just the expense of the paper but also of photocopying and filing.
>
> *(p. 581)*

Our history as a discipline during this period from the late 1800s until now, as seen through the lens of genre, reveals that it is distinguished by issues of gender, power, control, ethics, culture, technology and language—all topics worthy of continued research.

By looking at the history and role of the business communicator, then, three important topics emerge.

First, business communication has evolved from an entry-level position within a company. But, second, that evolution has been characterized by the fact that much of the communication work has been done by women—or, in other words, secretaries—as new economic opportunities developed. Finally, factors such as globalization, digital tools, and a reorganization of the labor force present opportunities for research that can help define and situation business communication as a discipline.

Addressing the Influence of the Technical Communication Field

In 2003, Locker wrote a piece titled "Will Professional Communication Be the Death of Business Communication?" in which she argues that mergers between business communication and technical communication are problematic. While she acknowledges the reasons for the merger are largely political—and largely a result of those factors mentioned earlier, such as globalization, digital tools, and a reorganization of the labor force—she also believes there are reasons connected to "a common base in theory and research" (p. 122). Locker notes that there are many parallels to business and technical communication but worries that new programs titled "professional communication" will emphasize the technical over the business. For instance, she cites the first issue of the *Journal of Business and Technical Communication* and its guest editorial by Dobrin as deeply troubling. Dobrin writes:

> Perhaps, though, business practices do differ essentially from technical practices. Perhaps, for instance, technical writers are essentially honest and straightforward because they're concerned with facts, while business writers are essentially greedy and deceitful because they're concerned with money. On the other hand, perhaps business writers are practical and sensible because they're concerned with getting things done while technical writers can never free themselves of their jargon to make things clear. Perhaps, but I doubt it.
>
> *(1987, p. 6)*

Locker is right to critique such a statement, especially since she points out that "businesses are not the only organizations whose effects have sometimes been malign: schools, universities, and even churches have also supported repressive status quos and hurt groups and individuals" (p. 130). Further, she argues that technical communication is not "purer" than business communication by giving the examples of critical scholarship by Katz (1992)—who researched how Nazi engineers communicated gassing human beings in concentration camps—or Winsor (2000)—who researched the communication surrounding the NASA Challenger disaster.

As mentioned earlier, with the premise for this chapter, communication related to the technical has had the opportunity to overtake that of the business because our history has remained told largely through our pedagogy—what we do versus who we are. Further, a research-based approach to our history lets us examine how the discipline originated as different workplace genres developed. As mentioned in the previous section, business communication has evolved from the responsibility of someone in an entry-level position within a company to one that is the responsibility of all employees in a global, distributed, and technology-mediated workplace. However, it has also been characterized by the fact that much of the communication work was done by women—or, in other words, secretaries—as new economic opportunities developed. Further, the more recent introduction of communication technologies into the workplace only helped to marginalize business communication as a field since such work was often viewed as "technical" rather than the perhaps "old-fashioned" rhetorical approach to secretarial labor—the female who, according to that quote from the *Today's Secretary*, knows "words."

A historical, critical approach to scholarship has acted as a legitimizing force in technical communication. Longo's (2000) germinal work, titled *Spurious Coin*, opens with the argument that the field has "a more active social role than being merely a neutral conduit for information" (ix). In the years leading up to this publication, other technical writing scholars called for the same kind of critical approach. For instance, Slack, Miller, and Doak's (1993) "The Technical Communicator as Author: Meaning, Power, Authority" discusses how it is "impossible to recognize the real power of technical discourse without understanding its role in the articulation and rearticulation of meaning and power" (p. 135). Or, Ornatowski's (1992) "Between Efficiency and Politics: Rhetoric and Ethics in Technical Writing"—the article explains how textbooks in technical writing emphasize objectivity, clarity, and neutrality in communication. However, these skills "are unable to accommodate a notion of ethics and responsibility" (p. 91). Further, Grabill and Simmons' (1998) "Toward a Critical Rhetoric of Risk Communication: Producing Citizens and the Role of Technical Communicators" builds on arguments in risk communication that the "predominant linear risk communication models are problematic for their failure to consider audience and additional contextual issues" (p. 415). While some scholarship, such as Tebeaux's (1996) "Reaffirming our Foundations," combines technical writing with business communication, the borrowing between the two fields only serves to emphasize the lack of scholarship specific to the latter.

In their introduction to this book, Paula Lentz and Kristen Getchell talk about the ways in which the discipline of business communication has engaged in "friendly subversion" (p. 24) to map its pedagogy using historical and pedagogical research in disciplines such as technical communication. Likely, this "friendly subversion" will continue, but as Lentz and Getchell argue, as a unique field, business communication needs its own distinct map. Historical research offers one point on this map.

Critiquing History as Rhetorical Approach to Business Communication

A quick search with the term "history" in the academic journals sponsored by ABC—the *International Business Communication Journal* and *Business and Professional Communication Quarterly*—provides few results. Locker's research, as might be expected, surfaces, along with the well-known bibliography of Hildebrant (1985). Other results include Thomas (2003), who focused on the medieval letter writer by Sampson in 1396, and Lund (1998), who wrote on the importance of Defoe's *The Complete English Tradesman* from the eighteenth century. Carbone's (1994) piece, titled "The History and Development of Business Communication Principles: 1776–1916," might appear to take a purely historical approach but instead traces the importance of the first acknowledged college business communication textbook by Hotchkiss. Only one result by Yates (1985) seems to yield a true, historically based research article about the development of genre in business communication from an American perspective.

The genre that Yates focuses on is the graph, and, in her article, she examines its use as a managerial tool at the beginning of the twentieth century. In particular, she uses the case example of DuPont to show how graphs became an efficient way to analyze and communicate data within American business. As she points out, graphs have evolved from the "chart room" at DuPont to now appear in other workplace genres—such as in reports, memos, and presentations. While most business communication instructors would agree that graphs are an important component of our classes, fewer would probably acknowledge that a critical history of the graph—as Yates presented it—may not at first seem relevant. However, after further reflection, Yates' work helps business communication instructors to contextualize *why* we use graphs at all in business communication and, therefore, is quite helpful as we prepare students for the workplace. Dale Cyphert's Chapter 9 discussion of Big Data reinforces this historical perspective that visuals are an inherent part of a rhetor's argument, not simply a means of delivering data.

To find another critical example of business communication, one would need to go to the *Journal of Technical Writing and Communication* with Zachry's (2000) article on the historical examination of genre development at a meat packing company in Waterloo, Iowa. In his article, he argues that while "professional communication" has provided insight into the ways professionals use writing to negotiate tasks in workplace settings, these studies lack "a historical perspective on the communicative practices of these professionals" (p. 58). Further:

> We know little about how the rhetorical choices of professionals are enabled and contained by prior communicative practices in their places. How did the varied textual forms come to be used in these professions? How have the practices for producing and receiving those forms developed? And, what work do these long-standing communicative practices make possible and what do they delimit. [. . .] We do not yet have a fully developed sense of our genre history in the twentieth century. The potential work for researchers is staggering given the scope of professional communication and the long history of its practice.
>
> *(p. 58)*

His examination of the genres used at the meat packing company highlights how communication adapted to the growing and expanding business. Zachry traces the company's employees as they developed habits for handling their repetitious tasks, which caused a standardization to occur as part of the work and ultimately developed forms to facilitate routine communication exchanges. He writes,

> Rath [the meat packing company] was able to coordinate activities across its dispersed organization through frequent generic exchanges. These exchanges, however, were not discrete activities. The genres that employees circulated across the organization were linked to still other—and often more elaborate—networks of genre-mediated activities.
>
> *(p. 66)*

For instance, Zachry gives the example of salesmen using their own genres to communicate with branch managers who would have overseen their daily activities.

Likewise, Amy Devitt's work in *Writing Genres* (2004) shows how tax accountants chose which genre conventions of their field to use. She also explains how those genres adapted and adjusted to conventions as they worked within (and thus created) their localized discourse community.

Another example of studying how organizations change genre to suit their needs is Orwig's (2014) work on military reports in *Connexions: International Professional Communication Journal*. In it, she traces the "genreology"—or, the genealogy of generic forms—used in World War I to efficiently report information within the command structure of the United States Army. Orwig found three major reports developed during the course of the war—Daily Operations Reports, Special Operations Reports, and After Action Reports. These reports differed greatly in terms of structure from earlier military communication, which took a much more narrative, letter-like approach to describing intelligence and actions.

While such historical research is promising, it also showcases some of the current problems with the critical scholarship in our field. First, Yates' work was published more than 30 years ago, which speaks to the gap in ABC's journals devoted to historical research, and Devitt's, while addressing workplace genres, is not extensively devoted to the study of business communication. Further, some of the older historical research mentioned above—such as Locker, Thomas, or Lund—tends to take a British perspective and does not specifically analyze an American approach to business communication. Second, while Zachry's article is fascinating, it does overlook the potential role of secretaries in the development of such workplace genres. Third, a study like Orwig's on military reports is useful when considering how genre changes within an organization, but it is based on the traditionally masculine subject of war—which again reinforces the marginalization of understanding a woman's role in the communication process.

Opportunities for Historical Research

There are, as mentioned earlier, uncomfortable realities in the history of business communication research—such as the unexplored role of women in creating workplace genres, the preference for technology over a rhetorical sensibility, or a prejudice of favoring historical research from a British perspective. However, research that explores these uncomfortable realities is important since it will help the field legitimize. If a history of business communication can take a critical approach, rather than a purely pedagogical one, then instructors can be more informed in their classrooms, and their research can help the field better understand itself.

For many business communication instructors, there is a chasm between pedagogical approaches to business communication as a skill and as rhetorical knowledge. As shown through the early history of business education, communication—or penmanship—was viewed as a largely mechanical skill of mastering different "hands" and types of genres, such as wills or sales letters. The second interpretation of business communication takes a much more rhetorical approach—as shown through the description of secretarial work. As a result, for most of the twentieth century—and, to some extent, today—business communication pedagogy has largely varied between the approaches that (1) students should know basic skills, such as shorthand or typing, with the other approach that (2) they should also be prepared to think in a general, analytical manner.

Hagge's 1989 essay argues that any approach other than a rhetorical one to business communication is problematic because it will continue to marginalize the field. As a result, Brooks explains, researchers taking a rhetorical perspective "have been investigating the role of writing in the workplace. Attempts to apply research findings in the classroom may be influencing business communication instruction" (1991, p. 14).

Indeed, scholarship dedicated to how genres function in the workplace and best practices for their use abound in the academic journals associated with ABC. For instance, a recent search in *Business and Professional Communication Quarterly* with the term "genre" yielded over 20 results and included research ranging from the use of infographics in annual reports (Toth, 2013) to the use of bad-news messages in business (Creelman, 2012). There were fewer results in the *International Journal of Business Communication* but Bremner's (2014) article on genres in the public relations industry was still included, as was Bruce's (2014) article on the genre of the fund manager commentary. So, again, our field seems to acknowledge that how genres function in the workplace and how best to use them is important. But the historical approach needed to help us understand how business communication has always been a rhetorical endeavor—something that Hagge argues—seems largely absent. If business communication is viewed as a rhetorical tradition—especially from a critical, historical perspective—it also says much about approaches to the role of invention.

Invention is the first of the rhetorical canons and is generally defined as the process of developing and refining argument. In the case of business communication, if our courses are teaching formulaic genres, then that first step of invention is a challenge. But, through a rhetorical approach to business communication pedagogy, students can begin to realize that the genres they use in the workplace are part of the invention process. As Devitt (2004) argues, instructors should attempt to generate critical genre awareness in students by leading students to see genres as (1) "created by people to achieve aims, not just as pre-existing and irrevocable constructs into which they must fit" (p. 348); (2) processes which emerge and change, which is as important as (3) serving the aims of groups, institutions, and cultures. When combined, these three elements help students to understand genres as created, dynamic, and ideological construct(s).

Devitt's work on critical genre awareness was largely influenced by Miller's 1984 piece titled "Genre as Social Action." Miller's work provided a way of looking at an artifact as a social response to a set of recurrent rhetorical exigencies rather than a collection of formal, generic elements. For most of the twentieth century, scholars used the tradition of Aristotle's formal features to analyze texts. However, Miller argued that "rhetorical criticism has not provided firm guidance on what constitutes a genre" and that a "rhetorically sound definition of genre must be centered not on the substance or the form of discourse but on the action it is used to accomplish" (p. 151). Rethinking genre from her sociocultural perspective involves, most essentially, a move away from defining genre primarily as a class or category. This view also suggests that genres function as activity structures and that these genres are continually mutating (Jasinski, 2001, p. 275). The development of the sociocultural approach helped scholars rethink genre theory and, most notably, takes the traditional view of genre in Aristotelian and literary classification systems and relocates it to the communicative behaviors of actors in everyday life (p. 155). Unlike literary studies, where the object of study is the literary canon, the objects of study in business communication research are what Berkenkotter and Huckin (1995) call "everyday texts" (p. 50). They continue to argue that genres should been seen as "dynamic rhetorical structures that can be manipulated according to the conditions of use, and that genre knowledge is therefore best conceptualized as a form of situated cognition embedded in disciplinary activities" (p. 3). Understanding genre apart from historical research is simply not possible.

Part of teaching critical genre awareness, then, is to help students perceive the ideological impact of genre and to make deliberate generic choices. An outline of the theoretical underpinnings of genre pedagogies, in which Devitt makes no claim to comprehensiveness, include a few insightful and essential points:

- Genres are social and rhetorical actions: they develop their languages and forms out of rhetorical aims and contexts shared by groups of users.
- The spread of a genre creates shared aims and social structures.
- As new users acquire genres, that process reinforces existing aims and structures.
- Existing genres reinforce institutional and cultural norms and ideologies.
- To change genres, individually or historically, is to change shared aims, structures, and norms.

Although she acknowledges that instructors may share these theoretical under-standings, specific pedagogies emphasize different components at different levels (p. 343). For many business communication instructors, as noted above, there is a chasm between pedagogical approaches—which are seen as either a largely mechanical skill of mastering different "hands" and types of genres, or a rhetori-cal approach to understanding genres and how to adapt, when needed, to those genres in the workplace.

Herndl (1993) further explains in his article, titled "Teaching Discourse and Reproducing Culture: A Critique of Research and Pedagogy in Professional and Non-Academic Writing":

> Once we abandon the current traditional rhetoric's notion of writing as a neutral, apolitical skill, we must recognize that discourse is inseparable from institutions, from organizational structures, from disciplinary and profes-sional knowledge claims and interests, and from the day-to-day interaction of workers.
>
> *(p. 353)*

McKee and Porter (2017) support that a rhetorical view of business communica-tion should be viewed as posited by Quintilian of "the good man speaking well." Or, in other words, the "good corporations (or organization or group) speaking well—and now, too, the good machine speaking well" (p. 15). For example, the authors explain how the rise of artificial intelligence (AI) has influenced the gen-res used in business communication.

For example, McKee and Porter (2017) cite Constine and Perez (2016, p. 139) statistic that Facebook's Messenger platform has been cited as having over 30,000 bots actively communicating as AI agents. Another example is Google and its feature of the Gorgias templates for email—which, ironically, is named after the well-known rhetorical work of the same name. Google claims that it will enable users to write emails quickly using keyboard shortcuts, templates.

The role of rhetoric, then, in the future of business communication is very important because artificial intelligence (AI) will continue to influence the invention of genres. Rather than revert to the boilerplate language in different "hands"—as was the tradition during the early era of the secretary—our field must emphasize the role that rhetoric should play as the businessperson adapts new, emerging technologies to specific communication situations. Furthermore, as Ashley Patriarca discusses in Chapter 10, social media is a primary player in the discipline of business communication and plays a significant role in creating organizational memories, which then become or organizational histories. A his-torical approach, then, to understanding how our field has developed is even more necessary as the field moves forward.

The major accrediting agency for schools of business, the AACSB, emphasizes the importance of business communication by listing it as the first bullet point under "General Skills Areas." That bullet point is phrased with: "Written and oral communication (able to communicate effectively orally and in writing)." If the AACSB lists business communication at the top of its list, then as researchers in the field, it is our responsibility to conduct and publish critical, historical scholarship that helps our field move forward.

References

AACSB International. (2018). *Standards*. Tampa, FL. Retrieved from www.aacsb.edu/accreditation/standards.

Berkenkotter, C., & Huckin, T. (1995). *Rethinking genre from a sociocognitive perspective*. Hillsdale, NJ: Lawrence Erlbaum Associates.

Bremner, S. (2014). Genres and processes in the PR industry: Behind the scenes with an intern writer. *International Journal of Business Communication*, 259–278.

Brooks, R. (1991). *Rhetorical theory in business communication curricula from 1900 to 1980: An historical critique*. Purdue University, Dissertation.

Bruce, I. (2014). Enacting criticality in corporate disclosure communication: The genre of the fund manager commentary. *International Journal of Business Communication*, 315–336.

Carbone, M. (1994). The history and development of business communication principles: 1776–1916. *Journal of Business Communication*, 173–193.

Creelman, V. (2012). The case for "Living" Models. *Business Communication Quarterly*, 176–191.

Cyphert, D. (2009). Who we are and what we do. *Journal of Business Communication*, 262–274.

Devitt, A. (2004). *Writing genres*. Carbondale, IL: Southern Illinois University Press.

Dobrin, D. (1987). Guest editorial: Writing without disciplines. *Journal of Business and Technical Communication*, 5–8.

Douglas, G., & Hildebrant, H. (1985). *Studies in the history of business writing*. Urbana, IL: Association for Business Communication.

Du-Babcock, B. (2006). Teaching business communication: Past, present, and future. *Journal of Business Communication*, 253–264.

Dvorak, E. (1961). *Informal research by the classroom business teacher*. Bloomington, IN: National Business Teachers Association.

Fisk, M. (1942). A chronological account: The history of business education in the United States. *The Journal of Higher Education*, 131–158.

Gordon, R. (2016). *Rise and fall of American growth*. Princeton, NJ: Princeton University Press.

Gorgias Templates. (2017). Google. Retrieved from https://chrome.google.com/webstore/detail/gorgias-templates-email-t/lmcngpkjkplipamgflhioabnhnopeabf?hl=en-US.

Grabill, J., & Simmons, M. (1998). Toward a critical rhetoric of risk communication: Producing citizens and the role of technical communication. *Technical Communication Quarterly*, 74–415.

Graham, M. (2006). Disciplinary practice(s) in business communication, 1985 to 2004. *Journal of Business Communication*, 268–277.

Hagge, J. (1989). The spurious paternity of business communication principles. *Journal of Business Communication*, 261–233.

Herndl, C. (1993). Teaching discourse and reproducing culture: A critique of research and pedagogy in professional and non-academic writing. *College Composition and Communication*, 443–349.

Jasinski, J. (2001). *Sourcebook on rhetoric: Key concepts in contemporary rhetorical studies*. Thousand Oaks, CA: Sage.

Johnson, M. (1980). *The changing office environment*. Reston, VA: National Business Education Association.

Katz, S. (1992). The ethic of expediency: Classical rhetoric, technology, and the holocaust. *College English*, 255–275.

Knepper, E. (1941). *History of business education in United States*. Ann Arbor, MI: Edwards Brothers.

Locker, K. (1985). "Sir, This Will Never Do": Model dunning letters, 1592–1873. *Journal of Business Communication*, 179–200.

Locker, K. (1987). As per your request: A history of business Jargon. *Journal of Business and Technical Communication*, 27–47.

Locker, K. (2003). Will professional communication be the death of business communication? *Business Communication Quarterly*, 118–132.

Locker, K., Miller, S., Richardson, M. Tebeaux, E., & Yates, J. (1996). Studying the history of business communication. *Business Communication Quarterly*, 109–127.

Longo, B. (2000). *Spurious coin: A history of science, management, and technical writing*. New York: SUNY Press.

Lund, R. (1998). Writing in the history of business communication: The example of Defoe. *Journal of Business Communication*, 500–520.

McKee, H., & Porter, J. (2017). *Professional communication and network interaction*. New York: Routledge.

Miller, C. (1984). Genre as social action. *Quarterly Journal of Speech*, 151–167.

Miller, C. (1998). Learning from history: World War II and the culture of high technology. *Journal of Business and Technical Communication*, 123–288.

Moshiri, F., & Cardon, P. (2014). The state of business communication classes. *Business and Professional Communication Quarterly*, 773–312.

Ornatowski, C. (1992). Between efficiency and politics: Rhetoric and ethics in technical writing. *Technical Communication Quarterly*, 11–91.

Orwig, M. (2014). The "Genreology" of U.S. army World War I reports: An exploration of historical genre change. *Connexions: International Professional Communication Journal*, 33–55.

Porter, G. (1973). *The rise of big business, 1860–1910*. Arlington Heights, IL: Harlan Davidson.

Schindler, I. (1984). Is shorthand dead, terminally ill, or just ailing? *Business Education Forum*, 3–7.

Slack, J., et al. (1993). The technical communicator as author: Meaning, power, authority. *Journal of Business and Technical Communication*, 7–12.

Tebeaux, E. (1996). Reaffirming our foundations. In A. Duin & C. Hansen (Eds.), *Nonacademic writing: Social theory and technology*. New York: Routledge.

Thomas, M. (2003). Textual archaeology: Lessons in the history of business writing pedagogy from a medieval Oxford scholar. *Business Communication Quarterly*, 98–105.

Today's Secretary. (1959a). 1899 to 1958: These were the years when. *Today's Secretary*, 18–23.

Today's Secretary. (1959b). 1899 to 1958: These were the years when. *Today's Secretary*, 40–41.

Toth, C. (2013). Revisiting a genre: Teaching infographics in business and professional communication courses. *Business Communication Quarterly*, 446–457.

Twentieth Century Fox. (1980). *9 to 5*.

Winsor, D. (2000). Ordering work: Blue-collar literacy and the political nature of genre. *Written Communication*, 155–184.

Yates, J. (1985). Graphs as a managerial tool: A case study of DuPont's use of graphs in the early twentieth century. *Journal of Business Communication*, 5–33.

Yates, J. (1993). *Control through communication: The rise of system in American management.* Baltimore, MD: Johns Hopkins University Press.

Zachry, M. (2000). Communicative practices in the workplace: A historical examination of genre development. *Journal of Technical Writing and Communication*, 57–79.

Zunz, O. (1990). *Making America corporate: 1870–1920.* Chicago: University of Chicago Press.

2

INVENTIO THROUGH PRAXIS

Connecting Competencies with the Canon

Jacob D. Rawlins

The world of business communication has always been an ever-shifting mix of traditional genres and emerging genres. The written memos, letters, and reports that were the standards not too many years ago have been updated and replaced with electronic communication in the form of email, websites, and blogs, which in turn are quickly being superseded by quicker, more efficient forms of instant communication, such as social media, texting, and instant messaging. Some of these changes to how business people communicate have been driven by new technologies, others by a rapidly changing economy, with new businesses and new challenges. Still others are driven by the evolving attitudes of the people who create and receive business messages.

The constantly evolving landscape of business communication presents many challenges to business communication instructors. In order to adequately prepare their students for a competitive job market, instructors must teach their students to write, speak, and understand traditional genres, current genres, and emerging genres and to anticipate future genres that haven't been invented yet. Although it is challenging, it has never been more important. Employers in the United States consistently rate the "ability to verbally communicate with persons inside and outside the organization" as the most important skill for prospective employees, even more important than "technical knowledge related to the job" (NACE, 2017). Once a prospective employee gets a job, that person will spend most of his or her time communicating (Chui et al., 2012; Project Management Institute, 2013; Silverman, 2012). In fact, each year the average American worker will spend the equivalent of 111 work days reading, responding to, and managing email messages alone (Gill, 2013). Business communication instructors have the unenviable task of preparing their students for these realities of the modern workplace, usually in a single semester of coursework.

Many business communication instructors use one of a few major textbooks as the foundation for their course. These textbooks typically use rhetorical theory or communication theory to provide the basis for teaching essential communication skills (such as Adler, Elmhorst, & Lucas, 2013; Guffey, 2015; Locker & Kienzler, 2013; Rentz & Lentz, 2018). The theoretical foundation provides a starting point for examining the different genres of business communication through instruction, exercises, assignments, and assessment. This class structure is common throughout many universities. One recent analysis of the syllabi for business communication classes showed that courses include learning about good and bad news messages; understanding and following conventions of specific kinds of documents (such as email, letters, and reports); and learning the tools and practices of effective business speaking (Russ, 2009).

More recently, some business communication instructors have developed different approaches to preparing students for a competitive job market and a shifting business communication landscape. One of the approaches focuses on helping students develop communication to "[cultivate] a higher ordered mind-set about communication that transcends particular genres and persists within students long after they have left the business communication classroom" (Lucas & Rawlins, 2015, p. 168). Helping students develop specific competencies that aren't tied to particular genres can, in theory at least, prepare students to communicate in traditional, current, emerging, and future genres as soon as they enter the workplace. In contrast to other pedagogical approaches to business communication, the competency approach focuses almost entirely on *praxis* by connecting students with the terms, practices, and skills they will use in the workplace.

To respond to the challenging landscape of modern business communication, with its many different genres and ever-shifting expectations, some business communication instructors have become increasingly focused on the practice of business communication, particularly the forms, media, and current content that students will see when they enter the workplace. Some instructors may skip, downplay, or ignore discussions of the foundational theory included in traditional textbooks in favor of providing more instruction and practice in the many different genres of business documents, and rhetorical and communication theory may be lost entirely.

This focus on practice presents a new problem for both instructors and students. When the *praxis* of business communication is disconnected from or given primacy over the theoretical foundation in rhetoric, instructors run the risk of inadequately preparing students for shifts in technology, modes of communication, or workplace practices. On the other hand, when rhetorical theory is given the most emphasis without enough attention to praxis, practical-minded students may not see the connections to their day-to-day workplace communication problems.

This chapter proposes improving the balance of theory and praxis in business communication courses by foregrounding the canon *inventio*. After a brief discussion of *inventio* and its place as a foundation of modern business communication, the chapter gives an overview of one recent *praxis*-based approach, the competencies model designed by Lucas and Rawlins (2015). This essay then suggests foregrounding *inventio* in the Lucas-Rawlins model in order to better prepare students with communication tools to adapt to workplace situations. Connecting business communication competencies with the rhetorical canon may prove to be an important tool in helping students connect classroom instruction with workplace practice. The goal is to teach students to be more than simply skilled in creating certain types of messages or even to have developed specific skills; they need to be nimble rhetors who are prepared for shifting genres and changing communication demands. This nimbleness comes from a strengthened rhetorical foundation combined with a range of adaptable competencies.

Inventio as a Foundation

Modern business communication moves at lightning speed. Those who send messages expect instant responses and immediate answers to their questions and problems. In an ideal world, speed would not create problems with communication, because "absolute communication would be of every man's essence . . . it would be as natural, spontaneous, and total as with those ideal prototypes of communication, the theologian's angels, or 'messengers'" (Burke, 1969, p. 22). But in the real world, communication is "partly embodied in material conditions and partly frustrated by these same conditions" (Burke, 1969, p. 22). Because the conditions of business communication are focused on speed, the creation and use of modern communication technologies has focused on facilitating more instant communication. But the unrealistic expectation for speed can often lead to a lack of thought, careful consideration, or professional behavior in business messages.

Many problems in business communication (and in businesses themselves) can be attributed to this lack of care in composing and presenting messages. This is not a new problem, of course. Cicero wrote, "That controversies arise also on the interpretation of writing, in which any thing has been expressed ambiguously, or contradictorily, or so that what is written is at variance with the writer's evident intention" (*De Oratore* 1.XXXI). The problems or "controversies" associated with communication have, perhaps, been exacerbated by the expectation for speed that takes precedence over crafting rhetorically appropriate and powerful messages.

While each of the five canons of rhetoric is neglected or ignored in fast-paced communication, *inventio* is perhaps the most critical. After all, the receiver of an email may forgive convoluted organization, sloppy grammar, and poor formatting (arrangement, style, and delivery) if he or she is able to get the information required to take action. But without proper invention, the sender may fail to establish the purpose of the message, omit crucial information, or strike a tone inappropriate to the rhetorical situation, all of which can lead to misunderstanding, miscommunication, and lost time and effort.

In some views of classical rhetoric, invention is characterized by individual careful consideration, thought, and meditation. LeFevre (1987) wrote that classical invention focuses "on the isolated writer seeking inspiration within" (p. 17), while D'Angelo (1975), Miller (1974), and Gadamer (1982) describe invention as a work of genius, inspiration, or being touched by a creative muse. The classical rhetoricians, on the other hand, often describe invention as more complex than introspection. In his discussion of *inventio*, Cicero wrote,

> a constant and diligent habit of writing will surely be of more effect than meditation and consideration itself; since all the arguments relating to the subject on which we write, whether they are suggested by art, or by a certain power of genius and understanding, will present themselves, and occur to us, while we examine and contemplate it in the full light of our intellect.
>
> *(De Oratore 1.XXXIII)*

In other words, fully realized rhetorical invention is based on both internal thought and external suggestions—a rhetor's experiences and explorations, all of which combine to draw on "the full light of our intellect."

This approach to invention is further developed by scholars who focus on invention as a social or cultural construction, where rhetors create texts from sociocultural *topoi* and from existing texts and arguments. Kamberelis and Scott (1992) wrote, "We seldom, if ever, create our own language styles and texts anew. Rather, we use the styles and texts of other individuals and groups with whom we wish to be affiliated, have power over, or resist" (p. 363). Invention, therefore, should be a process of rhetorical identification, where by carefully crafting our language, style, delivery, and message we can signal our connections to and, according to Burke (1969), our divisions from the social, cultural, professional, and ideological communities with which we are communicating. A key to successful invention is understanding the social and professional expectations of the receivers in order to craft the appropriate message for the situation.

One challenge for business communication instructors, however, is that the traditional approach to teaching *inventio* in both high school and university writing courses is to instruct students on how to create original, creative content. Personal essays, reflection papers, and creative stories and poems all focus on originality, and much of the instruction surrounding them involves learning to harness the creative muse. Even research papers, term papers, and reports are focused on collecting data and sources into an original, critical argument. Secondary schools and universities teach *inventio* as originality.

In business communication, on the other hand, originality is much less of a priority. In fact, most communication in the workplace crafts existing ideas, text, or documents into rhetorically appropriate forms. Therefore, teaching invention to students of business communication needs to be more about refocusing their efforts away from originality towards understanding the situation and the receiver, making and achieving goals for the communication that align with business goals, and being efficient and ethical in their use of existing information. This approach is in line with classical concepts of *inventio*, which rely heavily on *imitatio* rather than original inspiration. Cicero wrote,

> Let this, then, be the first of my precepts, to point out to the student whom he should imitate, and in such a manner that he may most carefully copy the chief excellencies of him whom he takes for his model.
>
> *(De Oratore 2.XXII)*

Cicero goes on to warn against imitating "what is easy, or what is remarkable, or almost faulty; . . . But he who shall act as he ought must first of all be very careful in making this choice" (*De Oratore* 2.XXII). Like ancient orators, students of business communication need to be pointed toward those individuals, styles, and genres which they should imitate as they produce their own messages.

But simply imitating individuals, styles, and genres may not be enough to help students become both nimble and efficient as business rhetors. In workplace communication, *inventio*, and, by extension, *imitatio*, "is a complex process that allows historical texts to serve as equipment for future rhetorical production" (Leff, 1997, pp. 201, 203). Workers are often working with vast libraries of previously written texts. After all, a quarterly earnings report is produced every single quarter, and nearly every customer service email has been written in some form before. An efficient worker understands how to draw upon existing documents to create updated documents specific to the rhetorical situation. For most of the actual business communication that happens in the workplace, *inventio* is the process of assessing the situation and the receiver, gathering appropriate existing text, and modifying that text to meet the needs of both the situation and the receiver. While learning the forms and expectations of genres teach students *what* to imitate, teaching them to navigate and repurpose existing text teaches them to consider how to "most carefully copy the chief excellencies of [that which] he takes for his model" (*De Oratore* 2.XXII).

In teaching students *inventio* to "first . . . find out what [they] should say" (*De Oratore* 1.XXXI), instructors need to provide them with theoretical and practical tools to draw on "the full light of [their] intellect" (*De Oratore* 1.XXXIII). In the next section, this chapter discusses one such effort to provide a set of communication tools "that transcends particular genres and persists within students long after they have left the business communication classroom" (Lucas & Rawlins, 2015, p. 168). Later, the chapter will return to the discussion of *inventio* to show how introducing and foregrounding the rhetorical canons while instructing students in practical competencies can help students become better communicators who are more prepared for a shifting business communication landscape.

The Competency Approach

The idea of better preparing students for a world where genres are changing and being replaced has led some instructors to explore different approaches to teaching business communication. In 2015, Lucas and Rawlins proposed a pivot away from teaching documents and conventions and a move toward helping students develop core competencies in connection with setting specific goals for specific audiences. This approach grew out of a practical need—employers reported that graduating students were ill-prepared to communicate in the workplace. Lucas and Rawlins found that at least some of the problem of poor preparation was caused by terminology—business communication instructors and employers were simply using different terms, which caused confusion among students who were trying to adapt to new workplaces. But other parts of the problem were caused by the students' inability to transfer their skills to the workplace or to adapt their knowledge to different communication challenges.

Based on these findings, Lucas and Rawlins reworked the content of a genre-based approach to teaching business communication into a system that uses structure, language, and evaluation tools familiar to both business students and employers. It uses a simplified and consistent framework for teaching competencies, evaluating students, and assessing programmatic goals. While both Lucas and Rawlins have strong theoretical backgrounds (in communication theory and rhetorical theory, respectively), this pivot toward a competency-based approach was specifically focused on practicality for teaching, learning, and transfer into the workplace. This section provides an overview of the Lucas-Rawlins competency-based approach to teaching business communication.

Background

Competency-based education has been a rising trend in communication courses. The driving idea behind this trend is that students should be taught and evaluated on their development of specific skills, rather than their ability to complete certain assignments or documents. In competency-based courses, students focus on one competency at a time, and then are evaluated on it in different applications. Some competency-based systems allow students to move at their own pace until they are able to adequately demonstrate certain skills (Lynch & Murranka, 2002; Murranka & Lynch, 1999). Other systems are tied to the specific expectations of an industry, such as the accounting communication course created by Sharifi, McCombs, Fraser, and McCabe (2009). Lucas and Rawlins (2015), however, base their approach heavily on Dannels (2002), who identified five core competencies for speaking, which were used as the foundation for both instruction and evaluation in her classes. In all of the approaches, one goal is to "bridge the gap between school and the workplace" (Lucas & Rawlins, 2015, p. 169; Biemans et al., 2009) in a way that the competencies "[are] broad enough to apply to a range of business communication tasks and [are] specific enough that quality standards could be clearly defined" (Lucas & Rawlins, 2015, p. 170). Competency-based systems directly address the challenges associated with changing and evolving genres of business communication. Where genre-based approaches teach successful communication practices within the context of specific genres, the competency-based approach teaches genre-awareness as part of a larger system of communication competencies. The core idea is that rather than instructing students on how to create specific kinds of documents, a competency-based system helps students develop qualities that apply to any kind of document, presentation, or other communication task. In essence, the competency-based approach is a pivot that incorporates many of the ideas of a genre-based approach within a practical framework, which is described below.

Overview

Lucas and Rawlins (2015) propose a framework for teaching business communication based on two overarching principles and five core competencies (Figure 2.1). These principles and competencies are modeled on Dannels (2002) but are adapted for specific use in business communication. Lucas and Rawlins developed the content of the principles and competencies based on interviews with business professionals and reviews of job listings. The names for the competencies were also drawn from this research, based especially on the qualities that students were said to lack. The names of the principles and competencies were then assigned based on their ability to be "broad enough to apply to a range of

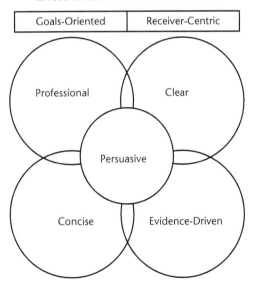

Effective Business Communication

Goals-Oriented	Receiver-Centric

Professional   Clear

Persuasive

Concise   Evidence-Driven

FIGURE 2.1   Lucas and Rawlins's (2015) Competency Model for Business Communication. This model shows two theoretical principles (goals-oriented and receiver-centric) and five core competencies (professional, clear, concise, evidence-driven, and persuasive) as part of an interconnected system of effective communication.

business communication tasks and specific enough that quality standards could be clearly defined" (Lucas & Rawlins, 2015, p. 170). Eventually Lucas and Rawlins settled on a set of seven adjectives that, while they present some grammatical difficulties, are easily understood by both students and employers: goals-oriented, receiver-centric, professional, clear, concise, evidence-driven, and persuasive. One additional advantage of these adjectives is that they are adaptable themselves. So, the competency professional can mean "professional demeanor," but it can also be used in *professional tone, professional document design,* or even *professional dress.*

The principles and competencies are taught in sequence and scaffolded in a way that each assignment incorporates the competencies that have been taught so far in the semester. In the final project and final exam, students are asked to demonstrate their skill in combining the principles and competencies by responding to a complex business situation in rhetorically appropriate ways.

Guiding Theoretical Principles

The starting points for this competency approach to teaching business communication are two overarching theoretical principles: goals-oriented and receiver-centric. These two principles provide the foundational ideas for developing competencies. The students are taught that they are not simply developing skills; they are developing the ability to achieve goals for specific receivers of their communications.

The first principle, that business communication is goals-oriented, connects students with the idea that communication is complex and multilayered. The senders and receivers of messages are working together to create meaning with the intent to accomplish business goals. Most importantly, this principle teaches that every message includes three interconnected layers of meaning: instrumental, relational, and identity (Adler et al., 2013). The *instrumental* meaning of a message focuses on what the message is intended to accomplish, such as conveying information or persuading someone to make a decision. The *relational* meaning of a message is the implied relationship between the sender and receiver, which is often communicated through tone and word choice rather than explicitly stated. The *identity* meaning is related to how the receiver of the message views the sender, based on the content, tone, and presentation of the message.

The goals-oriented principle, then, asks students to recognize the layers of meaning and to articulate specific, strategic goals for those layers. For each assignment in a competency-based approach, students complete an initial exercise where they answer these questions:

1. What do I hope to accomplish with this message?
2. What kind of relationship do I have with the receiver?
3. What kind of relationship do I want to create with the receiver?
4. How do I want the receiver to view me?

These questions help students understand that their communication tasks are doing more than simply responding to a question or providing a report. By taking time to set specific goals, students learn how to create a framework for their communications. This approach emphasizes that these same goals should be addressed for any kind of communication, from the shortest social media post to the longest, most complicated formal document.

The second principle, receiver-centric, operates in connection with the first, goals-oriented. In fact, the two principles are two sides of the same coin: Where goals-oriented business communication addresses the three communication goals of the sender of a message, a receiver-centric message addresses the interests, concerns, and goals of the receiver. One of the primary lessons students learn is that "the receiver of the message is the ultimate arbiter of meaning" (Lucas & Rawlins, 2015, p. 174). It is how the message is interpreted and acted on by the receiver that determines whether the message is successful. Therefore, students are taught to anticipate the needs and the reactions of the receiver (or receivers)—not as vague, amorphous potential receivers, but as targeted individuals or groups of individuals with specific needs, goals, and preferences. Again, for each assignment in the course, students are required to ask questions about their receivers:

1. Who are my intended receivers (primary, secondary, and tertiary)?
2. What information do my receivers need to process and act on my instrumental message?
3. What kind of relationship do the receivers have or want with me?
4. What kinds of expectations, biases, and sensitivities do the receivers have that could influence how they perceive my identity?

Being receiver-centric, then, takes the three goals senders set for themselves and refocuses them on the goals of the receivers. With a combination of carefully articulated sender's goals and the receiver's anticipated goals, students are better prepared to address most communication tasks.

Core Competencies

These two theoretical principles set the foundation for a set of core competencies that students in the course are asked to develop: professional, clear, concise, evidence-driven, and persuasive. While each of the competencies can stand on its own to enable effective communication, when developed as a set with the goals-oriented and receiver-centric principles as a foundation, they become powerful tools for business communicators to adapt to different communication situations. The competencies are always presented as part of a complete package (see Figure 2.1): visually in the syllabus and slides; conceptually in lectures and discussions; and practically in assignments and assessments. Additionally, the competencies are named with common business terms that are easily recognizable by students, faculty in other business classes, and future employers.

Professional

The first competency is professional, which means acting and communicating appropriately for the business context. While much of a person's professionalism is judged by outward expressions (e.g., the spelling, grammar, and formatting of an email message), the competency itself is a set of carefully cultivated internal and external attitudes and behaviors that find their expression in thoughtful, professional messages. The professional competency is about helping a student become (to paraphrase Quintilian), "a good person skilled at communicating" (Quintilian, 12.1.1). While many possible attributes could be connected to being professional, this competency focuses on three traits: (1) *care*, which involves an attention to details, such as grammar, punctuation, and formatting; (2) *courtesy*, which involves observing professional etiquette and demonstrating appropriate tact and emotional control (Fritz, 2013); and (3) *conventionality*, which is connected to understanding and conforming to professional expectations in any form of communication. The professional competency helps students connect their behavior and communication practices with their instrumental, relational, and identity goals.

Clear

The second competency is clear, which means making all messages easy to interpret and act upon. This competency is one of the traits nearly universally identified by academics, professionals, and employers as a necessity for effective business communication. For example, Garner (2012) writes that "anything that requires undue effort from [your readers] won't be read with full attention—and is bound to be misunderstood" (p. 44). When placed within the structure of the other competencies, however, clear takes on additional purpose as it connects with the students' abilities to meet their communication and business goals. In the course, the clear competency comprises four components: (1) identifying a central purpose, (2) adhering to an organizational pattern, (3) using clear language, and (4) creating a clear visual design. These four components help students understand that being clear requires a holistic approach to the message where every word, sentence, paragraph, and visual element is understandable and contributes to the goals of the message.

Concise

The third competency is concise, which means delivering all of the needed information in as efficient a message (in any written or oral genre) as possible (Garner, 2012; Jones, 2011; Morrone, 2013). The students are taught first to plan a comprehensive message, one that includes the information, background, and any other details that the receiver may need. They are encouraged to look for places where receivers may be confused or less informed. From that beginning, the students then edit the content for concision in order to deliver the required information efficiently. In the process, they are encouraged to continually address their own communication goals and the goals of their receivers. The central idea of this competency is that concise means much more than simply "short"; rather, it means "complete and efficient."

Evidence-driven

The fourth competency is evidence-driven, which means "selecting, interpreting, and presenting credible and relevant data" (Lucas & Rawlins, 2015, p. 179). Business communicators need to present convincing arguments supported by evidence in order to get others to act on their messages. In many cases, this evidence includes "numerically rich" (Dannels, 2002) data, but in business it also often includes extensive qualitative evidence. Students must learn to base their messages on solid evidence and to present that evidence effectively and efficiently. The evidence-driven competency includes three components: (1) using better evidence, which focuses on helping students identify and analyze credible data sources; (2) using evidence better, which focuses on the incorporation, explanation, and presentation of evidence in a written or oral message; and (3) citing sources appropriately. These three components help students to see evidence as a vital part of communicating better.

Persuasive

The final competency is persuasive, which is the culmination of all of the other competencies. In the course, students are taught that they are always being persuasive, both explicitly, such as when they are asking for a specific action, and implicitly, in their day-to-day messages and behaviors. The persuasive competency focuses on helping them identify opportunities for persuasion and to make strategic plans to accomplish their goals. This includes combining and employing the other four competencies effectively in every message. Additionally, the students are taught three specific tools for persuasion: (1) making points, which involves going beyond simple discussion into actual rhetorical arguments; (2) connecting evidence, which means strategically using data and other evidence in connection with the overall rhetorical arguments; and (3) being ethical in their approach to persuasion by using complete information and avoiding deceptive practices.

When taught and used together, the two theoretical principles and five core competencies of business communication provide students with a comprehensive framework for addressing real communication situations. This practical approach helps bridge the classroom and the workplace by preparing students to operate in traditional business communication genres as well as in current and emerging genres.

Connecting *Inventio* to *Praxis*

The Lucas and Rawlins (2015) framework for teaching business communication through a competency approach is a practical way to help prepare students for constantly changing genres of communication. The Lucas-Rawlins focus on *praxis* rather than rhetorical theory shows early promise of improving how students internalize and transfer communication knowledge from the classroom to the workplace. This focus on praxis is an increasing trend in university business communication courses, with a wide variety of genres for instructors to cover and an increased focus across academia on preparing students for employment. Some may even argue that a rhetorical approach to business communication is outdated or too theoretical for practical-minded business students. But business communication courses, perhaps more than even basic composition courses, need to be founded on sound rhetorical principles. As Burke (1969) wrote,

> For rhetoric as such is not rooted in any past condition of human society. It is rooted in an essential function of language itself, a function that is wholly realistic, and is continually born anew; the use of language as a symbolic means of inducing cooperation in beings that by nature respond to symbols.
>
> *(p. 43)*

While Burke was writing about language in society as a whole, his argument that rhetoric's "wholly realistic" function is a means of "inducing cooperation" perfectly describes the goals of modern business communication classes. Students are not taking business communication courses to learn to write essays, poetry, or even research papers. They are taking the courses to learn about using language to do business in order to get jobs, develop their professional *ethos*, contribute value to their company and community, and earn a good living. This purpose of business communication courses—which is generally agreed upon and often explicitly discussed in classes—is entirely practical, "wholly realistic," and fundamentally rhetorical. All business and, therefore, business communication, is conducted with other people who need to be convinced to act in a certain way. In other words, the praxis of business communication is entirely in line with this theoretical rhetorical foundation.

Competency-based curriculum, in particular, could meld theory and practice in a way that makes sense to students, instructors, and administrators. In the Lucas-Rawlins system, students understand the wording of the competencies, since they are drawn from research into actual workplace usage. The students also appreciate the focus on developing skills and applying them in a variety of workplace situations. But the two principles and five competencies could also be firmly based in rhetorical theory, which would help students to understand the rhetorical power of becoming competent in communication. For instructors and administrators, the competency approach can provide a practical framework to create assignments and program assessments that are tied to rhetorical theory but can be quantified in their successful implementation in the classroom and transfer into the workplace. For all three groups, the competencies could provide an accessible connection between ancient rhetorical principles and modern business communication practices, if the foundational principles of the rhetorical canon were more explicitly discussed and connected to the practical materials.

There are already elements of rhetorical theory in the Lucas-Rawlins competency-based approach to business communication, particularly in its increased attention to the rhetorical canon of *inventio* (although it is not called that in the system). The system's design requires students to go through a formal process of invention for each in-class exercise, assignment, and exam. During the first week of the semester, after being taught the principle of being goals-oriented, the students are expected to articulate three goals for every piece of communication they produce during the course. They are also shown examples of unsuccessful and successful messages and asked to analyze what the goals of the communication should have been for the situation and how well the piece of communication met those goals. For example, during the first week the students are given a situation where a student has a grade complaint for a college course. In small groups, they discuss what they want to accomplish in their instrumental, relational, and identity goals by sending an email to the professor. Generally, they decide they want to get their grade changed (or at least explained); they want to build or repair their relationship with the professor, which means they will be respectful and professional in their email; and they want the professor to view them as competent and worthy of a grade adjustment. With the goals set, the students are then shown an actual grade complaint email, which they evaluate according to the goals they have set. The class discusses the potential outcomes of the example email and compares those against the desired outcomes. This exercise proves to be a powerful lesson in how basic preparation can produce much better practical results.

Students are taught to do similar exercises for the second principle, receiver-centric. For this principle, they work through another side of invention by analyzing their receivers to understand the receivers' goals and concerns. When paired with the communication goals the students have already set, receiver-centric communication deepens their understanding of what content should be in a message.

As the course moves on to the competencies, each of the five competencies is explicitly connected back to being goals-oriented and receiver-centric. For example, students learn that their level of professionalism and overall tone in an email depends on their goals and on their relationship with the receiver. They learn that being clear is not something to do simply because it is subjectively better but to be clear because clarity is objectively proven to help them achieve better outcomes. They learn similar lessons about being concise, evidence-driven, and persuasive. The overall goals are to help the students learn the benefits of a formalized writing process and to develop habits of planning out messages with clear goals, targeted receivers, and focused plans for employing the five competencies to their best effect.

One of the key lessons for the students is that the process is beneficial no matter the length or complexity of the piece of communication. They are encouraged to go through the same process for the shortest social media post and the longest formal document. The complexity of their analysis differs, of course, but the basic steps are the same. For example, if a student is given the situation of responding to a customer's angry tweet, his or her invention process could look like the following:

Set Goals

1. Instrumental: I need to respond to this customer's complaint about service times with an apology and explanation.
2. Relational: I want to repair the relationship with this customer by properly addressing the complaint.
3. Identity: I need to make sure I represent my company well to everyone who reads this tweet.

Analyze Receivers

This customer is angry but seems reasonable. But other people are paying attention to the problem, because they are retweeting it, and the national news has picked it up. It may be hard to satisfy everyone, but my first priority needs to be this one customer.

For longer documents, the goals may be much more detailed, and the receiver analysis may contain a breakdown of specific goals for each of the different groups who may get the message. As the process is repeated in class and in the assignments, students become more accustomed to doing it naturally and often report their own experiences of stopping to think before sending an email or even a personal social media update.

The goals and the receiver analysis create the foundation for writing a message, but they also provide a tool for self-analysis and grading. The students are taught to set their goals and analyze their receivers before writing their message but then to use those goals and that analysis to review the message before finalizing it. Instructors use the student's articulated goals and receiver analysis as part of grading the assignment, first giving feedback on the goals and the analysis and then assessing the message on how well it meets the specific goals the student defined, rather than how the message meets a more arbitrary set of goals defined by the instructor.

The Lucas-Rawlins competency approach is already employing elements of solid rhetorical theory, though without acknowledging the theoretical elements in the classroom. The system provides students with practical applications of the rhetorical canon, particularly in the focus on *inventio* as a central element of successful communication. In its current framework, however, the competency approach emphasizes the practice of communication as the primary focus, especially with businesslike terms, actual workplace examples, and a practical approach to every communication problem. In the next section, this chapter examines the possible benefits of foregrounding *inventio* in a competency-based approach to teaching business communication.

Foregrounding *Inventio* in *Praxis*

A competency-based approach to teaching business communication can be a successful strategy for students, teachers, and administrators. The balance of practical approaches to workplace problems with sound rhetorical theory strengthens students' preparation for a rapidly shifting communication landscape. The system may be made even more effective, however, by foregrounding some rhetorical principles in instruction, exercises and assignments, and assessment.

As outlined above, the competency approach is already implicitly connected to the rhetorical canon, particularly *inventio*. When presented without the context of the canon, however, the competencies may appear to both students and administrators as a trendy—but effective—pedagogical approach. Connecting the competencies to the rhetorical canon, even in subtle ways, shows that it is a system that can stand on theoretically sound, universal principles of rhetoric that can be applied in any situation. It lifts the competency approach from being simply another pedagogical strategy to being a tool that bridges the ancient rhetorical canons with modern business practices.

For the Lucas-Rawlins competency-based approach, incorporating the canons involves a simple revision to the visual representation of the principles and competencies by adding a third level representing the foundational rhetorical principles (see Figure 2.2). The graphic clearly shows the relationships between the elements while preserving the visual emphasis on the core competencies. As this graphic is included in syllabi, presentation slides, assignment sheets, and other materials, students expect to see the connections among the canons, the competencies, and the communication principles.

The graphic cannot stand on its own, of course. Instructors would need to enhance their discussions of the competencies with introductions connecting them to the rhetorical canons. As shown in earlier sections of this chapter, those connections are especially relevant to the canon *inventio*. The various activities of the two principles and five core competencies that need to happen before composition of the message could be grouped together under the term *Invention*. This not only grounds the activities in rhetorical theory but also provides students with an understanding of when certain actions should take place, such as setting clear goals, analyzing receivers, and planning strategies for the other competencies. The

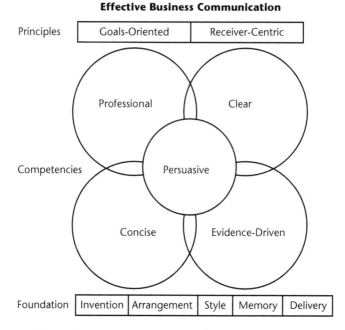

FIGURE 2.2 With a slight revision, the Lucas and Rawlins (2015) model foregrounds the rhetorical canon as the foundation of the principles and competencies, thereby better connecting students to the theoretical basis of the practical skills they are learning.

grouping of actions by canon creates a clear structure that is both theoretically sound and practically applicable.

Because the competency-based approach is designed to help better prepare students for workplace experiences—particularly those that involve different and changing genres of communication—rhetorical theory should be taught and incorporated into assignments and assessments as a means of enhancing the *praxis*. Students should be able to connect with rhetorical theory through practical approaches to business communication. In other words, the rhetorical canons are employed in the classroom to provide a foundation and support for the practice of communication rather than communication being employed as a viewfinder into the depths of rhetorical theory.

Conclusion

This chapter has explored how the competency-based approach to teaching business communication can be linked with the rhetorical canons to provide a richer communication experience for students. Connecting Ciceronian rhetoric with the Lucas and Rawlins (2015) system of principles and competencies creates opportunities for both instructors and students. Foregrounding rhetorical principles in classroom discussions, assignments, and assessments provides a stronger foundation for developing core competencies. The goal is for the principles and the skill-sets based on the principles to connect, thereby guiding students to be stronger communicators who can adapt to any situation or audience. In addition, helping students understand the nuances of *inventio* in connection with developing practical competencies can help them navigate the tricky waters between the efficient reuse of business communication content and the unethical practice of plagiarism.

Business communication instructors are tasked with preparing their students to be skilled, nimble rhetors who can respond to difficult situations and changing genres with professionalism and understanding. Clearly articulating the existing connections between *inventio* and *praxis* in an explicitly rhetorically based core competency approach can better prepare business communication students for constantly changing workplace environments in the modern world.

References

Adler, R. B., Elmhorst, J. M., & Lucas, K. (2013). *Communicating at work: Strategies for success in business and the professions* (11th ed.). New York: McGraw-Hill.

Biemans, H., Wesselink, R., Gulikers, J., Schaafsma, S., Verstegen, J., & Mulder, M. (2009). Towards competence-based VET: Dealing with the pitfalls. *Journal of Vocational Education & Training, 61*, 267–286.

Burke, K. (1969). *A rhetoric of motives*. Berkeley, CA: University of California Press.

Chui, M., Manyika, J., Bughin, J., Dobbs, R., Roxburgh, C., Sarrazin, H., . . . Westergren, M. (2012). *The social economy: Unlocking value and productivity through social technologies*. New York: McKinsey Global Institute.

D'Angelo, F. J. (1975). *A conceptual theory of rhetoric*. Cambridge: Winthrop.

Dannels, D. P. (2002). Communication across the curriculum and in the disciplines: Speaking in engineering. *Communication Education, 51*, 254–268.

Fritz, J. M. H. (2013). *Professional civility: Communicative virtue at work*. New York: Peter Lang.

Gadamer, H. G. (1982). *Truth and method* (Barden, G., & Cumming, J., Eds. and Trans.). New York: Crossroad.

Garner, B. A. (2012*). HBR guide to better business writing*. Boston, MA: Harvard Business Review Press.

Gill, B. (2013). E-mail: Not dead, evolving. *Harvard Business Review, 91*(6), 32–33.

Guffey, M. E. (2015). *Business communication: Process and product* (8th ed.). Boston, MA: Cengage.

Jones, C. G. (2011). Written and computer-mediated accounting communication skills: An employer perspective. *Business Communication Quarterly, 74*, 247–271.

Kamberelis, G., & Scott, K. D. (1992). Other people's voices: The coarticulation of texts and subjectivities. *Linguistics and Education, 4*, 359–403.

LeFevre, K. B. (1987). *Invention as a social act*. Carbondale, IL: Southern Illinois University Press.

Leff, M. (1997). Hermeneutical rhetoric. In W. Jost & M. J. Hyde (Eds.), *Rhetoric and hermeneutics in our time*. New Haven, CT: Yale University Press.

Locker, K. O., & Kienzler, D. (2013). *Business and administrative communication* (10th ed.). New York: Mc-Graw Hill.

Lucas, K., & Rawlins, J. D. (2015). The competency pivot: Introducing a revised approach to the business communication curriculum. *Business and Professional Communication Quarterly, 78*(2), 167–193.

Lynch, D. H., & Murranka, P. (2002). Competency-based instruction in business and management communication courses taught by Association for Business Communication member faculty. *Journal of Education for Business, 77*, 159–163.

Miller, J. E. Jr. (1974). Rediscovering the rhetoric of imagination. *College Composition and Communication, 25*, 360–367.

Morrone, M. (2013, April). Measuring conciseness in business writing: Process and implications. Association for Business Communication Midwestern/Southeastern U.S. conference. Louisville, KY.

Murranka, P. A., & Lynch, D. (1999). Developing a competency-based fundamentals of management communication course. *Business Communication Quarterly, 62*(3), 9–23.

NACE. (2017). *Job outlook 2017*. Bethlehem, PA: National Association of College and Employers.

Project Management Institute. (2013). *The high cost of low performance: The essential role of communications*. Newtown Square, PA: Project Management Institute.

Russ, T. L. (2009). The status of the business communication course at U.S. colleges and universities. *Business Communication Quarterly, 72*, 395–413.

Rentz, K., & Lentz, P. (2018). *Business communication: A problem-solving approach*. New York: Mc-Graw Hill.

Sharifi, M., McCombs, G. B., Fraser, L. L., & McCabe, R. K. (2009). Structuring a competency-based accounting communication course at the graduate level. *Business Communication Quarterly, 72*, 177–199.

Silverman, R. E. (2012, February 14). Where's the boss? Trapped in a meeting. *Wall Street Journal*. Retrieved from http://online.wsj.com/news/articles/SB10001424052970204 64260457721501350456 7548.

3

RHETORICAL GRAMMAR IN THE BUSINESS COMMUNICATION CLASSROOM

Cultural Capital vs. Privileged Rhetoric

Paula J. Lentz

Introduction

Since the middle of the twentieth century, grammar instruction has been a point of contention, particularly in composition classrooms. Questions of what constitutes a standard English, who gets to decide the standard, the marginalization of dialects and culturally specific Englishes, the gendered nature of some grammar rules, and research indicating that grammar knowledge does not improve students' writing all contribute to the argument that grammar instruction has little (if any) place in the composition classroom. In fact, to advocate for a standard for English is contrary to promoting equality in the classroom and instead promotes the notion of a privileged rhetoric. As a former director of composition told me,

> When you teach that there is a standard English grammar in business communication, you are teaching a privileged rhetoric, you are telling students that their use of the language to express themselves is inferior to that of your own, and you are undermining the purpose of a liberal arts education.

That is an accusation that we as business communication instructors should take seriously. The teaching of a standard English at the expense of marginalizing others' use of the language is bad pedagogy and does, indeed, wrongly perpetuate the idea of a privileged rhetoric. But is that what we are really doing when we teach grammar in the business communication classroom? The goal of a business communication course is to prepare students for the communication competencies they need to enter the workforce as either an intern or entry-level employee and to prepare them to meet the communication demands of their upper-division business courses, many of which require them to communicate via the genres (and thus follow the genre conventions) in their business disciplines. Common to all business communication is that it is audience-centered, builds goodwill, adapts to the context, and promotes a professional image for writers and speakers and their companies; consequently, teaching the grammar that supports students' abilities to function in these business contexts is not only helpful but necessary for enabling students to adapt to the various Englishes, cultures, rhetorics, and language demands of the workplace.

This chapter traces the history of grammar instruction and contextualizes its value in the development of the rhetorical canon of style (*elocutio*) and the projection of a professional *ethos*. Also discussed are the reasons for the decline of grammar instruction in the field of composition. The primary focus of this chapter, however, is how the explicit, rhetorical instruction of grammar as a means of developing students' competencies in the rhetorical canon of style enables them to develop the social, cultural, and economic capital required for success in the workplace (Bourdieu, 1986). The outcome of this discussion is a presentation of a pedagogical strategy of grammar as rhetoric that instructors may find useful in their business communication classrooms.

For the purpose of this chapter, "grammar" is used a blanket term that refers to language competence in the workplace sense—the ability to present written and oral communication in a way that communicates a message, builds a positive business relationship with the audience, and enhances the speaker's or writer's professional image. Consequently, any language feature, including but not limited to spelling, punctuation, mechanics, and word choice, falls under the term "grammar" in this chapter.

The Traditional Role of Grammar Instruction in a Liberal Arts Education

Martineau (2016) describes grammar instruction—part of the classical liberal arts curriculum that also includes instruction in logic and rhetoric—as "a 2,500-year-old course in clear thinking" (p. 3). In fact, Martineau notes that from the era of the classical Greeks and Romans to medieval times to the present day, grammar, logic, and rhetoric (the "trivium") were once considered central to a classical liberal arts education along with math, science, and the arts. Of special note is that a classical Greek understanding of this trivium is that these liberal arts disciplines "train and refine the core faculties of the learner" and that "mastery of these special subjects 'liberates' a person into rational, intellectual, and civic life . . . and provides a foundation from which all other subjects are learned" (p. 2). Grammar, as the first of the subjects taught in the trivium, provides students with the understanding of the structure of the language they need to engage in the study of logic and then rhetoric (McGlinn, 2002). Thus, the ability to effectively deploy rhetorical strategies that result in clear and persuasive communication does not (and cannot) exist apart from a student's grammatical competence, as grammatical knowledge provides people with options for making rhetorical choices; students must learn and practice the interrelatedness of grammar, logic, and rhetoric to be competent communicators (Joseph, 2002).

Although grammars date to ancient Sanskrit (Holley, 2016), Aristotle classified words in what we would recognize today as parts of speech (e.g., nouns, verbs, and adjectives) and saw them as necessary tools for the study of logic (Aristotle, 1889); the study of logic would be followed in a classical liberal arts education by the study of rhetoric (McGlinn, 2002). The connection between grammar and rhetoric, then, is clear and in fact essential in Aristotle's use of *logos, ethos,* and *pathos* in the practice of "persuasion by all available means." His concern was primarily the invention or mapping of an argument using these three means of persuasion, and it is this interconnectedness among grammar, logic, and rhetoric that leads us to the rhetorical canon of style (*elocutio*) and its connection to a writer's or speaker's professional *ethos.*

Grammar Instruction in the Rhetorical Canon

Aristotle's work was fundamental nearly 300 years later in Cicero's development of the five rhetorical canons: invention, arrangement, style, memory, and delivery. Style, the canon of discussion in this chapter, is primarily associated with the features of language that impact how a message is delivered. Nicgorski (2013/14) notes that as a result of study of and access to the works of Aristotle, Cicero was described by Dante as "Rome's best Aristotelian" (p. 34). Indeed, Aristotle's attention to *pathos* and the impact of the speaker's character (*ethos*) on an audience were of particular interest and utility to Cicero in his development of the five canons (May & Wisse, 2001), particularly in the canon of style: correct Latin and clarity. Of the importance of grammar to style, Cicero (2001) says "we cannot hope, if someone cannot speak correct Latin, that he will speak with distinction" (p. 235). He establishes the need for correct Latin, saying that to appear credible, people must "use [words] in proper case, tense, class, and number so that there is no confusion, want of agreement, or incorrect order" (p. 235). Regarding clarity, Cicero also advises that if speakers want to be effective, they will adapt their words to their audience:

> And really, let us not spend more time on the second point, on discussing in what ways we can see to it that what we say will be understood—obviously by speaking correct Latin, by employing words in common use, that properly designate the things we want to be signified and indicated, by avoiding ambiguous words or language, excessively long periodic sentences, and spun-out metaphors, by not breaking up the train of thought, confusing the chronology, missing up people, or muddling the order.
>
> *(p. 237)*

Quintilian, approximately 50 years after Cicero, used these five canons in his work to describe the ideal education. Quintilian specifically tied the study of grammar to style, saying, "The grammarian has need of no small portion of eloquence that he may speak fluently and aptly on [music, astronomy, and philosophy]" (Quintilian, 1987, p. 29, Book 1). But Quintilian also advises that speakers and writers choose wisely in elements of style. He says that

> style is revealed both in individual words and in groups of words. As regards the former, we must see that they are Latin, clear, elegant, and well-adapted to produce the desired effect. As regards the latter, they must be correct, aptly placed and adorned with suitable figures.
>
> *(Book 8, pp. 196–197)*

But he cautions that grammar must be adaptable and appropriate for the audience, saying "our words should have nothing provincial or foreign about them" (Quintilian, pp. 196–197, Book 8). While it is true that Cicero and Quintilian were concerned with grammar primarily as it regards oral communication, Quintilian also includes written communication in his many books in *Institutio Oratoria*, in which he details the ideal education for preparing students to become engaged and impactful citizens. Furthermore, both frequently refer to the importance of applying the features of good grammar/style to written communication. Cicero (2001), for instance, says that "writing perfects the ability of actually arranging and combining words, not in a poetic, but in a kind of oratorical measure and rhythm" (p. 91), while Quintilian says

> It is in writing that eloquence has its roots and foundations, it is writing that provides that holy of holies where the wealth of oratory is stored, and whence it is produced to meet the demands of sudden emergencies. It is of the first importance that we should develop such strength as will not faint under the toil of forensic strife nor be exhausted by continual use.
>
> *(Book 10, p. 93)*

The grammar instruction established by Aristotle, Cicero, and Quintilian as foundational to the development of style largely still informs what and how we teach in business communication today. You-view, active and passive voice, agreement, parallel structure, coordination and subordination, and even word choice—all are rhetorical strategies related to style, and all require a student to have a fundamental understanding of English grammar that is sufficient to apply them. And, like the educators of Aristotle's, Cicero's, and Quintilian's times, we teach our business communication students grammar with the intent of making them more impactful and engaged citizens in both their communities and their workplaces.

The Shift from Grammar as Rhetoric to Grammar as Linguistics

The classical Greek model was the standard for a liberal arts education in the United States through the early twentieth century, with the trivium (grammar, logic, and rhetoric) as a central component. Interestingly, while logic and rhetoric are still central to composition instruction today, grammar is not. Mulroy (2003) traces the beginning of the demise of grammar instruction in the United States to the 1925 doctoral work of prominent linguist Charles Fries. Mulroy asserts that while Fries's approach to the scientific study of language was groundbreaking for the field of linguistics, it led to (1) the study of grammar as one of rules governing the use of language rather than as a means of expression in rhetorical context and (2) the conventional wisdom that these rules were only born of scientific study rather than emerging from "intuitive judgements" (p. 5). The result was the teaching of grammar from a highly prescriptive, rule-governed perspective that fell out of favor by the middle of the twentieth century.

However, as teachers abandoned the linguistic approach to teaching grammar in their composition courses, they did not return to the classical approach to grammar instruction as a means of deploying rhetorical strategies. Instead, they largely abandoned grammar instruction altogether, as several microhistories in the field illustrate (Hinson, n.d.; see Table 3.1).

Of course, all of these microhistories are reflected to some extent in both composition and business communication classrooms today. And none of these theoretical frameworks foreground grammar instruction, though Thomas Kent, a key figure in the post-process framework, acknowledges that grammar knowledge is essential background knowledge for writing (Kastman Breuch, 2002); however, as I argue throughout this chapter, grammar must be foregrounded in writing instruction because of its profoundly powerful rhetorical effects.

The absence of any mention of grammar instruction is not surprising. Many in the field of composition are familiar with the NCTE's "Research in Written Composition" report (Braddock, Lloyd-Jones, & Schoer, 1963), which was the first major publication by a national organization to review the research on grammar instruction in the composition classroom and conclude that it had no place there. In fact, the report refers several times to the "harmful effects" of doing so (e.g., pp. 22, 38, and 82). Furthermore, statements throughout the report, such as "if the teacher has been emphasizing rhetorical matters as well as grammar and mechanics, objective tests simply are not valid—they make little or no attempt to measure the larger elements of composition" (p. 45) clearly show that grammar instruction was considered separate from the instruction of rhetoric—a concept completely antithetical to the teaching of writing little more than a half century earlier.

The National Council of Teachers of English (NCTE) has, for the most part, sustained the rhetoric of the "harmful effects" of grammar instruction for nearly 60 years via several position statements. In a position paper from 1985, the NCTE "[affirms] the position that the use of isolated grammar and usage exercises not supported by theory and research is a deterrent to the improvement of students' speaking and writing" ("Resolution," para. 1). A position paper from 1994 ties the "harmful effects" of grammar instruction to the potential marginalization of social groups and encourages that instead of grammar instruction, students "[examine] how 'correctness' in language reflects social-political-economic values; examining how the structure of language works from a descriptive perspective" ("Resolution,"

TABLE 3.1. Microhistories in Rhetoric and Composition* (Hinson, n.d. unless otherwise noted)

Framework and Origin	Theoretical Focus	Pedagogical Practice
Current Traditionalism (1940s–1970s)	Texts have "fixed meanings that can be discovered through close reading and explication" ("Current Traditionalism," para. 3).	Students used models to learn "correct" writing. The five-sentence paragraph essay is the model for writing.
Expressivism (1960s–1970s)	Writing is an art, which makes writers, artists. The teacher facilitates the writer's ability to express him/herself.	Instructors and students engage in freewriting, clustering, and peer review.
Cognitivism (1970s–1980s)	Writing is an individual effort, and writing processes can be judged as correct or incorrect.	Instructors and students recognize that each student's writing process may be unique. Instructors model "ideal" writing processes ("Cognitivism," para. 4).
Cultural Studies (1970s–1980s)	Writing must recognize "marginalized and/ or oppressed groups and the importance of their voices" ("Cultural Studies," para. 3).	Writing is "less about 'correct' grammar and standard English and more about student identity and voice" ("Cultural Studies," para. 4).
Social Constructionism (1980s)	Writing, knowledge, and meaning are a reflection or product of the standards in their discourse community.	Instructors use class discussion, collaborative writing, and assignments that include contextual information.
Critical Pedagogy (1980s–1990s)	The pedagogy is rooted in the work of Paulo Friere and focuses on the role of power and social activism.	Instructors and students discuss "power dynamics, social issues, and activism. Students are urged to write to effect social and political change" (Hinson, n.d.).
Post-Process (1990s)	The theory espouses that writing cannot be reduced to a process. It is often referred to as not having a pedagogical framework.	Teachers are mentors who focus on interaction and discussion with students. Peer tutors also play a role (Kastman Breuch, 2002).

para. 1). A position paper from Shoffner et al. (2017) entitled "What Is English Language Arts Teacher Education?" discusses the language competencies required in an English language arts curriculum but stops short of specifically mentioning grammar instruction as essential to teaching English language arts.

Even when the NCTE's position papers rightly remind us that grammar should never be used to marginalize audiences (NCTE, 1994; Prosenjak, Harmon, Johnson, Bloodgood, & Hazlett, 2002; Shoffner et al., 2017), they ignore the foundational role of grammar in ensuring that we do not. For example, in its paper on gender-inclusive language (Prosenjak et al., 2002), the NCTE advises that "an editor's task is to rewrite whenever necessary to eliminate language that is awkward, inconsistent, or inaccurate. In the case of language inconsistent with these guidelines, the editor's duty is to question the author's vocabulary or usage" ("Implementing the Guidelines," para. 2). But a writer's or editor's ability to accomplish this writing task without an understanding of English grammar and usage—pronoun case, first-person, second person, pronouns, indefinite pronouns, agreement, antecedents, and so on—is surely limited.

It is encouraging, though, to read the NCTE's "Some Questions and Answers About Grammar" position paper (Haussamen et al., 2002), in which its authors state that

> grammar is important because it is the language that makes it possible for us to talk about language . . . We can all do grammar. But to be able to talk about how sentences are built, about the types of words and word groups that make up sentences—that is *knowing about* [sic] grammar . . . But *knowing about* [sic] grammar also helps us understand what makes sentences and paragraphs clear and interesting and precise . . . And *knowing about* [sic] grammar means finding out that all languages and all dialects follow grammatical patterns.
>
> *("Why Is Grammar Important," para. 1 and 2)*

Contextualizing this 2002 position paper on grammar knowledge with the rest of the NCTE position papers provides insight to the reasons for the Council's resistance to grammar instruction. When seen through the lens of rules and prescriptions, grammar instruction does have the potential to marginalize and discriminate, and the NCTE's position that grammar instruction through this lens produces "harmful effects" is understandable. But the 2002 position paper, in reframing "grammar instruction" as "grammar knowledge," returns grammar instruction to its traditional role in the study of language—as essential for developing rhetorical strategy. This one position paper, however, seems to be a relatively small voice among the NCTE's other publications.

Toward a Rhetorical Instruction of Grammar

A rhetorical approach to grammar requires writers and speakers to think first about what they want to accomplish with their communication and then to choose the words, punctuation, voice, sentence structures, and so on that best help them make their argument. In this approach, the traditional rules or standards are fluid and may vary with the audience, context, and purpose of the message, and they ultimately determine the tone, style, and appropriateness of the argument, as well as the speaker's or writer's professional *ethos*. Micciche (2004) describes how she teaches rhetorical grammar by having her students analyze the ways content and grammar come together to make a text meaningful. Because of the inter-connectedness of thought and expression and the extent to which grammatical choices and rhetorical strategies reflect social and cultural practices and beliefs, students must see that

> the grammatical choices we make—including pronoun use, active or passive verb constructions, and sentence patterns—represent relations between writers and the world they live in. Word choice and sentence structure are an expression of the way we attend to the words of others, the way we position ourselves in relation to others.
>
> *(p. 719)*

In other words, the rhetorical focus helps students be aware of the connection between what they say and how they say it. Kolln and Funk (2012) further define the instruction of grammar as teaching a system of choices and then analyzing their rhetorical effects on an audience. The goal of the rhetorical approach to grammar instruction becomes "consciousness raising" regarding students' use of language. That is, "the more that speakers and writers know consciously about their language, the more power they have over it and the better they can make it serve their needs" (Kolln & Funk, 2012, p. xviii). Kolln and Gray (2017) advise students to think of themselves as a "repository" of grammar knowledge (p. 1), which they acquired when they learned a language, and to understand the impact of their grammatical choices on their audience. Kolln and Gray say that "to study grammar in this way—that is, to consider the conscious knowledge of sentence structure as your toolkit—is the essence of rhetorical grammar" (p. 3). Unlike the linguistic approach to grammar instruction that was popular from the first quarter to half of the twentieth century where students learned structures and rules that govern the use of language, the rhetorical approach draws on students' inherent competence and focuses on the patterns that emerge or apply to the rhetorical context or exigence.

Reframing Rhetorical Grammar as Social and Cultural Capital

I hope that by now the need for us to teach grammar as a rhetorical pursuit is clear. Asking students, for example, to memorize 30 rules for comma usage or to always choose "he" or "she" to refer to a singular antecedent or to never end a sentence with a preposition runs counter to basic principles of business communication. Asking students to make grammatical choices based on their business and communication goals is exactly what we want our students to do. Business communication requires that writers and speakers be adaptable and flexible—that the only "correct" grammar is the one that resonates with audience, helps writers and speakers achieve their business goals, and enables them to build their and their companies' professional *ethos*. It is advice that, as we've learned, has remained constant since the time of Aristotle, Cicero, and Quintilian.

So, what are business communication students doing when they make grammatical choices based on their audience and context? They are acquiring what Bourdieu (1986) referred to as "capital" or, in our students' language, the "street cred" that leads an audience to believe that what speaker or writer says is true or right. Bourdieu's (1999) describes these human interactions as an "economy of practice" (p. 45). Within these interactions, an individual's objective is to gain or assert power. Individuals gain and assert power by accumulating or deploying various types of capital.

Types of Capital

Bourdieu (1986) outlines four types of capital. *Social capital* refers to the power or credibility an individual has by virtue of the individual's social network, which could include, for example, a family name or a connection to high-powered or well-known business people. *Economic capital* refers to an individual's worth—the monetary value of all of a person's goods or possessions. *Cultural capital* exists both within and outside the individual. *Embodied cultural capital* includes factors internal to the individual—personality, knowledge, language use, speaking style. *Objectified cultural capital* would be what we call "status symbols": the size of our house, the type of car we drive, or even the cell phone we use. Yes, these items may also be a type of economic capital when viewed in terms of their dollar value, but when viewed as cultural capital, it is what these objects represent (the possession of wealth or social standing) rather than the actual dollar value of the item that gives them their value. *Institutional capital* is the third type of cultural capital, and it refers to academic degrees or professional credentialing that afford people their *ethos*. For example, consider a job posting requiring an individual to have a bachelor's degree. Embedded in that requirement is the assumption (and expectation) that an individual with a bachelor's degree will possess other types of capital (e.g., communication skills, technical aptitude, team skills) as well that make them a better candidate than those, say, with an associate's degree or those with work experience but no degree. A fourth category, *symbolic capital*, refers to an individual's authority or status in the overall social hierarchy; individuals with symbolic power will likely be able to more easily take advantage of the other types of capital they hold.

Social Fields

The interesting thing about capital is that its value is not static. It is arbitrary, ever-changing, and completely dependent on what Bourdieu refers to as "social fields" (1999). These fields are the contexts in which interactions occur. The types of capital valued in one field may or may not hold the same status in another. If individuals want to achieve status, success, or power—in any field—they will have to acquire the necessary capital or strategically deploy the capital they have; and then when they enter other social fields, they must be flexible to adapt, deploy, or acquire capital for that context. In other words, the acquisition of capital is never enough for success; individuals who want to be successful in any social field (including business) must continually assess their capital relative to their audience and adapt or acquire additional or other capital accordingly.

Habitus

One of Bourdieu's (1999) key contributions to understanding capital is the concept of *habitus*, which, simply put, refers to an individual's tendency to act a certain way in a particular social field. Bourdieu (1999) specifically addresses linguistic competency relative to habitus, saying it

> [implies] a certain propensity to speak and to say determinate things (the expressive interest) and a certain capacity to speak, which involves both the linguistic capacity to generate an infinite number of grammatically correct discourses, and the social capacity to use this competence adequately in a determinate situation.
>
> *(p. 37)*

He further notes that a linguistic approach to or understanding of the use of grammar is limited: "Grammar defines meaning only very partially: it is in relation to a market that the complete determination of the signification of discourse occurs" (p. 38). He also says that

> the paradox of communication is that it presupposes a common medium, but one which works . . . only by eliciting and reviving singular, and therefore socially marked, experiences. The all-purpose word in the dictionary, a product of the neutralization of the practical relations within which it functions, has no social existence: in practice, it is always immersed in situations, to such an extent that the core meaning which remains relatively invariant through the diversity of markets may pass unnoticed.
>
> *(p. 39)*

Bourdieu reflects what scholars of rhetoric have been espousing since the time of Aristotle: that language and rhetoric and the grammar that informs them are all context dependent and are meaningful only if people adapt them to the audience; social context; and their rhetorical, business, or communication goals. Our goal, as Kolln and Hancock (2005) say, should be that "we would aim at a program embracing deep and wide knowledge of grammar as highly useful, perhaps proclaiming that ignorance of grammar is far more limiting than knowledge, that it creates a vacuum within which dysfunctional prescriptive norms are enforced" (p. 29).

Exploring the Disconnect

Why, then, with scholarship from all directions that spans over 2,000 years (i.e., classical rhetoric, Kolln and others who advocate for a rhetorical approach to using grammar, Bourdieu), do we let the master narrative of composition theory—that grammar instruction yields only "harmful effects" (Braddock, Lloyd-Jones, & Schoer, 1963) and does not improve the quality of student writing—be the one that dominates? Why do we allow what amounts to a historical blip in which a linguistic model of grammar was inappropriately applied to the teaching of grammar undo the work of the last 2,300 years? We can only imagine how the scholarship on the teaching of grammar would be different over the last 90 years had the lens been a rhetorical one. And we can only speculate on the reasons the field of composition has stuck to its master narrative that grammar instruction does not improve student writing.

Perhaps the reason for adherence to this master narrative is what Veblen or Burke would call "trained incapacity" (Wais, 2005). That is, the composition field sticks to this master narrative because it is one that appears to work well for them. It is so entrenched in the culture of the field that few question it; many loudly and stubbornly promote it; and some may even be relieved that this master narrative releases them of the responsibility for learning, teaching, and assessing grammar altogether. Certainly, not devoting time to the direct instruction of grammar has allowed room in the curriculum for cultural studies, critical pedagogies, and so forth. As Veblen and Burke would say, this master narrative drives what they can "think and know easily" (Wais, 2005, para. 7). Composition instructors and business communication instructors alike would agree that decontextualized instruction of grammar does not work, but it will take a major (and likely difficult and slow) shift of the master narrative to return grammar to its rightful place in composition pedagogy.

In some ways, none of this discussion of the master narrative in composition matters. We are, after all, the field of business communication, not composition, and our student writers have much different rhetorical contexts and exigencies than students in a composition class. And yet, it matters greatly. Some business schools require no writing beyond the freshman composition course. Other business schools require students to take business communication courses offered in English departments that may or may not be taught by instructors with expertise in business communication. Even business communication instructors within business schools will frequently have advanced degrees in English or composition. Thus, this master narrative has the potential to drive what we do in business communication, and consequently, we need to know why we must challenge that narrative at every possible turn when we develop curricula, pedagogy, disciplinary identity, and scholarship specific to business communication as an academic discipline. As I discuss in the next section, businesses require their employees to use a standard English grammar (albeit the standard is a flexible one) for distinct rhetorical purposes; therefore, business communication instructors—whatever their degree or academic department—must be able to teach and ensure that their students learn grammatical standards of the workplace discourse communities they encounter.

Bringing It All Together: Rhetorical Grammar, Bourdieu, and Business Communication

As you have read through this chapter, you may have nodded several times in recognition of the connections among rhetorical grammar, Bourdieu, and business communication. In doing so, you likely connected your teaching of business communication to the many social (i.e., workplace) contexts in which your students use what you are teaching—including grammar. The reason is likely that, as a discipline, business communication has not so much struggled with whether to teach grammar but how and to what extent given all of the other content we teach in our courses. A quick review of journal articles in the Association for Business Communication's *Business and Professional Communication Quarterly* (*BPCQ*) and a quick review of journal articles in *College Composition and Communication* reveal an interesting take on how the fields of business communication and English composition study grammar instruction. By and large, the articles in *BPCQ* contextualize the study of grammar in surveys of what employers want. Articles in *CCC* largely address grammar as nonessential to the acquisition of writing skills or rhetorical competence; its absence is conspicuous in numerous other articles that appear to focus only on rhetorical competence, language competence, or writing competence without reference to grammar instruction at all.

In other words, to my mind, business practitioners have long recognized the importance of grammar to rhetorical contexts and have long sought to teach grammar as the capital students need to acquire to be successful in the workplace, largely because written communication (and oral communication) has long been considered essential for success in in business (e.g., Locker's (1985) study of dunning letters in the sixteenth through twentieth centuries). It is also true, though, that a command of the English language has also historically been associated with membership in middle- or upper-class social standing and that business and commerce themselves have driven the idea that there is a "right" way to use the English language (Longaker, 2015; Bartolotta, 2013). Of course, we should question the value of studying grammar to promote elitism, as doing so marginalizes other culturally, contextually, and rhetorically appropriate uses of the language in business and ignores that a rigid understanding of a standard English is no longer compatible with a global twenty-first-century workplace.

But without an understanding of the English language and its syntax and generally (though not rigidly) applied guidelines for usage, students cannot begin to know how to adapt the use of the English language to the many rhetorical exigencies of the workplace. It is this adaptability that requires an understanding of grammar as rhetorical choice. We already know rhetoric as it applies to business communication; our knowledge of rhetoric is how we know when to be direct or indirect or how to write a persuasive message or how to choose or create the right visual. We are fully poised to get to the place where we apply grammar rhetorically as well.

Aristotle, Cicero, Quintilian, Bourdieu—they all provide a framework for understanding what makes business communication a distinct rhetorical field and thus a distinct academic discipline in which students must use grammar strategically for unique, varied, and distinct rhetorical purposes. Understood at the intersection of classical rhetoric and Bourdieu, grammar instruction becomes an opportunity for business communication instructors to teach students to think less about hard-and-fast rules and more about how the structure of the language rhetorically impacts their audience, their message, and their professional *ethos*. The outcome, ideally, is that students are prepared to navigate the social fields and types of capital required for their success.

A Workplace Definition of Grammar

The linguistic and rhetorical definitions of grammar are largely academic in nature and seek to uncover the optimal way (or "right" way) to use grammar in a particular context. In the workplace, however, grammar is defined more broadly and more colloquially than it is in academic settings and generally in terms of a reader's opinion than by rules that determine what is correct or appropriate. Whether you do a quick Google search of the top grammatical errors that bother employers or whether you look for what employers define as "good" grammar, you will likely get the same results—lists of what bothers employers, not any idea of what they consider "right." Furthermore, what is considered "right" frequently depends upon the rhetorical exigence. Beason (2001), for example, found that employers are bothered by word choice and spelling errors, sentence fragments, comma splices, and fused sentences, but the extent to which they are bothered depends on many factors, such as formality (e.g., a letter vs. a sticky note). Additionally, the impact of the error depends on both textual features (e.g., the resulting lack of clarity or causing the audience to reread a sentence) and extra-textual features that include the reader's "assumptions, memories, and preferences" (p. 47). However, many subjects in Beason's study also commented on the impact of errors on the writer's professional *ethos*: the writer as hasty, careless, uncaring, or uninformed; the writer as a business person who is a faulty thinker, not detail oriented, a poor communicator, poorly educated, or unaware of the tone; and the writer as a representative of the company to customers or in court. Likewise, Coffelt, Baker, and Corey (2016) note that communication competence takes on many different meanings in the workplace but found, generally, that employers expect "good grammar and spelling" and define writing competence much differently than do college instructors (p. 311). Coffelt, Baker, and Corey conclude that employers' expectations "may challenge English educators at a time when pedagogical shifts to analysis and critical thinking skills trump fundamental skill development or reinforcement" (p. 311).

In summary, employers largely define grammar broadly to include any element associated with use of writing or speaking, including spelling, word choice, punctuation, sentence structure, parallelism, and so on. And what we know is that even though they themselves may not know the difference between a dangling modifier and faulty parallelism, or be able to distinguish a gerund from a participle, or even use the grammatical term to describe the error, they know an error when they see it, and errors bother them for reasons of both textual accuracy and professional *ethos*.

The Rhetorical Context of the Workplace

In addition, employers primarily associate "correct" communication with two outcomes relative to professional *ethos* and what Bourdieu would refer to as social, cultural, and symbolic capital: image and the bottom line. Consultant Celia Scaros (2016) provides seven reasons for good grammar in business communication, three of which address first impressions, reputation, and competitive edge and the rest of which address efficiency, productivity, and the avoidance of lawsuits. And Kyle Wiens (2012) is well known for saying:

> Good grammar is credibility, especially on the internet . . . If it takes someone more than 20 years to notice how to properly use 'it's,' then that's not a learning curve I'm comfortable with . . . I've found that people who make fewer mistakes on a grammar test also make fewer mistakes when they are doing something completely unrelated to writing.

Likewise, Grammarly (2013) reviewed 100 LinkedIn profiles and found that individuals whose profiles contained fewer grammar errors were more likely to achieve higher positions in their companies, be promoted more frequently within their companies, and change jobs frequently—a clear connection to social, cultural, economic, and symbolic capital.

Additional research, as well, supports that companies hire students either as interns or entry-level employees based primarily on students' communication skills (e.g., Gilsdorf & Leonard, 2001; Bacon & Anderson, 2004; Brandenberg, 2015; Clokie & Fourie, 2016; Coffelt, Baker, & Corey, 2016; Low, Botes, David, & Allen, 2016; Gray & Koncz, 2017; Mozafar, El-Alayli, & Kunemu, 2017). The relevant question, then, is not "Does grammar knowledge make students good writers?" as composition instructors have been asking for nearly a century but rather "What grammar knowledge helps students make rhetorical choices that enable them to communicate clearly and concisely in the workplace?"

An Instructional Method for Teaching Rhetorical Grammar

For my part, as a business communication instructor, I have used a rhetorical approach to grammar instruction with my students in which we daily ask not only *what* we are doing (e.g., using the objective pronoun case, putting a comma after an introductory clause, or making all items in a series grammatically parallel) but also *why* we are doing it (e.g., to use active vs. passive voice, to subordinate or coordinate information, to be clear and promote smooth reading). In other words, the grammatical rules are not so much rules as they are reasons. And when my students make choices for a reason, they become much more intentional in their use of the language and how their choices impact the success of their message.

My approach is largely informed by the work of Kolln and Gray (2017) and their premise that grammar instruction starts with an acknowledgement that students already come to the classroom with a fair amount of linguistic competence acquired when they learned the English language itself. While I do not cover their full curriculum, this philosophy along with a practice that focuses on what their writing is supposed to accomplish has transformed how I teach grammar in my Advanced Business Writing course.

Before I describe my approach, I have two caveats: (1) I am not a linguist, and I recognize that some of the terminology may not be as fine-tuned or precise as a linguist might use, but my students are not linguists, either. I am more concerned that they can recognize the difference between a clause and a phrase than I am, for example, that they can label a clause as introductory or elliptical. Our curriculum has only so much room and time, and in truth, we stick with learning the very basics of grammar terminology that help them act rhetorically. (2) I have only anecdotal feedback about the effectiveness of my approach from my students and alums who tell me they are more confident not just about their grammar knowledge but also about their writing skills in general. Empirical research on the effects of rhetorical grammar instruction is a topic rich with possibilities.

Setting the Stage

Before they begin their study of phrases and clauses—the heart of rhetorical grammar in my mind—students need to readily recognize the parts of speech. A quick game such as You've Been Sentenced, Mad Libs, Jeopardy, or bingo would work well for a parts of speech review. Again, as people who have learned the English language, students likely come to the classroom with this knowledge; the review helps them call attention to what they already know and does not take a lot of class time. You could also review parts of speech while explaining phrases and clauses.

That said, my students struggle to recognize verbs, particularly linking verbs and helping verbs. Because verbs are the heart of any sentence and because of their importance in recognizing phrases, clauses, active and passive voice, and other rhetorical constructions, I generally do a more intensive review to increase verb recognition, using a worksheet that I have downloaded from the internet that requires students to find a verb in a sentence and match it to its subject.

Moving On to Phrases and Clauses

Once students can identify verbs and their subjects, we move on to distinguishing between phrases and clauses, the two main components of a sentence. Specifically, we discuss the material seen in Table 3.2.

As students see the sample sentences, they begin to see possibilities for how clauses and phrases might come together to form sentences. As a knowledge check, I use a brief worksheet of phrases and clauses that students work in small groups to complete and then share answers with another group or the entire class. From there, we begin our study of rhetorical grammar with the introduction of punctuation patterns.

TABLE 3.2

Clauses: Defined by the presence of a subject + verb combination

Independent:	Example:
Subject + verb = complete thought	The employees attended the training.
Dependent:	Example:
Subject + verb ≠ complete thought	Because they were recently hired
Relative dependent:	Examples:
that + verb	that was on Tuesday
which + verb	which was on Tuesday
who + verb	who attended the training

Phrases: Defined by the absence of a subject + verb combination

Prepositional:	Example: in the employee handbook
in, on, of, with (and many more)	
Infinitive:	Example: to learn the policies
to + verb	
Verbals	Examples:
gerunds, participles	*Filing* is my least favorite task. (Gerund)
	Having finished my filing, I went to lunch. (Participle)

Identifying Punctuation Patterns

I was first introduced to punctuation patterns as a doctoral student when I received a punctuation pattern sheet (Underwood & Kett, 1981) from the instructor who had done her doctoral work at Iowa State. This pattern sheet is publicly available for download at www.public.iastate.edu/~bccorey/105%20 Folder/PuncPatternSheet.doc, and it is one that has served my students and me well. I have added patterns over the years to further enable my students to respond to rhetorical exigencies, but the original 11 patterns offer instructors a great place to start.

The patterns on Iowa State's punctuation pattern sheet are arranged to show how phrases and clauses are combined and punctuated, with the extra spacing providing a visual break between the sentence elements:

#1 Independent clause.
#2 Independent clause ;   independent clause.
#3 Independent clause ;   therefore,   independent clause.
                           however
                           nevertheless
                           consequently
                           furthermore
                           moreover
#4 Independent clause,   and   independent clause.
                           but
                           or
                           nor
                           for
                           yet
                           so
                           (then)
#5 Independent clause,   on the other hand,   clause.
                           of course
                           it seems

Additional patterns address punctuation with phrases, quotations, items in a series, and colons. Once students are oriented to the patterns and how they work to illustrate basic punctuation, they are ready to move to the discussion of their rhetorical applications.

Applying this Model Rhetorically to Sentences

These patterns open the discussion to two foundational concepts in business communication: coordination and subordination. For example, we discuss what rhetorical purpose is served by choosing the Independent Clause, + coordinating conjunction + Independent Clause pattern vs. the Dependent Clause, + Independent clause or Independent Clause + Dependent Clause pattern.

Discussion of the patterns leads to several questions: How does punctuation impact which ideas are foregrounded or de-emphasized? What does the presence or absence of a comma after or between clauses or phrases do? When might a writer choose a semicolon over a period between two independent clauses? When would a writer want to use a relative dependent clause or embed information in a prepositional phrase? How does the presence of commas with nonrestrictive or nonessential relative dependent clauses impact the reader? What happens when punctuation is used incorrectly to create a comma splice, fragment, or run-on—and how might that impact the reader? What difference does it make if you have a complete sentence before a colon or not? Students' answers vary, but when they make some kind of intuitive sense on an individual level, students are able to punctuate for meaning, regardless of whether they know formal grammatical terms or "rules."

In other words, this rhetorical approach requires students to pay attention to what they are trying to do with their message rather than pay attention to rules. In fact, when a student asks, "Do I need a comma there?" my likely response is, "You tell me …Why are you thinking you might want to use one?" Or if they ask, "Can I use a semicolon here?," my likely response is "What is that going to accomplish for you that using a period would not?" It is true that we work through some structured editing assignments to familiarize students with what the patterns look like in the context of a routine, bad-news, or persuasive message, but once they are writing their own documents, they choose the patterns they use to accomplish their rhetorical intentions. I am always surprised and impressed that when they punctuate for meaning, students are often following formal rules for punctuation anyway—but with a lot less guesswork and a lot more intentionality. Fortunately, in business communication, our messages are short, usually less than half a page, which makes for a doable in-depth examination of punctuation. In-class peer editing or drafting time and a flipped classroom have also helped me to remind students to be rhetorical in their sentence structures and punctuation.

Almost always, the discussion of the serial (Oxford) comma generates the most interest. Students will tell me that they have been taught that it is not necessary. When I ask why, they either do not know or they just say that it's the rule they learned. Once we review cases in which the presence or absence of the comma had dire consequences for the audience, students once again must look past the rule to the rhetorical intent. One case we have discussed is that of the Balanced Budget Act of 1997, in which there was a $1940 cap on "occupational therapy, physical therapy and speech therapy," which meant that the cap for occupational therapy was $1940, while the cap for BOTH physical and speech therapy was $1940, or $970 each (NARA: National Association of Rehabilitation Providers and Agencies, 2015). We also consider the more recent example of the Oakhurst

Dairy having to pay $5 million in overtime wages as a result of a missing serial comma in its overtime policy (Gonzalez, 2018).

Beyond punctuation, implications for rhetorical grammar instruction extend to several other concepts. For example, in teaching parallelism, students may not know the grammatical term, but they will be able to tell you that the non-parallel items joined by conjunctions just don't sound or look right. Allowing students to explore what is happening in terms of flow will frequently lead them to discover, for example, that by changing all of the words in the series so that they end in –ing, they have made the sentence clearer and more readable. Once they understand the concept rhetorically, the term "parallelism" then makes much more sense and becomes part of their vocabulary.

Likewise, when the grammatical requirement for singular pronouns to reflect the singularity of their antecedents vs. popular usage of "they" and "their" as a gender-neutral alternative, students will have several strong opinions on the need for gender equity and inclusiveness. But then we play devil's advocate and ask ourselves when and where the singular "he" or "she" would be necessary or whether writing around the issue (e.g., changing the singular antecedent to a plural one) accomplishes the same rhetorical intent.

The possibilities for introducing and teaching grammar as a rhetorical effort are many. The question is not whether to teach grammar. The question is how to teach grammar, and one way to teach it is to return grammar instruction to its original place in writing instruction—in particular, business writing. It is true that business communication textbooks are not set up to teach grammar rhetorically. Most come with grammar guides that include common rules and explanations and some practice exercises. These guides are certainly a useful reference, and they also offer students a great jumping-off point for exploring the rhetorical implications discussed above.

Ultimately, students must understand that using grammar rhetorically means using the standard English grammar expected in the workplace and recognizing its implications for their professional success—and recognizing that the "standard" is fluid and includes possibilities for the "multiple Englishes" (Dubinsky, foreword, p. xii) they encounter in the workplace. Business communication cannot, as a discipline, subscribe to any master narrative that rejects grammar instruction based mostly on tradition and history that says the study of grammar does not make students better writers. This view of grammar instruction fails to account for the rhetorical effects of grammar and does not acknowledge that these errors are more than flaws in a piece of text Beason (2001). As Beason says, "defining error as simply a textual matter fails to forefront the 'outside' consequences of error, especially the ways in which readers use errors to make judgments about more than the text itself" (p. 35). Rather, business communication needs to claim grammar instruction as part of its identity as an academic field that works with one foot in the academy and the other in the workplace. We need to consider Bordieu's framework for habitus and capital and ensure that our students have a command of grammar that enables them to meet the demands of the workplace—to communicate in a way that conveys their message and cultivates their professional *ethos*.

References

Aristotle. (1889). *The Organon or Logical Treatises* (Owen, O. F., Trans.). London: George Bell & Sons.

Bacon, D. R., & Anderson, E. S. (2004). Assessing and enhancing the basic writing skills of marketing students. *Business and Professional Communication Quarterly, 67*(4), 443–454. doi: 10.1177/1080569904271083.

Bartolotta, J. P. (2013). *Laboring literacy: Rhetoric, language, and sponsors of literacy in workers' education in the international ladies garment workers' union, 1914–1939*. Doctoral Dissertation. Retrieved from https://conservancy.umn.edu/bitstream/handle/11299/152425/1/Bartolotta_umn_0130E_13828.pdf.

Beason, L. (2001). Ethos and error: How business people react to errors. *Business and Professional Communication Quarterly, 53*(1), 33–64.

Bourdieu, P. (1986). The forms of capital. In J. G. Richardson (Ed.), *Handbook of theory and research for the sociology of education* (pp. 241–258). New York: Greenwood Press.

Bourdieu, P. (1999). *Language and symbolic power*. Cambridge, MA: Harvard University Press.

Braddock, R., Lloyd-Jones, R., & Schoer, L. (1963). *Research in written composition*. Champaign, IL: National Council of Teachers of English.

Brandenberg, L. C. (2015). Testing the recognition and perception of errors in context. *Business and Professional Communication Quarterly, 78*(1), 74–93. doi: 10.1177/2329490614563570.

Cicero. (2001). *De Oratore* (May, J. M., & Wisse, J., Eds.). New York: Oxford University Press.

Clokie, T. L., & Fourie, E. (2016). Graduate employability and communication competence: Are undergraduates taught relevant skills? *Business and Professional Communication Quarterly, 79*(4), 442–463. doi: 10.1177/2329490616657635.

Coffelt, T. A., Baker, M. J., & Corey, R. C. (2016). Business communication practices from employers' perspectives. *Business and Professional Communication Quarterly, 79*(3), 300–316. doi: 10.1177/2329490616644014.

Gilsdorf, J., & Leonard, D. (2001). Executives' and academics reactions to questionable usage elements. *International Journal of Business Communication, 38*(4), 439–475.

Gonzalez, R. (2018, February 8). *Maine dairy drivers settle overtime case that hinged on an absent comma*. Retrieved March 3, 2018 from NPR www.npr.org/sections/thetwo-way/2018/02/08/584391391/maine-dairy-drivers-settle-overtime-case-that-hinged-on-an-absent-comma.

Grammarly. (2013). *Good grammar will get you promoted*. Grammarly. Retrieved December 28, 2017 from www.grammarly.com/press-room/research/docs/Good%20Grammar%20Will%20Get%20You%20Promoted_03.2013.pdf.

Gray, K., & Koncz, A. (2017, February 16). *Employers seek teamwork, problem-solving skills on resumes*. Retrieved December 1, 2017 from National Association of Colleges and Employers www.naceweb.org/about-us/press/2017/employers-seek-teamwork-problem-solving-skills-on-resumes/.

Haussamen, B., Doniger, P., Dykstra, P., Kolln, M., Rogers, K., & Wheeler, R. (2002). *Some questions and answers about grammar*. Urbana, IL: National Council of Teachers of English.

Hinson, L. (n.d.). *A history of composition studies theory.* Retrieved March 3, 2018 from Sutori www.sutori.com/story/a-history-of-composition-studies-theory.

Holley, R. (2016). Grammar: The structure of language. In J. Martineau (Ed.), *Trivium: The classical liberal arts of grammar, logic, and rhetoric* (pp. 55–114). New York: Bloomsbury.

Joseph, M. (2002). *The trivium: The liberal arts of logic, grammar, and rhetoric* (McGlinn, M., Ed.). Philadelphia: Paul Dry Books, Inc.

Kastman Breuch, L.-A. M. (2002). Post-process "pedagogy": A philosophical exercise. *JAC: A Journal of Composition Theory, 22*(1), 119–150.

Kolln, M. J., & Funk, R. W. (2012). *Understanding English grammar* (9th ed.). Upper Saddle River, NJ: Pearson.

Kolln, M., & Gray, L. (2017). *Rhetorical grammar: Grammatical choices, rhetorical effects* (8th ed.). New York: Pearson.

Kolln, M., & Hancock, C. (2005). The story of English grammar in United States schools. *English Teaching: Practice and Critique, 4*(3), 11–31.

Locker, K. (1985). "Sir, this will never do": Model dunning letters 1592–1873. *International Journal of Business Communication, 22*(2), 39–45.

Longaker, M. G. (2015). *Rhetorical style and bourgeois virtue: Capitalism and civil society in the British Enlightenment.* University Park, PA: The Pennsylvania University Press.

Low, M., Botes, V., David, D., & Allen, J. (2016). Accounting employers' expectations: The ideal accounting graduates. *e-Journal of Business Education & Scholarship of Teaching, 10*(1), 36–57.

Martineau, J. (Ed.). (2016). *Trivium.* New York: Bloomsbury.

May, J. M., & Wisse, J. (2001). Introduction to De Oratore. In *De Oratore.* New York: Oxford University Press.

McGlinn, M. (2002). Editor's introduction. In M. Joseph (Ed.), *Trivium* (pp. 11–13). Philadelphia: Paul Dry Books, Inc.

Micciche, L. R. (2004). Making a case for rhetorical grammar. *College Composition and communication, 55*(4), 716–737.

Mozafari, A., El-Alayli, A., & Kunemu, A. (2017). Impressions of businesses with language errors in print advertising: Do spelling and grammar influence the inclination. *Current Psychology.* doi: https://doi.org/10.1007/s12144-017-9735-0.

Mulroy, D. D. (2003). *The war against grammar.* Portsmouth, NH: Heinemann.

NARA: National Association of Rehabilitation Providers and Agencies. (2015, February 11). *Capping problems: More than just a dollar amount.* Retrieved March 3, 2018 from NARA www.naranet.org/blog/post/capping-problems-more-than-just-a-dollar-amount.

National Council of Teachers of English. (1985). *Resolution on grammar exercises to teach speaking and writing.* Urbana, IL: National Council of Teachers of English.

National Council of Teachers of English. (1994). *Resolution on language study.* Urbana, IL: National Council of Teachers of English.

Nicgorski, W. (2013/14). Cicero on Aristotle and Aristotelians. *Hungarian Philosophical Review, 57*, 34–56.

Prosenjak, N., Harmon, M., Johnson, S., Bloodgood, P., & Hazlett, L. (2002). *Guidelines for gender—fair use of language.* Urbana, IL: National Council of Teachers of English.

Quintilian. (1922). *Institutio oratoria: Book 8* (Butler, H. E., Ed.). Cambridge, MA: Harvard University Press.

Quintilian. (1922). *Institutio: Book 10, Chapter 3* (Butler, H. E., Ed.). Cambridge, MA: Harvard University Press.

Quintilian. (1987). *Institutio Oratoria: Book 1* (Murphy, J. J., Ed.). Carbondale, IL: Southern Illinois University.

Scaros, C. (2016, May 2). *The importance of good grammar in business communication.* Retrieved December 26, 2017 from LinkedIn www.linkedin.com/pulse/importance-good-grammar-business-communications-cecile-scaros/.

Shoffner, M., Alsup, J., Garcia, A., Haddix, M., Moore, M., Morrell, E., . . . Zuidema, L. (2017). *What is a language arts teacher education?* Urbana, IL: National Council of Teachers of English.

Underwood, V., & Kett, M. (1981). *College writing skills.* Columbus, OH: Charles E. Merrill Publishing Company.

Wais, E. (2005). Trained incapacity: Thorstein Veblen and Kenneth Burke. *K.B. Journal: Journal of the Kenneth Burke Society, 2*(1). Retrieved March 3, 2018 from http://kbjournal. org/wais.

Wiens, K. (2012, July 20). *I won't hire people who use poor grammar. Here's why.* Retrieved December 30, 2017 from Harvard Business Review https://hbr.org/2012/07/i-wont-hire-people-who-use-poo.

4

EXAMINING THE ROLE OF THE WRITER'S SELF IN BUSINESS COMMUNICATION PEDAGOGY

Holly Lawrence

Traditionally, in business communication classes, students are assigned writing tasks that are reader-centered. The student writer is encouraged to craft an argument that focuses on the reader's concerns and appeals to his or her needs. For example, in a cover letter, writers offer reasons why they are viable candidates in hopes the reader can *see* them on the job. However, this emphasis on the reader tends to remove the writer from the equation, an odd omission given that a cover letter is one of the most personal documents a business person writes. Content is about the writer as an individual, as someone who can make a difference in an organization, contribute to a team, and get work done. As a result, student writers can benefit from taking a step back from the initial writing task to focus on their own needs, values, and goals and to imagine themselves as members of an organization. As a business communication instructor, I believe that our students should be taught how to use writing as a tool of self-exploration so that they can make connections between who they are (them*selves*) and who they hope to be in relation to the organizations they work for. As a result, I believe that instruction in business communication should pay more attention to the writer's self. In this chapter, I hope to persuade other instructors and scholars to see business communication as a discipline uniquely positioned to embrace a pedagogy that is both writer- and reader-centered. To do this, I adopt scholarship from composition and rhetoric that would support a more writer-centered approach in our business communication pedagogy as well as offer classroom applications for bringing the writer's self into the curriculum more directly and intentionally.

I have organized this chapter into several main sections that are designed to make a case for what I am proposing. First, I offer a brief history of the reader- or audience-centered approach in business communication instruction. As I will discuss throughout this chapter, business communication pedagogy tends to favor the reader because of the practical nature of business communications.[1] Business communications are typically produced with a reader in mind and are, therefore, born out of a relationship between the writer and reader, whether that reader is a well-known individual or a body of readers, a mass, homogenized group. Business communications are almost always practical because they are primarily designed to get the organization's work done, work that almost always relies on relationships among constituents of the organization. Therefore, effective business communications aim to preserve, if not further, the relationship between those who produce messages on behalf of an organization and those who receive those messages. A positive relationship between an organization and its constituents is fundamental to an organization's success, which means, as a general rule, organizations cannot afford to have communications negatively affect its various relationships. As a result, we wisely teach our students to approach a business writing task by first analyzing the audience as a way to meet the objectives of the communication. This approach is so pervasive in business communication that even when writing employment communications—messages that are almost entirely about the writer's self—students are taught to approach the writing task by first analyzing the job description and doing research on the organization and the industry so that they can respond to the needs of the organization and, in turn, present them*selves* as a desirable applicant, as aligned with the organization's needs, and as a match with the position. With this backdrop in mind, I discuss the theory and practice that has informed business communication pedagogy as primarily reader-centered. I then turn to scholarship in composition and rhetoric to find a model or way of thinking about audience that accommodates both a writer-centered and reader-centered pedagogy.

My argument for making business communication pedagogy more writer-centered is grounded in critical rhetorical theory as well as research and scholarship from management and organization studies. Through a discussion of research and theory from management and organization studies, I make a case for the need to bring more of the writer's *self* and the writer's point of view into our business communication instruction. I posit that self-exploration in business communication classes is especially crucial because of challenges our students face today for finding and keeping a job. Specifically, I look at the demand for students to package themselves as a personal brand and then feed that packaged, actually commodified, self to others as a way to expand professional networks and be a part of an organization. In short, their personal brand is at the core of many of the assignments we help them draft, polish, and disseminate. Those pieces include a cover letter, elevator pitch, and LinkedIn profile. Each is part of a career toolkit business students are encouraged, if not required, to develop. By bringing in a pedagogy that allows for more self-exploration and an examination of ones' values and goals, we can help them make thoughtful, meaningful decisions as they extend their brand and core career pieces to various audiences. To support this claim, I pull from a rich tradition in composition and rhetoric of using a writer-centered ped-agogy; in addition, I discuss theory and research from management and organiza-tion studies to show the value of self-exploration as part of a student's preparation for working in organizations. As business communication instructors, I contend we are in a unique position to help our students produce work that has immediate implications for their careers as practitioners of management. As a result, we want to help them think carefully and deeply about the selves they want (and hope) to be at work. I conclude my chapter with applications in the classroom.

Business Communication, Reader-Centered Writing, and a Place for the Writer's Self

In their attempts to document the history of the discipline of business communi-cation, several scholars have discovered the emergence of core principles that still exist today (Weeks, 1985; Hagge, 1989; Reinsch, 1996; Locker, 1998). Through an examination of J. Willis Westlake's *How to Write Letters* (1876), Hagge finds what he calls "canonical 'C's'" (p. 42); they are correctness, clarity, and conciseness. Westlake also instructs writers to adapt their style "to the person and the subject" and suggests, for example, the letter be "respectful and deferential" to "superi-ors" and "courteous" to "inferiors" (as cited in Hagge, p. 44). Through Westlake's instruction, we see origins of you attitude and the development of a pedagogy that is reader-centered. In 1911, in his *Business Correspondence*, George Hotchkiss codified the "Five Cs" of "good business letters" by adding "character" and "cour-tesy" to Westlake's list (as cited in Hagge, p. 37). Following in 1914, Lomer and Ashmun argued for the inclusion of courtesy and character. They write, "Prompt-ness in replying and courtesy in the tone of the letter are essential in business letters . . . and are an indication of the character of the writer" (as cited in Hagge, p. 40). In this very early instruction, we see the emergence of principles that are product-focused and reader-centered.

In their "Special Topics of Argument in Engineering Reports" (1985), Miller and Selzer argue for a "third kind of [Aristotelian] special topic for contemporary theory, a kind based on the specialized knowledge of disciplines" (p. 313). Miller and Selzer analyze technical reports produced by engineers and build on other scholarship that analyzed writing produced by professionals in law, science, tech-nology, and business. Findings suggest that professionals produce writing that they understand as prescribed, institutionalized by professional norms or requirements. As such, the content of memos, reports, and other documents is determined by institutionalized norms that, in turn, affect the writer's perceptions of the reader's needs. As Locker (1998) and Reinsch (1996) have shown, Miller and Selzer's research, along with similar studies from Toulmin, Rieke, and Janik (1979), were highly influential, affecting how we teach business communication today, with the primary focus on the product and the audience.

Shelby and Reinsch (1995) and Locker (1999) study the effects of you attitude and positive emphasis on letters and reports in real-world business situations. In each study, the researchers find you attitude to be a necessary component of a successful business letter, further solidifying the reader-centered approach to teaching business communication that is alive and well in today's textbooks. Leading business communication textbook authors Bovee and Thill (2016) offer a contemporary definition of you attitude as, "speaking and writing in terms of your audience's wishes, interests, hopes, and preference" (p. 82). The authors go on to suggest practical ways that students can convey you attitude in their messages, including the technique of replacing first person pronouns with *you* and *your* (p. 82). Instructions for writing with you attitude certainly rest on more than a simple pronoun switch and involve guidelines for protecting the audience's ego, demonstrating a genuine interest in the audience's feelings, and respecting the audience's intelligence. The major takeaway for the student is to put the reader first.

Audience and Writer-Centered Models in Composition

In the late twentieth century, composition studies was emerging as a field separate from rhetoric. Scholars such as Bartholomae, Berlin, Elbow, Macrorie, and Murray, many of whom were trained in classic rhetoric, argued for and against a new pedagogy of writing instruction that was writer-centered. I will be discussing several pedagogical theories from compositionists, but for now I would like to look at two models for teaching composition that were introduced in the late 70s and early 80s. One model is almost entirely audience-centered; the other is more inclusive and offers an approach that is both audience-centered and writer-centered. The latter, I think, is especially useful for thinking about how to bring more of the writer's self into business communication pedagogy.

In their 1979 article "The Integrating Perspective: An Audience-Response Model for Writing," Mitchell and Taylor lambast the writer-centered model for teaching college composition and argue for an audience-centered writing process. They propose an audience-response model for teaching writing and ground their claims in the kind of writing that is done in the professional disciplines. Specifically, they suggest the need for reader-centered writing in engineering for reasons similar to what Miller and Selzer found years later—that institutional frameworks and reader-expectations dictate the kind of writing practitioners produce. At the risk of oversimplification, I see Mitchell and Taylor's model as one in which the writer responds to both internal and external stimuli to produce writing that meets the demands, needs, and expectations of the intended audience. In their article, Mitchell and Taylor go on to show how this model of instruction can be employed in university settings for teaching writing in the disciplines, including business.

Shortly after Mitchell and Taylor's publication, Ede and Lunsford (1984) offered a different model that hinges on two main categories of audience: audience invoked and audience addressed. The self is included in each category. What I appreciate and find helpful about their model is how it relies on the following understandings about audience. They write:

> The term *audience* refers not just to the intended, actual, or eventual readers of a discourse, but to *all* those whose image, ideas, or actions influence a writer during the process of composition. One way to conceive of "audience," then, is as an overdetermined or unusually rich concept, one which may perhaps be best specified through the analysis of precise, concrete situations.
>
> *(p. 168)*

I find this definition useful to those of us teaching business communication because it is inclusive and allows us to think more broadly about the complicated relationship writers in business communication have with their audiences (both real and imagined). It also creates space for the self to sit alongside other audiences (again, both real and imagined). And, finally, their definition provokes analysis of business situations that might call for additional self-awareness or self-exploration. That is, as we teach our students to write for a business audience, we can push them to explore their own understandings of their relationship with the audience as well as their goals as the writer for responding to a given business situation. In this way, as Ede and Lunsford argue, there is a place for both a writer-centered and audience-centered approach to teaching composition and drafting the communications our students produce in a business communication class.

With this theoretical and historical backdrop in mind, I would like to move next to a discussion of rhetorical principles that contextualize and further support the value of including a more writer-centered pedagogy in business communication. Specifically, I am interested in Burke's concept of identification. His work on identification helps us think theoretically about the rhetorical situation that can occur in organizational settings in which the writer/speaker must identify with an audience to communicate objectives and goals of the organization.

Identification and Our Students as Future Managers

In *A Rhetoric of Motives* (1969), Kenneth Burke defines "the basic function of rhetoric" as "the use of words by human agents to form attitudes or to induce actions in other human agents" (p. 41). We persuade, according to Burke, by identifying with our audience. Discussing Burke's theories of identification as presented in his article "Rhetoric—Old and New" (1951), Marie Hochmuth (1952) writes, the key term of the "new" rhetoric is *identification* and this may include partially "unconscious" factors in its appeal. Identification, at its simplest level, may be a deliberate device, or a means, as when the speaker identifies his interests with those of his audience.

(p. 136)

For Burke, identification is an essential rhetorical concept because it serves as a device for unifying divided groups (Hochmuth, p. 137). As Hochmuth writes, "Put identification and division ambiguously together . . . and you have the characteristic invitation to rhetoric" (p. 137). In business communication, we ask students to unite their interests—personal and professional—with the imagined, assumed, or known interests of their audience; we ask them to employ the rhetoric of identification, to identify with their readers and, very likely, use that identification to persuade their readers. What is unique about identification in business communication is the type of situations that occur. Specifically, in business communication, our students encounter rhetorical situations that are very often real and immediate, such as developing content for an active LinkedIn profile or drafting a cover letter for an internship that will soon commence. As a result, students in business communication find themselves in the position of trying to identify with a reader so that they may write about themselves from what they understand is the reader's point of view.

In his essay "The Rhetoric of Identification and the Study of Organizational Communication" (1983), George Cheney calls for a greater "application of identification in rhetorical criticism to include other domains of discourse (in this case, organizational communication)" and offers "the individual-organization relationship as an exemplar for understanding and examining the rhetoric of identification" (p. 144). Using Burke's idea of "Administrative Rhetoric," Cheney argues that persuasion is "inherent in the process of organizing" and that in organizations, managers, as representatives of the organization, communicate the messages of the corporate body (p. 144). For Burke, one reason the rhetoric of identification works is that "people earnestly yearn to identify themselves with some group or other" (as cited in Hochmuth, p. 136). In this vein, managers use identification to bridge divided groups that are typical in an organizational hierarchy. As a result, in organizations, we find "the requisites for Burke's rhetorical situation: segregation and congregation" (Cheney, p. 145) and can see how managers use communication to bridge this divide.

Personal Values of Managers and Organizational Strategy

At this stage, we need to understand how the rhetoric of identification and its subsequent theories and interpretations influence business communication, and to do that, I would like to continue to look at the role of managers as agents who simultaneously communicate and influence a corporate message and corporate strategy. In their article "Corporate Strategy, Organizations, and Subjectivity" (1991), Knights and Morgan treat "corporate strategy as a set of discourses and practices which transform managers and employees alike into subjects who secure their sense of purpose and reality by formulating, evaluating and conducting strategy" (p. 252). Using a framework developed largely from Michel Foucault's work on knowledge and power, the authors compare and contrast other methods researchers have used in management to evaluate "subjectivity" and the manager-employee (or staff) relationship to corporate strategy. They reach this conclusion:

> Managers and staff are not just passive victims of the power of strategic discourse; through it they are constituted as subjects either in support of, or in resistance to, its plausibility. Insofar as strategic discourse would seem to facilitate general concerns with personal as well as organizational well-being and control, individuals readily participate in its practices and internalize its discipline. In this respect they are transformed into subjects who secure their sense of meaning, identity and reality (Knights, 1990) through participation in the discourses and practices of strategy. Again, this participation is not passive: individuals and groups exercise power to elaborate some and resist other elements of the discourse.
>
> *(p. 269)*

Within this framework, Knights and Morgan show that strategy is produced by managers and employees who act as agents of the organization and engage in the actions of the corporation and, as a result, shape and inform its strategy. In this view, corporate strategy is not a static thing handed down to subjects of the organization and is, instead, a living result of the rhetorical situation created by constituents of the organization.

As instructors of business communication, we can and should assume that the majority of our students will become managers who will deal daily with dynamic relationships that require them to identify with other groups as well as act on behalf of the organization. According to Holt (2006), "managers have to be aware of the conditions to which epithets of good and bad apply" (p. 1661). Holt argues against prevailing management theory[2] to use Aristotle's phronesis to describe a middle ground or way that is "the good life" that managers can achieve; within a management context, this "middle way" is managers' ability "to recognize that [their] voice is one amidst others and that what can be said and done by us as individuals can be said and done differently by others" (p. 1663). "The resultant 'good life'" is one that is *led* through active and public engagement in local contexts (p. 1663). In keeping with Holt's position, I contend that our students, as future managers, will engage in a variety of rhetorical situations that involve their public and private selves and that require decision making that can be seen as good and bad. In this way, our students' education should include elements that help them prepare for the roles they will assume and for bridging public and private and for achieving "the good life."

Within organization studies and management, researchers have linked the relationship of one's personal values to ethical management practices. As Stackman, Connor, and Becker (2005) show in their article "Sectoral Ethos: An Investigation of the Personal Values Systems of Female and Male Managers in the Public and Private Sectors," researchers in management have been studying the personal value systems of managers and other employees and the effect their values have on the organization for decades. Citing Schwartz and Bilsky (1987), Stackman, Connor, and Becker summarize the literature on personal values in managers and define values thusly: "(a) concepts or beliefs, (b) about desirable end states or behaviors, (c) that transcend specific situations, (d) guide selection or evaluation of behavior and events, and (e) are ordered by relative importance" (p. 579).

Business people, especially managers, are the mouthpieces for an organization, communicating important initiatives, policies, change, or other news. To convey that information successfully, managers must find a way to meet the needs of the audience and make the content of the message palatable. From a business communication point of view, if the message is potentially unsettling to its readers, for example, the organizational spokesperson or manager tries to deliver that news in a way that bridges the needs of the organization (e.g., to effect some sort of organizational change) with those of the audience (to feel reassured and secure during said time of change). Our students will be in the position of spokesperson for an organization, producing communications on behalf of their employers. In our classes, they are producing communications that meet an immediate exigence—getting an internship or fulltime job. They are also producing scenario-based communications that help them anticipate future exigencies—getting work done in the name of the organization. In both cases, our students need to be able to recognize the rhetorical situation and identify with the needs of their audience as a way for getting work done and moving forward the objectives of the organization and the writer. Our dominant business communication pedagogy helps our students recognize the situation and prepare an appropriate communication for the audience. As I have tried to show, producing a response that connects the writer and reader through the process of identification requires writers to pull from their own personal values and beliefs. It is this need for identification with an audience through one's personal values and beliefs that legitimates an analysis of the writer's role, needs, and goals as part of a bigger analysis of the rhetorical situation that includes analysis of the needs of the audience.

Within the business communication framework, I believe we can serve our students best by assigning writing tasks that allow them to express their personal values and goals and see themselves as private individuals within the public context that organizations impose on them. In short, by engaging in writing exercises that push them to explore them*selves*, we help them articulate personal values and goals to be expressed within a broader business context. As they explore their individual values and goals, for example, through personal writing exercises in our classes, they can use that self-information to try to identify and align themselves (their values and goals) with the organizations of their choice. As students, they are actively interacting with those organizations through job applications, career fairs, networking events, and social media. In short, there is a direct link between what I am proposing they need space and time for in our classes and the employment communication assignments we teach in business communication. In addition, a more tangential (but, I contend, vital) link lies between the self-exploration they can do through writing in our classes and that exploration's effect on how they position themselves rhetorically as interns, entry-level employees, and, eventually, managers.

Personal Brand and Meeting Organizational Expectations

Rhetorical frameworks from LeFevre (1986) and Knights and Morgan (1991) allow us to see the individual or self in relation to a larger social construct and interpret that relationship as reciprocal and not necessarily one of power in which a larger entity dominants and subjugates another. However, within management and organization studies, a considerable body of work expresses concern about organizational control over the individual (see DuGay, 1996; Alvesson and Willmott, 2002; and Vallas and Cummins, 2015 for research and discussion on organizational control, individual identity, enterprise theory, and corporate culture). One aspect of that research I would like to focus on is the emergence of personal branding and the message our students receive from business educators, career coaches, and their larger professional network that they should create a personal brand.[3] In short, a personal brand is the essence of our students' career "toolkit" and feeds the core career pieces they work on in our classes—resume, cover letter, LinkedIn profile, and elevator pitch.

The research and discussion of personal brand or self-branding in marketing, management, and organization studies is extensive, fascinating, and, at times, disturbing.[4] No matter how we may feel about the push or need for students to create a personal brand, we are currently in the position of helping them create a set of employment communications that ultimately rely upon or contribute to a personal brand. To this end, part of our own training as business communication instructors should include understanding the implications of personal branding and knowing how we can best assist our students as they navigate the tricky terrain of packaging themselves for corporate others.

Personal brand is defined as "a planned process in which people make efforts to market themselves" (Khedher, 2014, p. 29, abstract) and as "the process by which an individual activity tries to manage others' impression of their skills, abilities and experiences" (Johnson, 2017, p. 21, abstract) and as "the deployment of individuals' identity narratives for career and employment purposes" (Brooks & Anumudu, 2016, p. 24). Concerned about personal branding as an act that commodifies the self to make it available for corporate consumption, Lair, Sullivan, and Cheney (2005) describe it this way:

> Rather than focusing on self-improvement as the means to achievement, personal branding seems to suggest that the road to success is found instead in explicit self-packaging: here, success is not determined by individuals' internal sets of skills, motivations, and interests but, rather, by how effectively they are arranged, crystallized, and labeled—in other words, branded.
>
> *(p. 308)*

Personal branding, they write, is used "to market persons for entry into or transition within the labor market" (p. 309).

In 1997, Tom Peters' *Fast Company* article "The Brand Called You" popularized the concept of personal branding and concretized it in the trade press (Vallas and Cummins, 2015). Additionally, developing a personal brand is a part of student education in marketing and career and professional development courses and training in business schools (Johnson, 2017). How-to guides and persuasive treatises on the necessity of managing one's career and brand are easily found on the internet. (A quick search in the *Harvard Business Review* database alone yields many hits.)

For business communication instructors, the intense demand on our students to develop a personal brand as a step in "self-presentation" (Johnson, 2017) presents a special challenge for us. We are in the position of developing a rhetorical framework that allows us to teach students the value of self-exploration and self-discovery as a step in the process of writing their brand. I suggest we use personal writing as a practice that encourages our students, at the start of their careers as they initiate their brand, to investigate and explore what they care about and, in turn, to test their core values and goals against/within the socially constructed contexts that surround them.

As business communication instructors, we have a responsibility and an opportunity to help our students use writing as a means of self-exploration that allows them to think through their values, beliefs, and goals and, therefore, potentially become better equipped to identify with organizations in which they will work and ultimately in which they will make decisions as managers. Personal writing, mostly in the form of prewriting activities and freewriting, has the potential to serve as a mechanism for that kind of self-exploration.

Prewriting

Gordon Rohman and Albert Wlecke (1965) are credited with research that "launched the term 'prewriting,' which they called the 'initial and crucial stage of the writing process'" (Lauer, 2004, p. 78). Rohman and Wlecke characterized prewriting as an act of discovery, "of a personal context, of self-actualization through writing" (Lauer, 2004, p. 79), and recommended strategies of invention that involved prewriting. As an act of self-discovery, Rohman and Wlecke's claims about the way prewriting works are grounded in humanist psychology and in the idea that subject matter could easily originate from the self if students were given the opportunity to explore themselves as legitimate subjects.

Karen LeFevre (1986) argues that invention is a social act, as humans are socially constructed creatures that cannot exist outside of the context in which they exist. We therefore "build on a social legacy of ideas" and "are influenced by social collectives, such as institutions, bureaucracies, and governments" (Lauer, 2004, p. 183). LeFevre's position is in keeping with Knights and Morgan as both see a partnership between the social construct as the context in which we exist and our *selves* as agents who act.

Treated as an early stage in the writing process, Rohman and Wlecke's prewriting, as an inventional strategy toward self-discovery, self-exploration, and self-actualization, serves as step in the writing process that ultimately becomes social as most of our second-stage or final-stage writing tasks in business communication require our students to define themselves within a socially constructed context. That context, for example, may be a job description and set of requirements for an internship. After conducting a prewriting exercise, such as journaling, students can, theoretically, use some of that self-exploration to position themselves within the defined framework the organization has provided. The prewriting task has, hopefully, helped students articulate details and ideas about themselves that they will openly express to their readers in the next step of the writing process—for example, drafting the cover letter. Or, conversely, they may use the self-discovery to inform decisions about what not to share with their readers. Either way, the students have had the opportunity to explore values and goals that affect their thinking about their engagement with and within a specific context—in this case, a job in a prospective organization. As a former student of Rohman (1965) put it, journaling as a form of personal writing offers the act of "discovering myself for myself" (p. 109).

In my business communication classes, I have used prewriting as a way to ask my students to think about challenges they are facing regarding a writing assignment. For example, I give them five minutes of prewriting at the start of class, before we begin a peer-response activity, to articulate and grapple with their struggles as writers when drafting the assignment. After prewriting, I ask them to review their drafts and make any changes the prewriting exercise may have prompted. I also use the exercise as an opportunity to shape the peer response. I solicit challenges and concerns the students have about the drafts and custom-build a peer response plan. In short, we use the prewrite as a way for them to reflect on the writing process, the assignment, and them*selves* as writers. Invariably, we end up in a discussion of the rhetorical situation they have found themselves in vis-à-vis the assignment constraints, and that discussion is usually typified by the relationship of the writer to the reader.

Freewriting

Another kind of personal writing I use in my business communication classes is freewriting. Ken Macrorie's *Uptaught* (1970) laid the foundation for using free-writing in composition classes. Borrowing from Macrorie and others, I define freewriting as stream-of-conscious, judgment-free, non-stop writing, assigned for a designated amount of time. Freewriting and journaling are forms of personal writing that are also often called expressivist. Fundamental principles of expres-sivism are often attributed to theories of Abraham Maslow, Carl Rogers, and other humanist psychologists. An expressivist approach tends to support personal writing as a part of the writing process, oftentimes at the prewriting stage, in which the creative act of writing (the expression) is as important as, if not more than, the product (Berlin, 1988). In this vein, expressivist rhetoric has close ties to the humanist psychological theories of self-discovery and self-actualization that also inform the theory and practice of management education, especially the use of reflection as a tool for experiential learning (Rohman, 1965; Waddock, 1999; Albert and Grzeda, 2015; Cunliffe, 2016). In short, the practice of writing as a means of self-discovery and reflection on one's experience is grounded in the pedagogical literature of both composition and management education.

In composition, freewriting is often used as a prewriting strategy for helping students overcome writer's block (Oliver, 1982), developing writing strategies and habits (Li, 2007), "getting started" (Elbow, 1989), and tapping into a reservoir of ideas (Lawrence, 2013). All of these reasons for assigning freewriting are as relevant to a business communication class in a business school as they are to a composi-tion class in an English department. That is, freewriting can be liberating for a stu-dent writer, and students of business communication can benefit from its effects.

I sometimes use freewriting as a way to simply get the juices flowing in my busi-ness communication class. Business students often enter my classroom after exiting an accounting or finance class where they have been handling difficult equations or analyzing data. Despite their enjoyment of these other subjects, students may also feel drained after intense study or lectures. Their heads are in a different world, one of data and equations. As a result, freewriting, even for five minutes, at the start of class can help a student shift from that world to a world of words.

In a recent business communication class, I assigned a five-minute freewrite. I told the students the exercise was a form of private, personal writing. In the free-write, the topic is unassigned, so it may be personal or not, whatever flows from the students' minds. The writing is private because I assured them they would not have to share their writing with anyone. After five minutes, I asked for a bit of reflection on the practice. What follows is a summary of their comments.

- Several found the practice relaxing, calming.
- One student said he does not think of himself as a good writer and generally does not like to write, but in the freewrite, he used the note function on his phone, and the writing came much more easily. He attributed this shift in

experience with using a more comfortable, easier technology; writing on his phone was like texting, almost like second nature.

- Another student said his writing style in the freewrite was different. He said that he normally writes in long, complicated sentences and with freewriting he wrote short, declarative statements. He felt a bit like he was yelling because he was writing about something that was really bothering him. He felt more clear (and more angry) after writing about the problem.

- Other students said they wrote about things that were on their minds and were glad to have cleared their minds a bit.

- One student said he wrote about something that had been troubling him, and in his writing, he elucidated more details and reached new understandings.

Wow. I was delighted, to say the least. Of course, not everyone shared, and some probably did not like the task, but so many raised their hands and wanted to reflect on their freewrite that I have to think of it as generally positive.

For freewriting to be truly free, teachers only have to give the task structure, specifically when to start and when to end, and general guidelines about how it works (judgment-free, private, no stopping, whatever comes to mind, and so on). Instructors have to be prepared for pushback, as students can complain that they do not know what to write about, or they may even claim the practice makes no sense. My best advice about freewriting is to be comfortable assigning it and clear about why we are doing it. In my experience, business students can be skeptical about a practice that may seem non-business-oriented, and they may associate freewriting with an English class. For some instructors, this perception issue may cause a bit of discomfort regarding authority in the classroom. I recommend that, when using freewriting, instructors set up the activity by stating its purpose and hoped-for benefit. In my class, I let them know how long we will write, that the writing is private, that the topic is open and can, therefore, be personal or not, that they can say anything (including that they hate writing or that they are not enjoying the freewrite), and that the only rule is to keep writing.

I participate in the freewrite at the same time. In class, I shared a few insights about my own experience of the freewrite exercise. I noted two things in particular. I didn't use punctuation (a surprise for me); I had trouble not editing (not a surprise). I also told them that part of the purpose of the freewrite was to get the writing juices flowing. I felt that the freewrite helped me sink into class and be fully present.

As a bonus, debriefing the freewrite was incredibly useful when it came to a self-edit we did later in that same class. By talking about our freewrites, we also learned who we are as writers and thinkers. In essence, the freewrite served as a bit of self-discovery in the quest to know ourselves as business writers facing a type of writing that was new to the class. Examining the self, the writer as an individual with emotions and needs, allows the writer to think of the self as a real person behind the writing and, hopefully, in turn, imagine the real person, with equally important emotions and needs, on the other end receiving the communication.

Personal Writing and Ethical Communications

As we have seen, in management and organizational studies, there is a considerable body of scholarship devoted to the study of personal values and morals of managers. Many argue that a manager's moral code and personal values are relied upon to make decisions and communicate as well as propagate the corporate identity and that, in turn, the manager is both a subject and agent of corporate identity (Stackman et al., 2005; Holt, 2006; Wieland, 2010; Bardon, Brown, & Peze, 2017). Additionally, there is an enormous body of literature on business ethics in management education and the importance of teaching our students to act as ethical agents of an organization. The Association to Advance Collegiate Schools of Business (AACSB), the primary accreditation body for business schools, requires colleges and schools of business that seek accreditation to teach business ethics.[5] In the spirit of ethical communications, we instruct our business communication students to produce communications that are honest and sincere. We encourage students to tell the truth, to create original materials and to provide sources and references when they lean on the ideas of others. We also know from Hotchkiss' very early *Business Correspondence* the writer's character became a major "C" of effective messages. I posit that we can use personal writing as a way to help our students explore their ethics and morals. By engaging in personal writing exercises that require students to think through and articulate their probable behavior or response to a given situation, students are prompted to articulate personal values, beliefs, or morals that they would invoke in a tricky or questionable situation, a situation that might occur in an interview or on the job. Simple ten-minute personal writing exercises in which students respond to a "what-would-you-do" prompt can help them articulate thoughts that could be useful to them when they need to rely on their personal values to make decisions on the fly in the future.

Conclusion

In the age of the personal brand, elevator pitches, and online social networks, our students, perhaps more than ever, are being asked to articulate who they are and what they care about for a variety of professional audiences—real, imagined, known, and assumed. Competition for jobs and internships is high, and demand for effective communication skills is status quo. (In a 2017 National Association of Colleges and Employers' survey, employers ranked attributes they are looking for on college students' resumes. Effective written communication skills is the number three desired attribute, and oral communication skills is number five.) Additionally, business students are under scrutiny to be ethical communicators, and universities and colleges are required by governing bodies, such as the AACSB, to teach our students business ethics. While I by no means am suggesting that personal writing is a panacea that can treat all things, I do firmly believe that personal writing, as a means of self-exploration, offers our students an opportunity to think deeply and meaningfully about their futures, about where they want to work and how they want to present themselves to their current and prospective professional audiences. Personal writing can also help them articulate personal values, beliefs, and goals that can, in turn, help them identify who they are in relation to their audience and, therefore, address their audience's needs as well as attend to the work and needs of the organization. In other words, while audience-centered writing is a necessity for crafting effective business messages, the writer must understand her own position first, and I contend that our pedagogy is flexible enough to include both a writer-centered and audience-centered approach. Drafting employment communications is perhaps the most obvious starting point for using personal writing and self-exploration in a business communication class. Additionally, personal writing, in the form of guided prewriting, for example, can offer students an opportunity to think through and articulate their personal values and morals as part of their preparation and training as managers and agents who contribute to and help shape an organization's identity and corporate strategy. What follows are a few prompts and exercises that can be used in business communication to achieve self-exploration. The exercises can remain personal and private or can become material for sharing and class discussion.

The Personal Statement

The purpose of the personal statement is to focus on the writer's experience and goals. The statement directions ask writers to articulate who they are background and experience) and who they wants to be (goals) and why. The prompt is intentionally broad, and the idea is to get the students to write about their experience and what is important to them in terms of their background and their goals. The material can be used for working on employment communications, such as the LinkedIn profile or elevator pitch, or can be stored as self-knowledge. As an outcome, students can check the content of their public communications, those such as LinkedIn that are intended to reach a wide professional network, *against* the private writing in their personal statement. Questions to ask them include Are you staying true to who you say you want to be privately? How are you merging and projecting your private identity with your public communications? Is there a difference between the two selves? If so, why? Does the difference matter? In other words, we can push our students to think as deeply and carefully about them*selves* as the class curriculum and course execution allow. Formatting, audience, and quality of writing are all secondary to content generation and attention to the writer's self.

What Would You Do?

What-would-you-do prompts put the writer in a situation and ask her to write about how she would respond to an issue. The situation can be student-based or job-related. Possible prompts follow below.

You are in a class and a student nearby is cheating on an exam. Do you say something to someone? If so, to whom and what do you say and why? Do you do nothing? If so, why?

You are in an interview and the interviewer asks you about an experience you have had that has not gone well. What do you say? How do you explain a negative experience? Try to think of a real experience you would rather not discuss in an interview—a poor course grade, a bad first semester in college, being let go from a job, or something similar.

You are on the job as a new employee or intern, and a colleague at your level has asked you to keep quiet about something she has done that is a problem for your team. What do you do?

Your boss asks you to shred a document you suspect should be kept as a permanent record. What do you do?

Some of the questions can be discussed in small groups or as a class. I have found that students value being able to talk about tricky situations in a small class with other students. As business communication instructors, we can link the prewrite and discussion to one of our assignments or simply treat the exercise as practice and an opportunity to use writing for self-exploration.

Notes

1 In this essay, I use three terms with similar and overlapping meanings and would like to define how I use each. By business communication, I am referring to the field of study and practice. By business communications, I mean both written and spoken messages produced in a business context and exchanged between one or more people. By business writing, I mean the genre of writing done at and for the workplace; business writing may also be the writing that we ask our business communication students to produce.

2 Holt argues against Alasdair MacIntyre's philosophical interpretation that "within every-day activities—such as management—one's moral responsibilities remain unattached to the specifics of that activity" (p. 1660) as appropriately applicable to managers because it suggests managers "have no concern for wider questions of impact or substantive questions of the good" (p. 1660). Of Milton Friedman's theory of managers, Holt writes, "Management is a particular activity with its own practical means which in and of themselves remain amoral insofar as they are concerned with effective and efficient ordering of material and knowledge resources within specific organizational offices" (p. 1661). As a result, for Friedman, Holt claims, managers act on their own principles to do good (or bad) as private individuals making the act of managing a technical amoral activity (pp. 1660–1661).

3 I loosely define larger professional network as recruiters, prospective employers, and organizations that engage with our students as they transition from student status to professional employee.

4 The loss of the self to a commodified, ready-for-corporate-consumption version of one's identity is discussed in much of the literature. In some cases, this commodification

is treated as a non-issue; in others, how to keep one's identity within this contemporary framework of careers and corporate culture is treated with concern.

5 The Association to Advance Collegiate Schools of Business website at www.aacsb.org offers numerous resources on how and why to teach business ethics as core management education curriculum.

References

Albert, S., & Grzeda, M. (2015). Reflection in strategic management education. *Journal of Management Education, 39*(5), 650–669.

Alvesson, M., & Willmott, H. (2002). Identity regulation as organizational control: Producing the appropriate individual. *Journal of management studies, 39*(5), 619–644.

Bardon, T., Brown, A. D., & Pezé, S. (2017). Identity regulation, identity work and phronesis. *Human Relations, 70*(8), 940–965.

Berlin, J. (1988). Rhetoric and ideology in the writing class. *College English, 50*(5), 477–494.

Bovee, C., & Thill, J. (2016). *Business communication essentials* (7th ed.). Hoboken: Pearson.

Brooks, A. K., & Anumudu, C. (2016). Identity development in personal branding instruction: Social narratives and online brand management in a global economy. *Adult Learning, 27*(1), 23–29.

Burke, K. (1951). Rhetoric—old and new. *The Journal of General Education, 5*(3), 202–209.

Burke, K. (1969). *A rhetoric of motives* (Vol. 111). Oakland: University of California Press.

Cheney, G. (1983). The rhetoric of identification and the study of organizational communication. *Quarterly Journal of Speech, 69*(2), 143–158.

Cunliffe, A. L. (2016). Republication of "On Becoming a Critically Reflexive Practitioner." *Journal of management education, 40*(6), 747–768.

Du Gay, P. (1996). *Consumption and identity at work.* Thousand Oaks, CA: Sage.

Ede, L., & Lunsford, A. (1984). Audience addressed/audience invoked: The role of audience in composition theory and pedagogy. *College composition and communication, 35*(2), 155–171.

Elbow, P. (1989). Toward a phenomenology of freewriting. *Journal of Basic Writing, 8*(2), 42–71.

Hagge, J. (1989). The spurious paternity of business communication principles. *The Journal of Business Communication (1973), 26*(1), 33–55.

Hochmuth, M. (1952). Kenneth burke and the "new rhetoric." *Quarterly Journal of Speech, 38*(2), 133–144.

Holt, R. (2006). Principals and practice: Rhetoric and the moral character of managers. *Human Relations, 59*(12), 1659–1680.

Johnson, K. (2017). The importance of personal branding in social media: Educating students to create and manage their personal brand. *International Journal of Education and Social Science, 4*(1).

Khedher, M. (2014). Personal branding phenomenon. *International Journal of Information, Business and Management, 6*(2), 29.

Knights, D. (1990). Subjectivity, power and the labour process. In *Labour process theory* (pp. 297–335). London: Palgrave Macmillan.

Knights, D., & Morgan, G. (1991). Corporate strategy, organizations, and subjectivity: A critique. *Organization Studies, 12*(2), 251–273.

Lair, D. J., Sullivan, K., & Cheney, G. (2005). Marketization and the recasting of the professional self: The rhetoric and ethics of personal branding. *Management Communication Quarterly, 18*(3), 307–343.

Lauer, J. M. (2004). *Invention in rhetoric and composition.* West Lafayette, IN: Parlor Press.

Lawrence, H. (2013). Personal, reflective writing: A pedagogical strategy for teaching business students to write. *Business Communication Quarterly, 76*(2), 192–206.

LeFevre, K. B. (1986). *Invention as a social act.* Carbondale, IL: Southern Illinois University Press.

Li, D. (2007). Story mapping and its effects on the writing fluency and word diversity of students with learning disabilities. *Learning Disabilities: A Contemporary Journal, 5*(1), 77–93.

Locker, K. O. (1998). The role of the Association for Business Communication in shaping business communication as an academic discipline. *The Journal of Business Communication (1973), 35*(1), 14–44.

Locker, K. O. (1999). Factors in reader responses to negative letters: Experimental evidence for changing what we teach. *Journal of Business and Technical Communication, 13*(1), 5–48.

Macrorie, K. (1970). *Uptaught.* Rochelle Park, NJ: Hayden.

Miller, C. R., & Selzer, J. (1985). Special topics of argument in engineering reports. *Writing in Nonacademic Settings,* 309–341.

Mitchell, R., & Taylor, M. (1979). The integrating perspective: An audience-response model for writing. *College English, 41*(3), 247–271.

Oliver, L. J. (1982). Helping students overcome writer's block. *Journal of Reading, 26*(2), 162–168.

Peters, T. (1997). The brand called you. *Fast company, 10*(10), 83–90.

Reinsch Jr, N. L. (1996). Business communication: Present, past, and future. *Management Communication Quarterly, 10*(1), 27–49.

Rohman, D. G. (1965). Critical theory and the teaching of composition, satire, autobiography. *College Composition and Communication, 16*(2), 106–112.

Rohman, D. G., & Wlecke, A. (1965). "Construction and application of models for concept formation in writing." US Office of Education Cooperative Research Project Number 2174.

Schwartz, S. H., & Bilsky, W. (1987). Toward a universal psychological structure of human values. *Journal of Personality and Social Psychology, 53*(3), 550.

Shelby, A. N., & Reinsch Jr, N. L. (1995). Positive emphasis and you-attitude: An empirical study. *The Journal of Business Communication (1973), 32*(4), 303–326.

Stackman, R. W., Connor, P. E., & Becker, B. W. (2005). Sectoral ethos: An investigation of the personal values systems of female and male managers in the public and private sectors. *Journal of Public Administration Research and Theory, 16*(4), 577–597.

Toulmin, S., Rieke, R., & Janik, A. (1979). *An introduction to reasoning.* New York: Palgrave Macmillan.

Vallas, S. P., & Cummins, E. R. (2015). Personal branding and identity norms in the popular business press: Enterprise culture in an age of precarity. *Organization Studies, 36*(3), 293–319.

Waddock, S. A. (1999). Letter to a friend: A personal reflection exercise. *Journal of Management Education, 23*(2), 190–200.

Weeks, F. W. (1985). The teaching of business writing at the collegiate level, 1900–1920. In G. H. Douglas & H. W. Hildebrandt (Eds.), *Studies in the history of business writing* (pp. 201–215). Urbana, IL: Association for Business Communication.

Wieland, S. M. (2010). Ideal selves as resources for the situated practice of identity. *Management Communication Quarterly, 24*(4), 503–528.

5

INVENTION IN BUSINESS COMMUNICATION AND COMMUNITY-BASED PROJECTS

Danica L. Schieber

Teaching students to write for client audiences is one of the main challenges for business communication instructors. Researchers such as Freedman and Adam (1996) have found that the kinds of writing expected at colleges and universities differ widely from what is expected in the workplace (p. 395). Business communication courses often give examples for various types of documents or use textbook-generated or teacher-created writing prompts but may not offer students the opportunity to practice writing for an audience outside of the classroom. One method for addressing this problem is by assigning project-based service learning assignments that involve an authentic client in the local community.

Many researchers have analyzed the benefits of these assignments, such as solving community problems, exposure to authentic writing situations and client feedback, and transfer of learning from the classroom to students' future workplaces (Blakeslee, 2001; Bourelle, 2012; Cyphert, 2006; Tuomi-Grohn, 2003; Wickliff, 1997). Although many different terms are used, service learning is often the umbrella term used to describe community or nonprofit writing projects. While these projects may mean different things to different instructors, here I use Dubinsky's (2002) description of the three key parts of any service-learning project: "*learning* (establishing clearly defined academic goals), *serving* (applying what one learns for the communal/societal benefit), and *reflecting* (thoughtful engagement about the service-learning work's value)" (p. 64, original emphasis). This description of service learning served as the background for all client-based projects that I assigned in my class. Each of these three pieces is integral for students to achieve the stated outcomes/objectives of the course and for students to process their experience through the reflection process. Service learning projects in the classroom give students the opportunity to write for a client but with the safety net of the classroom. Business majors in particular are expected to be able to communicate effectively when they get to the workplace. Many researchers have explored how service-learning pedagogies can prepare students to write for the workplace.

Because of the community focus of client-based projects, Ciceronian rhetorical principles can be applied to these types of writing projects as guiding principles. One researcher interested in incorporating classical rhetoric into writing classrooms was Corbett (1986), who indicated that the common rhetorical topics (*topoi*) can influence the way we teach writing. Leff (1983) defines topics as "a resource for an argument, or a seat of an argument, or a region in which the argument resides" (p. 24). In Latin rhetoric, topics were typically the basis of argumentative invention. In Aristotelian rhetoric, Leff (1983) notes, "in rhetorical argumentation, the required connectives are relative to the audience addressed, and thus they arrive from and are verified from social knowledge existing within a community" (p. 25). While Aristotelian topics are inferential, Latin topics are listed in a more detailed way in Cicero's *De Inventione*. While Cicero was obviously focused on the art of oratory and taught his students to be eloquent orators in works such as *De Inventione* (On Invention) and *De Oratore* (On the Character of the Orator), business communication instructors can extend the same principles to business communication pedagogy. In Book 1 of *De Oratore*, Cicero reminds his readers that practice is absolutely essential for students who want to achieve eloquence and effectively reach their audiences: "thus eloquence is not the offspring of the art, but the art of eloquence" (translated by E. W. Sutton & H. Rackham, 1962, p. 101).

Cicero argued that a philosopher and a rhetorician (or a business communication student) could both use the same kinds of topics for invention to make their arguments (this theory later inspired Quintilian's works as well). Quintilian later writes (through his creative use of metaphors) how invention and practice help writers and orators create better arguments:

> But it is only by constant practice that we can secure that, just as the hands of the musician, even though his eyes be turned elsewhere produce bass, treble, or intermediate notes by force of habit, so the thought of orator should suffer no delay owing to the variety and number of possible arguments, but that the latter should present themselves uncalled, just as letters and syllables require no thought on the part of the writer, so arguments should spontaneously follow the thought of the orator.
>
> *(p. V10 125, translated by H. E. Butler in the Loeb edition)*

Giving students the opportunity to practice client-based writing projects in the classroom should therefore give them the opportunity for more practice in writing on various *topoi* (topics or genres) they may encounter in the workplace. Our students will need to practice to write effectively in the workplace.

Therefore, employing Cicero's pedagogy of rhetorical *inventio* and *imitatio*, "the emulation of working models that embody the practice in question in all its nuance and specificity" (Mendelssohn, 2002, p. 166), this chapter applies the principles of *inventio* to business communication pedagogy. I argue that business students need the opportunity to practice and create their own discourse using *inventio*, facilitated by Ciceronian *imitatio* in client-based writing projects so they can learn workplace writing skills that will help them transfer learning to their future careers. In this chapter, I tackle these issues and endeavor to answer how business communication students contribute to the invention process (*inventio*) in their projects. I then outline the principles from the rhetorical canon relevant to how these client-based projects may help students transfer learning; specifically, I discuss ways that these client-based service projects can help students to better writing by using *inventio* as a guiding principle. I also provide examples from my own business communication classes and provide anonymous reflections from students describing their own experiences with these types of writing projects. As I will illustrate, these projects allowed students to participate in their communities and gain workplace writing experience.

Inventio

Imitation is important when students are first learning to write. In many contexts, they model their writing on samples, and this is typically the basic set-up of business communication textbooks. However, Mendelssohn (2002) points out that imitation can only be successful if "invention intervenes to reframe the original according to the demands of a new time and place. Second, the pedagogy of imitation highlights the role of interpretation in the process of rhetorical production" (p. 168). For students to be able to do model professional writing in many business contexts, they first need to be able to analyze the business problem so they can address it correctly with their writing. Without experience, this modeling or imitation can be difficult for students to do.

Cicero, a scholar who began his career as a lawyer known for his eloquent speaking style, synthesized much of what he had learned from other scholars and philosophers. Cicero was heavily influenced by Aristotelian rhetoric but also by the stoics and the skeptics, and one of his strengths was being able to incorporate what he learned in his own writings. Also, Cicero's descriptions of *inventio* changed over the course of his work, from very detailed in *De Inventione* to a more universal approach later in *De Oratore*. The universal approach in his more mature works encouraged the use of *inventio* in many different occasions and situations, rather than the strictly defined situations that he provided in *De Inventione*. As Cicero's works progressed, he focused on an *inventio* system that was based on "persons and actions" for "rhetorical practice" (Ochs, 1989, p. 217). Cicero also implemented a stasis system for arguments that had to do with the judicial system. The stasis system was originally developed by Aristotle and Hermagoras, as a method of invention, to help students research and prepare for their arguments. Ochs (1989) noted that "students in the several schools of rhetoric were taught a system of inventional topics more or less arranged under the stasis headings of conjecture (*an sit*), definition (*quid sid*), and quality (*quale sit*)" (Ochs, 1989, p. 218). These were the topics that became a part of the rhetoric core of invention for years.

Cicero describes his purpose in *De Inventione* as a textbook, writing, "Therefore let us consider what the character of invention should be; this is the most important of all the divisions, and above all is used in every kind of pleading" (p. 21, translation by H. M. Hubbell, 1962). The inventional schema laid out in Book II of *De Inventione* was the basis of rhetorical invention for many years and was even used by some Renaissance rhetorical writers.

Many years later, technical communication researcher Harkness Regli (1999) brought up the use of invention in modern day writing. She notes,

> The view of knowledge as a collaborative activity of meaning making across disciplinary boundaries seems much more accurate to describe a situation in which technical writers work as professionals with expertise in invention—because invention, in this context, is a matter of elaborate communication among a variety of specialists, and technical writers should be specialists in elaborate communication.
>
> *(p. 34)*

Although Harkness Regli was working with technical writers to explain how they can be masters of invention, the same ideas can be argued for business communication students. Business communication students need to be able to use invention in a variety of situations, as they do not know what kinds of writing situations they will be faced with in their future careers. Business communication therefore requires a kind of fluidity and flexibility.

This fluidity and flexibility can give business communication students an opportunity to use invention as a way to solve problems in the community. Because Ciceronian topics are focused on people and actions, his method of invention is a helpful way for students to become involved in the community.

Service Learning Projects

Service learning projects can be incredibly helpful, not only for the students but also for their clients. As Kenworthy-U'Ren and Peterson (2005) find, "at its core, service-learning is about creating opportunities for students to apply theory they learn in the classroom to real-world problems and real-world needs" (p. 272). Although these projects offer students the opportunity to develop workplace writing skills, students get to practice these critical skills from the relative safety of the classroom. Instructors hope to achieve many goals from these types of projects.

As Hill and Griswold (2013) note, some of the goals of service-learning projects can include these elements:

- Application of higher-level skill sets to real-world situations, made complex by virtue of their being real and requiring on-the-spot analysis and attention
- Professional writing planning, structure, design, and implementation
- Professional document production and communication
- Critical reflection of community problems and individual civic responsibility
- Direct participation within the community
- Hands-on learning through feedback and communication with working professionals at the community nonprofits.

(p. 56)

As instructors of business communication, we are fortunate in that many of our course objectives can directly relate to communication needs in the community. Service-learning opportunities are incredibly helpful to our students' writing development. While there is some research on service learning in the business communication classroom (Bush-Bacelis, 1998; Dubinsky, 2002; Hill & Griswold, 2013; Jones, 2017), more research in this area is needed.

Transfer

However, students still need to be able to transfer those skills to the workplace. Although there are many different definitions and descriptions of transfer, here I use Haskell's (2000) definition of transfer (also used by the Elon Statement of Writing Transfer):

Transfer refers to how previous learning influences current and future learning, and how past or current learning is applied or adapted to similar or novel situations. Transfer, then, isn't so much an instructional and learning technique as a way of thinking, perceiving, and processing information.

(p. 23)

Transfer of learning is the ultimate goal of every instructor—that their students will be able to transfer what they have learned in their classes to their future careers.

Traditionally, transfer theory has been dominated by the field of cognitive psychology. Early research includes work by Thorndyck (1924), who came up with the idea of participants being able to transfer effectively if the two contexts had "identical elements." Later, in 1939, this was challenged by Judd, who followed a theory of general principles, arguing that the students who had a knowledge of general principles were able to learn more quickly than those who did not. This idea was later used similarly by Bereiter (1995), who discussed a dispositional view of transfer, as a way of transferring habits of mind.

Later, many scholars were interested in the transfer of writing skills from one classroom to another in various contexts, from composition studies to professional and business communication studies (Artemeva, 2009; Dyke Ford, 2004; Downs & Wardle, 2007; Yancey, Robertson, & Taczak, 2014, etc.). As Downs and Wardle (2007), Wardle (2012), Butler, Black-Maier, Raley, and Marsh (2017), and many others have found in their research, students do not easily transfer skills from one context to another. We need to make that transfer more explicit for students, so they can become more aware of that process. How can instructors do that? Downs and Wardle (2007) suggest that we teach them transferable conceptions of the activity of writing rather than just "basic" writing skill and that we incorporate frequent reflective assignments (p. 578). Their FYC-based pedagogy can be easily applied to business communication, as it includes scaffolding assignments and encouraging students to build upon (and reflect upon) the genres and ideas they have learned. Learning and applying the rhetorical situation to new genres is a skill that all students must learn for effective communication.

In Gregory Wickliff's (1997) study of college students performing group projects, he noted that client-based group projects provide skills that have value in an actual work environment, but, "that the classroom setting and agenda often fail to simulate the workplace" (p. 171). Not only is there a lack of similarity between the two environments, but there is also a difference in the types of genres they are asked to write. Some researchers have analyzed class assignments that integrate discipline-specific writing genres into their writing courses (Artemeva, Logie, & St-Martin, 1999; Dyke Ford, 2004). Dias et al. (1999) followed participants from fields such as law, business, and architecture and found that the classroom, because of its situatedness, could never really replicate the activity system of the workplace. They noted that for business students, courses like business communication often use assignments such as case studies to encourage students to think about situations they may experience in future careers, but because case studies are merely abstractions from the real business environment, they can show only simplified versions of situations. The authors argue that social relations in workplaces are more complicated than those in university classrooms.

Some researchers analyze transfer with the situated/socio-cultural approach (such as Legitimate Peripheral Participation). This approach does not focus on what is transferred from one task to another but instead on the patterns of participants in new situations. These participants learn new skills and depend upon tools or artifacts to help them accomplish new tasks. Therefore, for participants to achieve transfer, the instructor should create activities that will translate to other situations that students may come across (Tuomi-Grohn & Engestrom, 2003, p. 26). Legitimate Peripheral Participation is a concept created by Lave and Wenger (1991) that describes the process whereby novices are able to participate only on the edge (or periphery) of a new community of practice. As time goes on and they communicate and participate more in that community, they eventually become full members. Lave and Wenger (1991) situate learning by mentioning that "peripheral participation is about being located in the social world. *Changing* locations and perspectives are part of actors' learning trajectories, developing identities, and forms of membership" (p. 36). This situated learning framework is helpful for us to analyze how novices learn to participate within their new communities of practice.

In a more community-based approach (Activity Theory, Russell, 1995), King Beach (2003) discussed the concept of "consequential transitions" as a way to look at and describe transfer (p. 3). In this process, Beach (2003) focused on the "changing relationship between individuals and sets of social activities" (p. 3). This can involve many different processes. The locus of learning then is not on the individual but more so on the communities that surround the individual and that he/she participates within, whether legitimately or peripherally. The organizations or communities and those who participate within them are constantly changing and moving, so participants also change within them. This experience is transformative for the participant, who becomes part of the community. However, for these transitions or changes to become actually *consequential*, the participant must be able to reflect upon them or be somehow changed because of their experience. If business communication students can actually participate meaningfully within their communities, that learning experience will be more likely to be something that they are able to transfer to future writing situations.

Discussion of the Client-Based Writing Assignment

In this section, I explain what I have assigned for my students, based on research in service learning and in Academic and Community Engagement scholarship (Wozniak, Bellah, & Riley, 2016). I will also provide examples that have worked well for my business communication students as well as reflection prompts.

Instructors should endeavor to find some writing assignments that have real exigencies for students. While it may be difficult for an instructor to make connections with many different businesses in the area, simply working with one company and asking for specific writing tasks that are typically given to their newest hires may be feasible. Students could then complete a real writing assignment for a real company. As Ann Blakeslee (2001) states, these professional genre projects and assignments can "act as useful transitional experiences for our students: Students can get a taste of workplace writing practices while still having the guidance and support of their instructor and classmates" (p. 190). One of the many benefits is that the company gives students actual feedback, which can help them make subsequent revisions. Similarly, Tomlinson (2017) notes that students who participate in client projects feel that they are better prepared to communicate in the workplace and may feel more confident doing so.

Many universities have a community engagement office that may offer instructors options for partnering with community businesses and nonprofit organizations. At my institution, Sam Houston State University, the school motto is "A measure of a life is its service." The university encourages and appreciates students' and faculty members' participation within the community and community-based projects. The university endeavors to make many connections between community members and students and has a center dedicated to helping instructors create assignments that will help a community partner.

If a university does not currently have an office with those connections, instructors can look for local nonprofit agencies, as they frequently need help with business documents and specific writing projects. Similarly, another place to start could be a small business development center, where entrepreneurs often start, or by talking to owners of small family-owned businesses in their area.

To give a better example of the kinds of projects that students in business communication classes can complete, I have included some excerpts from various assignments, as well as some examples of past projects. The following is an excerpt from an assignment sheet for a client-based report project that students completed in the author's business communication class. The client for this particular project was the university food pantry, which had recently opened a secondary location at the university. The business problem students were trying to address was that many students on campus were not aware of the food pantry's location, hours, or registration options.

> For this project, your group will conduct research on outreach for the Food Pantry. Your final report presents the findings of your research (interviews with the client, outside research, etc.) to the client. Your goal in writing the report is to help our client help students who may experience food insecurity. Note that your audience is not your instructor, but the client—this is why the assignment can also be referred to as an *external* report.
>
> **Visual Deliverable**—Your group will also create one visual document for our client, based on your research. This can include a flyer, a 3-fold brochure, a bookmark, or a poster. The visual can either be for soliciting donations or reaching out to students. If you would like, you can create a logo for the Food Pantry, as well as the visual document.

Because of the flexibility of business communication classes, there are many kinds of client-based writing projects that students can be a part of. Other examples of past projects students have completed for my business communication writing courses include the following:

- Re-design local restaurant menus;
- Design a new website for local coffee shop;
- Re-design promotional materials for a small Vietnamese restaurant (flyers and business cards);
- Set up a blog and email for a resale shop;

- Create a website and online scheduling tool for a new beauty salon;
- Create new flyers and business cards for a coffee shop that moved across town to a new location;
- Write a SWAT analysis and report to explore the possibility of expanding a small gas station to include a tire shop;
- Write a research report and create one deliverable for a local women's shelter.

While the instructor chose many of the clients for these projects, for some of the projects students found their own clients and created projects based upon the client's needs. For many students, these types of projects were incredibly meaningful, as they were able to see their hard work being put to use in the local community.

Benefits

These kinds of writing projects would fit Cicero's description of "working models that embody the practice in question in all its nuance and specificity" (Mendelson, 2002, p. 166). Professional genre writing for actual clients would also help emulate the environment of the workplace, giving course assignments/projects a more realistic feel. Another benefit of teaching these professional genres would be to allow students to address a wider variety of audiences than just their instructor. Writing for clients rather than their instructor gives students a sense of professionalism and responsibility that may motivate them to do better work (Ward, 2009). Students would not want to turn in subpar work to a client for fear of embarrassment.

Also, receiving authentic feedback from clients gives students the chance to tailor their work to their specific audiences, which is an important rhetorical skill. This type of writing would avoid what Clay Spinuzzi (1996) (and others such as Joseph Petraglia, 1995) calls *pseudotransactional writing*, which is "patently designed by a student to meet teacher expectations rather than to perform the 'real' function the teacher has suggested" (p. 295). Students have the opportunity to practice workplace writing for a workplace situation. Not only do client-based writing projects more beneficial for students than contrived writing prompts, but they also benefit local communities.

Cicero was heavily influenced by the stoics, who believed that helping others in their society was a moral obligation and, according to Ochs (1989) "enabled one to attain happiness" (p. 223). Therefore, Ciceronian principles are fitting to encourage students to participate in their communities through service learning. Cicero encouraged his peers to use their skills to help others. He wrote, "the wise control of the complete orator is that which chiefly upholds not only his own dignity, but the safety of countless individuals and of the entire state" (translation by E. W. Sutton & H. Rackham, p. 27). My business communication students were able to, as Dubinsky (2002) noted, "see their work as important to the communities in which they live" (p. 71). Because their work was important to their client, the students felt as though they made a difference and were participating in their communities as professionals rather than students.

In past studies, researchers found that students seemed to transfer some rhetorical skills when they were asked to write for clients. Artemeva, Logie, and St-Martin (1999) explained how a form of transfer was achieved when a writing course was tied to disciplinary activities that engineering students would use in their future communities. Artemeva et al. (1999) note that "by introducing these assignments, we are attempting to equip students with skills and strategies that can be applied to their other engineering courses and that will facilitate their transition to the workplace" (p. 313). By assigning students client-based writing assignments, we give students the practice that they will need to work with real life clients in their future careers.

Another benefit of client-based writing projects is that they can help students to achieve their business communication course objectives and actually are a natural fit for most business communication course goals. To illustrate my point, I have included the course goals from the Business Communication syllabus at Sam Houston State University in Appendix B.

Reflections

Reflection is an integral part of any client-based project and is something I always recommend for students to fully process their writing experience. Anson (1997) reminds us that

> theories of service-learning value reflection for helping to create the connection between academic coursework and the immediate social, political, and interpersonal experiences of community-based activities. Reflection is supposed to encourage a movement between observation and intellectual analysis or consciousness-raising, and conversely to apply abstract concepts . . . to contexts beyond the classroom.
>
> *(p. 167)*

In fact, having students reflect upon their experiences helps make the experience more meaningful for them (Astin, Vogelgesang, Ikeda, & Yee, 2000; Hatcher & Bringle, 1997). Another researcher, Lawrence (2013) claims that not only do personal reflections help students learn to be better writers, but they may also help them become better leaders and managers.

Reflections need to be tailored to the course assignment to be an effective tool of learning. The following are some reflection questions that I have used with my students to help them think through their process and how the project may have helped them to be more engaged citizens. They can be assigned to help students reflect upon their client-based writing project:

1.   Overall, can you describe your experience working on this project?
2.   Thinking about the link between theory and practice—how did this project help you use and practice business communication skills?

3. How did it affect your work ethic and product to actually work with a real client?
4. Did you feel that you improved upon certain topics that we covered in this class by completing this project? If so, how?
5. What are some specific areas that you feel you still need to improve upon?
6. Many articles note the importance of being an engaged citizen as a business professional. How did this project influence your idea of the impact of community engagement? Why should we be engaged? Why is it or is it not important?
7. What is one way that this project has made you more marketable to an employee?

Student Feedback

Students typically respond favorably to these types of client-based projects. Students appreciate the opportunity to complete a real-life project, instead of writing a paper for no other purpose than a grade. I have included some of the feedback I have received. The comments below are all from the most recent project that business communication students completed. This particular project was for the local women's shelter and addressed several issues. An excerpt from the assignment sheet is included, as well as some student reflections:

> This will be an ACE project for the SAAFE House here in Huntsville. The SAAFE House, started in 1984, is a nonprofit organization that provides "crisis intervention, advocacy, and support services empowering abuse survivors to seek new beginnings and rebuild lives free from the effects of violence. They provide services to all victims of family and sexual violence" (Barker, 2016, p. 36). The SAAFE House also runs Elite Repeat, the resale store that helps fund the organization through donations. The acronym SAAFE stands for Sexual Assault and Abuse Free Environment.
>
> Currently, the SAAFE House is understaffed and underfunded. One of their main needs is up-to-date research and materials that they can use when talking to various audiences. They need materials to give to teens, to women, to children, and to groups who are interested in volunteering. We will be gathering up-to-date secondary research for them.
>
> Your final report presents the findings of your research (interviews with the client, outside research, etc.) to the client. Your goal in writing the report is to help our client help women and children who may have been in domestic violence situations. Note that your audience is not your instructor, but the client—this is why the assignment can also be referred to as an *external* report.
>
> *(please see entire assignment sheet in Appendix A)*

After students handed in their completed reports, they were asked to write a reflection on their experience writing for this client in the local community.

Students were given reflection prompts, and IRB approval (IRB # 34158) for the written reflections was received in April of 2017. Students typed in their responses to the reflection prompts through the Blackboard system at the university, and all responses were anonymous. Blackboard compiled the responses to the various questions, and representative student responses are listed below.

When asked "How did this project influence your idea of the impact of community engagement? Why should be we engaged? Why is it or is it not important?" none of my students wrote that they felt it was not important. In fact, all student responses argued for the importance of these projects.

One student noted:

> Working on this project made me realize how important it is to get involved and help the community. Our client made it extremely clear of the needs of the organization. They need all the help they can get, but not a lot of people know that. Community engagement gives a feeling of personal accomplishment even if it is only a few hours of your time. Because in that short time you never know how you can make an impact in someone's life and it shows.

Another student wrote in his/her reflection: "Community engagement is crucial because the more people you have, the greater the outcome. With more people on board, no matter what the issue, problems can be dealt with accordingly."

A third student wrote:

> This project influenced the idea of community engagement in the aspect of helping a fellow person in need out. We need to be engaged because as this project shows, the situation of sexual abuse can happen to anyone. This is important because sexual assault/abuse is something that happens everywhere with or without knowing from those close to you.

Similarly, a fourth student reflected, "We should be engaged because we live in the community. If we all work to make the community better we are all making a huge difference."

Overwhelming, students were able to see not only how they were helping others in their community and participating within their local communities, but also how they were able to help others and to see how their writing skills can effect change. They were able to fulfill their social obligation and take an active role in their communities.

It is important for students to feel that they can make a difference, using skills that they have learned in their classrooms. These client-based projects have also been similar to that of Littlefield's (2006) service-learning experiences. She mentions that she found service learning to be satisfying, as students appreciated that they were filling an actual business need or solving a real-world problem, which seemed to motivate them to work hard on their projects (p. 320). My students also seemed to feel a sense of obligation to their clients and didn't want to let them down.

Conclusions and Recommendations for Instructors

When students are given the opportunity to make a difference, they can learn so much more. Students are able to contribute to the invention process when they write for a specific client in the community, using their invention process to solve a business need or problem. Students are able to participate in the community as their Ciceronian moral obligation to help others.

As an instructor, it is important to realize that doing client-based projects requires more work, not only for the students but also for the instructor. However, the benefits of these client-based projects far outweigh the extra time that goes into them. The integration of Ciceronian *inventio* can help students to better understand how to transfer their learning to new situations. *Inventio* gives the students and instructors a bigger purpose—to make a difference in their communities by using business communication writing skills. Influenced by the stoics' ideals of duty and obligation, students may develop an interest in becoming more involved in their communities.

I encourage instructors to continue to use reflection as a tool of learning in the business communication classroom to encourage and promote learning transfer and make students' writing experiences more meaningful. I would also like to urge my fellow instructors to not only try these types of client-based writing projects in their classrooms, but also to continue to research the effects and benefits of them. We need more research in this area of service learning, and we owe it to our students to do so.

I end with Cicero as he exhorts his readers to help people in their community:

> What function again is so kingly, so worthy of the free, so generous, as to bring help to the suppliant, to raise up those that are cast down, to bestow security, to set free from peril, to maintain men in their civil rights? . . . Go forward therefore, my young friends, in your present course, and bend your energies to that study which engages you, that so it may be in your power to become a glory to yourselves, a source of service to your friends, and profitable members of the Republic.
>
> (De Oratore, *Book I, 1962, pp. 25, 27*)

References

Anson, C. (1997). On reflection: The role of logs and journals in service-learning courses. In L. Adler-Kassner, R. Crooks, & A. Watters (Eds.), *Writing in the community: Concepts and models for service-learning in composition* (pp. 167–180). Washington, DC: AAHE.

Artemeva, N. (2009). Stories of becoming: A study of novice engineers learning genres of their profession. In C. Bazerman, A. Bonini, & D. Figueiredo (Eds.), *Genre in a changing world* (pp. 158–178). Fort Collins, CO: WAC Clearinghouse and Parlor Press. Retrieved from http://wac.colostate.edu/books/genre/

Artemeva, N., Logie, S., & St-Martin, J. (1999). From page to stage: how theories of genre and situated learning help introduce engineering students to discipline-specific communication. *Technical Communication Quarterly, 8*(3), 301–316.

Astin, A. W., Vogelgesang, L. J., Ikeda, E. K., & Yee, J. A. (2000). *How service learning affects students*. Higher Education Research Institute. 144. Retrieved from https://digitalcommons.unomaha.edu/slcehighered/144.

Beach, K. (2003). From transfer to boundary-crossing between school and work as a tool for developing vocational education: An introduction. In T. Tuomi-Grohn & Y. Engestrom (Eds.), *Between school and work: New perspectives on transfer and boundary-crossing* (pp. 1–19). Bingley: Emerald.

Bereiter, C. (1995). A dispositional view of transfer. In A. McKeough, J. Lupart, & A. Marini (Eds.), *Teaching for transfer: Fostering generalization in learning* (pp. 21–34). Mahwah, NJ: Lawrence Erlbaum.

Blakeslee, A. M. (2001). Bridging the workplace and the academy: Teaching professional genres through classroom-workplace collaborations. *Technical Communication Quarterly, 10*(2), 169–192.

Bourelle, T. (2012). Bridging the gap between the technical communication classroom and the internship: Teaching social consciousness and real-world writing. *Journal of Technical Writing and Communication, 42*(2), 183–197.

Bush-Bacelis, J. L. (1998). Innovative pedagogy: Academic service-learning for business communication. *Business Communication Quarterly, 61*(3), 20–34.

Butler, A. C., Black-Maier, A. C., Raley, N. D., & Marsh, E. J. (2017). Retrieving and applying knowledge to different examples promotes transfer of learning. *Journal of Experimental Psychology: Applied, 23*(4), 433–446. doi: 10.1037/xap0000142.

Cicero, M. T. (1962a). *De Inventione, De Optimo Genere, Oratorium Topica* (Hubbell, H. M., Trans.). Cambridge, MA: Harvard University Press.

Cicero, M. T. (1962b). *De Oratore, Books I-II* (Sutton, E. W., & Rackham, H., Trans.). Cambridge, MA: Harvard University Press.

Corbett, E. P. J. (1986). The *topoi* revisited. In Jean Dietz Moss (Ed.), *Rhetoric and praxis: The contribution of classical rhetoric to practical reasoning* (pp. 43–48). Washington, DC: The Catholic University of America Press.

Cyphert, D. (2006). Real clients, real management, real failure: The risks and rewards of service learning. *Business Communication Quarterly, 69*(2), 185–189.

Dias, P., Freedman, A., Medway, P., & Pare, A. (1999). *Worlds Apart, Acting and Writing in Academic and Workplace Contexts*. Mahwah, NJ: Lawrence Erlbaum Associates.

Downs, D., & Wardle, E. (2007). Teaching about writing, righting misconceptions: (Re) Envisioning "first-year composition" as introduction to writing studies. *College Composition and Communication, 58*(4), 552–584.

Dubinsky, J. (2002). Service-learning as a path to virtue: The ideal orator in professional communication. *Michigan Journal of Community Service-Learning, 8*, 61–75.

Dyke Ford, J. (2004). Knowledge transfer across disciplines: Tracking rhetorical strategies from a technical communication classroom to an engineering classroom." *IEEE Transactions of Professional Communication. 47*(4), 301–315.

Freedman, A., & Adam, C. (1996). Learning to write professionally: "Situated learning" and the transition from university to professional discourse. *Journal of Business and Technical Communication, 10*(4), 395–427.

Hatcher, J. A., & Bringle, R. G. (1997). Reflection: Bridging the gap between service and learning. *College Teaching, 45*, 153–159.

Haskell, R. (2000). *Transfer of learning: Cognition, instruction, and reasoning*. San Diego, CA: Academic Press.

Hill, S., & Griswold, P. (2013). Potential for collaborative writing in professional communication and health studies through service-learning. *Business Communication Quarterly, 76*(1), 54–71.

Jones, N. M. (2017). Modified immersive situated service learning. A social justice approach to professional communication pedagogy. *BPCQ, 80*(1), 6–28.

Kenworthy-U'Ren, A. L., & Peterson, T. O. (2005). Service-Learning and Management Education: Introducing the "WE CARE" Approach. *Academy Of Management Learning & Education, 4*(3), 272–277. doi:10.5465/AMLE.2005.18122417

Lave, J., & Wenger, E. (1991). *Situated learning: Legitimate peripheral participation (Learning in doing: Social, cognitive and computational perspectives).* Cambridge: Cambridge University Press.

Lawrence, H. (2013). Personal, reflection writing: A pedagogical strategy for teaching business students to write. *Business Communication Quarterly, 76*(2), 192–206.

Leff, M. C. (1983). The topics of argumentative invention in Latin rhetorical theory from Cicero to Boethius. *Rhetorica, 1*, 23–44.

Littlefield, H. (2006). Service learning in business communication: Real-world challenges develop real-world skills. *Business Communication Quarterly, 69*, 319–322.

Mendelson, M. (2002). On De Oratore. In *Many sides: A Protagorean approach to the theory, practice, and pedagogy of argument.* Dordrecht: Kluwer.

Ochs, D. J. (1989). Cicero and philosophic inventio. *Rhetoric Society Quarterly, 19*(3), 217–227.

Petraglia, J. (1995). Spinning like a kite: A closer look at the pseudotransactional function of writing. *Journal of advanced composition, 15*, 19–33.

Quintilian. (1921). *Loeb Edition* (Butler, H. E., Trans.). Cambridge, MA: Harvard University Press.

Regli, S. H. (1999). Whose ideas?: The technical writer's expertise in Inventio. *Journal Of Technical Writing & Communication, 29*(1), 31.

Russell, D. R. (1995). Activity Theory and its implications for writing instruction. In Joseph Petraglia (Ed.), *Reconceiving writing, rethinking writing instruction* (pp. 51–77). Mahwah, NJ: Lawrence Erlbaum.

Spinuzzi, C. (1996). Pseudotransactionality, activity theory, and professional writing instruction. *Technical Communication Quarterly, 5*(3), 295–308.

Thorndyck, E. L. (1924). Mental discipline in high school studies. *Journal of Educational Psychology, 15*(1–22), 83–98.

Tomlinson, E. (2017). Enhancing student learning through scaffolded client projects. *BPCQ, 80*(1), 29–51.

Tuomi-Grohn T., Engestrom, Y., & Young, M. (2003). From transfer to boundary- crossing between school and work as a tool for developing vocational education: An introduction. In T. Tuomi-Grohn & Y. Engestrom (Eds.), *Between school and work: New perspectives on transfer and boundary-crossing* (pp. 1–15). Bingley: Emerald.

Wardle, E. A. (2012). Writing and Transfer [Special Issue]. *Composition Forum, 26.*

Ward Sr., M. (2009). Squaring the learning circle: Cross-classroom collaborations and the impact of audience on student outcomes in professional writing. *Journal of Business & Technical Communication, 23*(1), 61–82.

Wickliff, G. A. (1997). Assessing the value of client-based group projects in an introductory technical communication course. *Journal of Business and Technical Communication, 11*, 170–191.

Wozniak, J. R., Bellah, J., & Riley, J. M. (2016). Building a community garden: A collaborative cross-disciplinary academic community engagement project. *Journal of Business Strategies, 33*(2), 95–115.

Yancey, K., Robertson, L., & Taczak, K. (2014). *Writing across contexts: Transfer, composition, and sites of writing.* Logan, UT: Utah State University Press.

Appendix A—Assignment Sheet for Documented Business Report

Business Communication
Final Project: Assignment #6 The Business Report (group project)
(200 pts)

This will be an ACE project for the SAAFE House here in Huntsville. The SAAFE House, started in 1984, is a nonprofit organization that provides "crisis intervention, advocacy, and support services empowering abuse survivors to seek new beginnings and rebuild lives free from the effects of violence. They provide services to all victims of family and sexual violence" (Barker, 2016, p. 36). The SAAFE House also runs Elite Repeat, the resale store that helps fund the organization through donations. The acronym SAAFE stands for Sexual Assault and Abuse Free Environment.

Upcoming dates to be aware of:

February—Teen Dating Violence Awareness month (orange)
April—Sexual Assault Awareness month (teal)—candle light vigil held on campus
October—Domestic Violence Awareness month (purple)

Currently, the SAAFE House is understaffed and underfunded. One of their main needs is up-to-date research and materials that they can use when talking to various audiences. They need materials to give to teens, to women, to children, and to groups who are interested in volunteering. We will be gathering up-to-date secondary research for them.

Possible research topics to choose from include but are not limited to:

Teen dating violence prevention
Teen dating violence statistics (e.g., basic information, economic factors, certain geographic areas like Texas, etc.)

Sexual assault awareness

Domestic violence prevention

Domestic violence statistics and information (e.g., basic information, various factors, certain geographic areas, etc.)

Your final report presents the findings of your research (interviews with the client, outside research, etc.) to the client. Your goal in writing the report is to help our client help women and children who may have been in domestic violence situations. Note that your audience is not your instructor, but the client—this is why the assignment can also be referred to as an *external* report.

The report should include a clear research objective, a description of your research methods, your major findings, implications of those findings, and a recommendations and conclusion section. The four major sections of the typical workplace report include—Introduction, Methods, Results, and Discussion. The example in the book that you will find most helpful will be figure 13.6 in the textbook. You should tailor your report to your particular audience.

Visual Deliverable—Your group will also create one visual document for our client, based on your research. This can include a flyer, a 3-fold brochure, a bookmark, or a poster. We will have access to the client's logo and colors, so we can match their branding. We will create these documents in Word, but then will transfer them to Microsoft Publisher so they can be printed and given to our client. I will take care of the printing and each group member will get to keep one copy of their group deliverable.

Reference

Barker, S. (2016). SAAFE House: Sexual assault and abuse free environment. *Postcards Magazine: Piney Woods Edition*, 36–40.

Appendix B—Course Objectives

The goals of BUAD 3335 (Business Communication) are to

1. Apply business communication strategies and principles to prepare effective messages for domestic and international business situations.
2. Identify ethical, legal, cultural, and global issues affecting business communication.
3. Use analytical and problem-solving skills typical in business communication.
4. Construct clear, logically organized messages using accepted standards of American English grammar, mechanics, and business style.
5. Select appropriate organizational formats and channels (including technology) for developing and presenting routine business messages.
6. Compose effective employment communication.
7. Conduct research and compose a documented business report.

6

THE OCCASION TO POST

Connecting *Kairos* to Entrepreneurship in an MBA Business Writing Blog Assignment

Kristen M. Getchell

Introduction

As the introduction to this volume indicates, the field of business communication has complicated theoretical underpinnings. Porter (2013), writing about rhetorical theory in the field of technical communication, explains the critical influence that theory has on pedagogy and indirectly provides support for a focused, operational use of theory in business communication:

> Theory should have heuristic and explanatory power: that is, it should help you *do* things, it should help you *see* things in a different way, it should enable you to *produce* things ... findings, conclusions, recommendations that have a real effect—an action—in the world.
>
> *(Porter, 2013, p. 129)*

He argues that rhetoric theory must be varied and transferable in order to have the most significant impact on the communicator.

To this end, business writing instructors need to consider how they can teach rhetorical theory in a way that is transformative, allowing students to view their own laboring through a lens of rhetorical process. Further, business communication instructors need to articulate a pedagogical arch for our classes that draws a connection for students from the introduction of rhetorical theory all the way to one or many applicable workplace writing contexts.

In this chapter, I describe my recent attempt to do just that. The following presents a blog writing unit (main assignment and scaffolding assignments) to demonstrate how rhetoric heuristics can provide students with a deeper understanding of the rhetorical theory and draw connections between entrepreneurship and opportunity in order to craft a more effective professional message. In this blog unit, students engage with rhetorical theory—specifically the traditional rhetorical notion of *kairos*—to support their writing work and see the connection between how writers craft and develop their message and how entrepreneurs think and approach problems.

Rhetorical Theory in the Business Writing Classroom: Weaknesses and Opportunities

Teaching business writing to graduate students is challenging for several reasons. Many graduate students have already been working in industry and, therefore, often (for better or worse) rely on their own professional experience to tell them what is important, useful, or correct. They see a division between the academic (theoretical) world and the real (practical) world that they recently have left to pursue a graduate degree. Removed from the academic classroom before returning for an MBA, they regard theory as less useful and more academic. Further, they demand assignments that look and feel like actual professional tasks. As business communication instructors know, creating authentic assignments can be complicated.

Scholars and professional writing practitioners argue for the importance of providing writing experiences that are relevant, realistic, and purposeful in order for students to find value in their coursework and develop the ability to apply knowledge across contexts. Relying on crafted case situations—which many instructors do out of necessity—doesn't get us there at the MBA level.

VanHoosier-Carey (1997), highlighting this problem in technical communication texts, complicates some of these crafted assignments by arguing that, while they seem authentic, the objectives of these assignments still "sever 'real-world' objectives and tasks from the situational matrices that give them significance and, thus, their 'real-world' quality" (398). While these assignments may be useful for teaching writing skills, VanHoosier-Carey argues that they are not furthering rhetorical knowledge. Assignments that meet these criteria are essential for students to develop their own rhetorical acuity. (Schieber, in this volume, provides an example of client-based writing projects that fulfills this requirement.)

Beyond practicality and usefulness, however, writing activities in any classroom need to prompt consideration of the rhetorical systems within which writing takes place, and a sound understanding of rhetorical theory is necessary to guide students—and instructors—toward a deeper understanding of practice. As mentioned in the introduction to this volume and several of the chapters within this text, business communication often relies on rhetorical theory to situate assignments in a plausible workplace context. VanHoosier-Carey (1997) notes that while rhetorical strategy is often discussed in technical writing courses, it is often reinforced through simulation assignments that are decontextualized, lacking an audience or purpose (p. 397). Thus, outside of their original organizational context, cases and simulations are limited by the lack of applied workplace contexts that give our communications meaning. What VanHoosier-Carey supports is that understanding the rhetorical nature of any interaction will help writers focus less on the correctness of genre conventions and begin to think like writers in a business context.

Business communication has a similar problem, and, further, often relies on an outdated notion of rhetorical theory. In addition to lacking plausible workplace contexts, textbooks in the field of business communication are behind in presenting what business communication instructors and theorists consider in communicative interactions. While some suggested assignments and activities introduce the notion of audience and context, they do so inside of a traditional understanding of a rhetorical situation: writer, reader, and the immediate space within which the communication act occurs.

In the past two decades, we've seen rhetoric scholars in writing studies move away from a traditional static situation model to more fluid conceptions of rhetorical interaction. Doug Downs (Wardle & Downs, 2016), in an overview of rhetoric for student writers, provides examples of some of the outer reaches of current rhetorical theory and helps us move beyond the rote rhetorical triangle. He encourages us to think of rhetoric like gravity for its ability to provide a ubiquitous framework for interactions, asking the writer to consider the implications of a communications act beyond the immediate situation.

Edbauer (2005), borrowing language previously used by Cooper (1986) to describe writing, argues a framework of these systems of interactions as *ecologies*—with the goal of moving away from the rhetorical situation or "sitemodel" toward an understanding of rhetoric as distributed and viral. She writes, "An ecological or *affective*, rhetorical model is one that reads rhetoric both as a process of distributed emergence and as an ongoing circulation process." This framework is particularly useful when considering not just an immediate rhetorical act, but the relationships and consequential response to a particular piece of public writing, adding the complex interaction with time and place. Our students need to consider themselves and their communication as part of a complex system of interactions, not a specific communication act with fixed place, time, and players. However, there has been some pushback on the prolific use of the term "ecology" among conservation and ecological scholars (see Polunin & Worthington, 1990), specifically as it is used in academic writing to describe a type of system. So, in my class, I have adopted the language of "rhetorical system" to help students understand some of these wider influences of their communication.

So, how can we get students to expand their view of each communication as part of larger rhetorical systems? For business communication instructors, getting students to understand requires developing assignments and heuristics that teach rhetorical knowledge as expansive, not limited to a particular situation. Porter (2013) highlights the usefulness that rhetorical theory can hold when developing a dynamic communication strategy. He notes that despite the perception that attention to theory is time wasted in the business world, rhetorical theory helps the technical writer focus less on the textual product and more on the audience, thus improving understanding of the context for communication. Because of this research suggesting the usefulness of rhetorical theory as applied to a specific task, it can provide a valuable conceptual framework for business communicators. This instruction first needs to be done with a robust discussion of rhetorical theory, using terms and applying them. We want students to think like business writers as they rhetorically negotiate or navigate genre conventions.

Much of the work of this unit happens within the invention period, when we use two heuristic activities to support process. Invention has been written about extensively across writing and communication studies; and practitioners are focusing on invention as part of the discovery, strategy, and reflection of the drafting process. Several chapters in this volume provide a new perspective on invention in the classroom, and this article furthers that emphasis on activities during the pre-composing process.

Specifically, in the discipline of business communication, invention is foundational in the business writing classroom. Bacabac (2015) built on the work of VanHoosier-Carey to present an argument for a focus on rhetorical strategy in the professional communication classroom through the application of "pedagogical practices approaches that emphasize rhetoric and usability to improve user satisfaction" (Bacabac, 2015, p. 117). In particular, Bacabac focuses on using concept mapping to promote invention in the writing process, and in this case, students are using heuristics in invention similarly to help them think like writers early in their process. Both heuristics focus heavily on the rhetorical notion of *kairos* as a method of invention.

Citing Bitzer (1968) and others, VanHoosier-Carey points to the importance of creating an exigence in communication assignments. Exigence is one part of *kairos*: the opportunity to write. The second part of *kairos* is the appropriateness of the response to the situation, which gives us a way to move students from the process of invention (finding an opportunity) to drafting (appropriately responding to the situation). According to Crowley and Hawhee (2012), *kairos* is a complex understanding of time, separate from linear time, that privileges the quality of opportunity: "*Kairos* is not about duration, but rather about a certain kind or quality of time, a period during which opportunities appear to those who are prepared to take advantage of them" (Crowley & Hawhee, 2012, p. 38). While traditional notions of rhetorical situation often focus on a specific time and place, Smith (2002) explains the importance of using *kairos* when interpreting events, specifically history, "because it points to their significance and purpose and to the idea that there are constellations of events pregnant with possibility (or possibilities) not to be met with at other times and under different circumstances" (p. 47). Miller argues that *kairos* draws attention "to the way situations change over time, to the relationship between past and future, to the way that one moment differs from the next" and allows us to consider "change, development, and progress—all notions central to the way we conceptualize technology" (Miller, 1994, p. 82). The term *kairos* is instructive for business students because it forces them move from writer-focused process to a more reader-focused process (a foundational process in business communication), a shift that can be particularly difficult for graduate students with little past formal writing instruction. In the next sections, I provide an overview of a professional blog assignment in an MBA course and the rhetorical heuristics that support the work of the unit during the invention phase.

Development of Rhetorical Language: Overview of Course and Unit

The class outlined in this chapter was taught in an on-campus MBA class at a business school with a high-ranking entrepreneurship program. The majority of students have left careers in finance, management, and accounting to pursue a graduate degree. A majority of them come from a corporate or family-business background, but many of them consider themselves entrepreneurial thinkers and chose the specific institution and program in order to develop and launch a venture.

The 1.5 credit course, titled *Strategic Writing for Managers*, is a once-per-week course that uses a portfolio of four major writing assignments along with several smaller assignments to provide students with experience considering genre conventions and evaluating audience and rhetorical contexts. The first three assignments are a revision email assignment, a rhetorical effectiveness report, and an executive summary.

These first three assignments have merit. These cases support the notion that rhetoric is transactional and are useful in helping students consider sentence-level issues and foundational questions when imagining an audience, such as how to organize and edit for clarity. In the end, they don't offer students an opportunity to access and practice writing in a rhetorical system as part of a complex and dynamic networked audience. They provide situations for students to consider and write to, but they don't have a robust rhetorical system for our students to engage with beyond the limited details of the assignment prompt. These assignments are used to consider some rhetorical elements with larger focus on the organization and correctness.

When I began teaching the course, I felt a need to provide students with more applied workplace writing experience with stakes and consequences that existed outside of the traditional classroom context. In order to create an assignment that provided a more accessible rhetorical system, I needed to develop a case that had an external audience and a semi-public context, with real stakes for students. Further, the goal was to design an assignment that would help me and my students explore the possibility of rhetorical theory in the business writing classroom. Finally, I wanted an openness to the assignment. I wanted students to have agency to make writerly decisions about conventions of the genre. To achieve these outcomes, I chose a blog post as a genre because it combines elements of public writing and a networked audience while allowing students flexibility of topic, purpose, and writing style.

A blog post gave students options for professional topics, although I did make some restraints on their decisions. I wanted to give students the freedom to make choices about genre and strategy, but with limited time, and in order to scaffold student efforts, I provided them with a specific blog platform. The decision to use a blog post, and specifically a LinkedIn blog post, is outlined in the next section.

Situating a Blog Post: Why Blog?

MBA programs, like most educational organizations, are trying to prepare students to operate in a constantly changing working environment. Currently, students are expected to meet traditional outcomes, in this case of business writing skills, while also responding to the technological demands of the social web. As Rice (2009) pointed out, professional blogs have been derided for often anemic editorial oversight. However, these very characteristics of blogs allow them to be useful in writing development, with similar characteristics to the personal writing assignments that Lawrence advocates for in her chapter in this book. Further, Rice (2009) indicated that the early view of blog writing as personal writing akin to journaling has changed over time and is a reductive assessment of contemporary blog usage. Now, we are seeing individual and corporate blogs become commonplace on the web. In their survey of entrepreneurs, Spartz and Weber (2015) found that almost a third of surveyed entrepreneurs reported writing a company blog during the opening stages of their business. This number is not overwhelming, but evidence suggests that blogging is increasing. For example, the Center for Marketing Research at UMass Dartmouth (Ganim Barnes & Pavao 2017) has been monitoring social media trends among Fortune 500 and INC 500 companies since 2006, and despite a slight dip in 2015 and 2016, there has been an eight-year upward trend in corporate blogging, with 42 percent of companies reporting using blogs as part of their social media strategy.

Considering the nature of social media activity, the question becomes how are business writing courses preparing students to write in this particular context? Both collaborative and individual blogs are being incorporated into the classrooms in various business-related disciplines, such as management (MacDuff, 2009, 2012) and economics (Cameron, 2012), in order to provide students with this type of communication experience. One challenge of incorporating social media writing such as blogging into a business writing course is to avoid doing so as a novelty or gimmick. Much like Kaufer, Gunawardena, Tan, and Cheek (2011) caution with undergraduate writing courses, graduate writing courses, such as business writing in an MBA program, must also incorporate social media in a way that preserves the foundations of writing pedagogy and improves on the instruction and learning in the course.

Choosing a platform for blogging in our particular case also involved a matter of convenience, since all of the students enrolled in our graduate programs are required to create a LinkedIn account during orientation. Surpassing one million unique users in June 2015, LinkedIn is a platform that encourages conversations among users (Roth, 2015). The posting feature is free with a basic account, and the platform also features a comments section that has the potential to be used for frequent interaction with other users. According to the Center for Marketing Research at the Charlton College of Business at UMass Dartmouth, "the use of LinkedIn is virtually universal among the F500 (97%). This is clearly a platform that provides undisputed utility for them in terms of access to vendors, customers, potential employees etc." The assumption, then, is that this platform is familiar to MBA students and that they will be able to focus on their writing as opposed to learning technical aspects of a platform.

Sites such as LinkedIn are making publishing easier than ever for students interested in sharing their ideas on the web. Samuel (2015) argues that these sites have the potential to inhibit creativity and expression with the limitations on format. This certainly may be true, specifically for experienced bloggers; however, sites such as LinkedIn provide a way for new bloggers to easily access the ability to demonstrate credibility through a connection to a virtual resume as well as a number of connections that would be difficult to build with an independent blog. Further, Samuel notes that sites such as LinkedIn are encouraging a focus on content that is strategic toward one's career goals, resulting in a focus on product over process that can potentially inhibit the kind of exploratory writing that can generate ideas and ignite creativity.

All of these pros and cons make for interesting strategic discussion with students, shifting the focus back to the fundamental rhetorical consideration of purpose and audience. The discussion of choosing an appropriate platform for blogging provides its own opportunity to continue to reflect back on their rhetorical strategy. We consider why looking at other platforms may be a good idea for students who want to become prolific posters and who plan to post on content outside of their professional area. For my students' purposes, LinkedIn has a number of advantages: all incoming students have LinkedIn pages; it offers a uniform, pre-determined, and simple format; conventions of the site don't demand frequent posting; and it gives students a specific, professional audience in their network.

Arch of Blog Unit

In an attempt to create a truly authentic writing assignment informed by rhetorical theory, which demanded students draw on their own understanding of opportunity, I assigned the LinkedIn professional blog post assignment as the culminating part of a final unit of activities. The three-week unit consists of three written assignments: the Reflective *Ethos* and *Kairos* assignment, the Opportunity Checklist in-class revision, and the Final Blog Post.

The major guiding criteria of the final blog assignment (see Appendix) are that students take a strategic approach to the development of a professional post and that they follow the formatting conventions of the LinkedIn platform. Specifically, I tell students that they can choose any topic they would like for their content, but the post needs to be professional and appropriate for their LinkedIn network. The following sections describe the progression of this unit and outline the major rhetoric heuristics that are used to support students' strategic design and production of an effective blog post.

During the course of the semester, students become familiar with the notion of credibility and other fundamental elements of persuasive writing such as rhetorical appeals and audience awareness. Through reading and class discussion, we discuss effective informative and persuasive writing and identify characteristics of effective professional communication through samples and cases. During this time, I encourage students to consider the notion of rhetorical system; I ask them to move away from an understanding of rhetoric as site and time specific and formulate an understanding of rhetoric within a larger networked system of interactions. In the blog unit, we examine the rhetorical system, which includes the defined audience but also the subsequent shares across the social graph.

Since we are dealing with a system that has the potential for wide circulation, students must choose a topic that they feel they have the credibility to write about. This is the first blog post for many of my students, and they often find that this assignment is more difficult for them than they anticipate because of the volume of options. So, to try to make it more accessible to them, I ask them to write what they know.

Invention for a Blog Post: Introducing *Kairos*

In addition to helping students consider their own credibility as they approach their writing, I also help them pick a topic with opportunity. Online, conversations are happening at rapid pace, and reader attention is a scarce commodity. Therefore, it is important for students to choose a timely and relevant topic in order to increase their chance of readership. Further, this type of work needs to happen within the invention period as they are developing their topic and their ideas about that topic.

In class, I give a lecture on the term *kairos* and its application to business writing. We look at how the term has been defined, consider how it could be applied to their own text production, and even examine some of the representations of *kairos* in art and literature, such as depictions of the god Kairos as two-faced, walking a razor's edge.

To begin to make the idea of *kairos* more applicable to their blog post, we focus on the way that *kairos* is connected to virality. In order to find the most effective topic, they need to identify situations of Bitzer's (1968) "exigence" and occupy that space while also considering the interconnectedness of rhetorical acts, specifically how different rhetors may read and interact with blog posts in an online environment after they hit "post."

At the end of the lecture, students will complete two heuristic assignments aimed at helping them understand and evaluate *kairos*. Both of these assignments (one for homework and one in-class activity) are described as personal prewriting. As a professional writing course, our class tends to have a focus on product. I tell students that these two assignments are writer-focused and compare them to the reader-focused drafts that they produce for their cases. It is worth emphasizing at this point the value of writer-focused activities during the invention phase. Lawrence, in this volume, provides an argument for this type of personal writing as a way for students to reflect and also highlights the reader-oriented results of a writer-focused process. Both of these assignments give students a chance to explore the possibility behind writing, thinking, and reflecting, with the hope that they will see the value of these early activities in creating an effective final product.

Heuristic I: Reflective *Ethos* and *Kairos* Assignment

The invention activity students complete after the first class of the unit is the Reflective *Ethos* and *Kairos* Assignment (REK) (see Appendix). Just as Blakeslee and Savage (2013) argue for the use of heuristics for technical communicators, students in the class were asked to use questions as a heuristic and to develop questions of their own as they worked on the assignments.

In my first three semesters of teaching this unit, I made this a classroom activity, but I noticed a lot of students choosing and then abandoning topics, so I created a more deliberate and longer period for students to choose a focus for their post. Students take an entire week to complete the REK assignment, during which I ask them to spend some time identifying online conversations in their areas of interest. I also encourage them to explore newsworthy items that they feel comfortable commenting on. These habits are important to the *invention* process.

At the end of the REK assignment, students are asked to list three to five preliminary topics for a blog post.

Once they have completed the REK assignment, students come to the following class with potential topics for their blog post. In this second class period, we start by putting these topics to the test. Still in the invention phase of their processes, we start to consider the rhetorical system within which these topics would interact. It is important at this stage that I help them see that writing is not just addressing the specifics of a genre correctly but thinking like a writer about their business and communication goals, identifying consequences of their communications, and making appropriate decisions as a result.

The goal of this early work is to model the types of decisions and considerations writers need to attend to as they develop any written communication. It is worth noting for students that sometimes the invention process is longer (for lower-stakes, short written communications) or longer (for higher-stakes, more complicated professional writing tasks).

As a way to start to make this early work more applicable to my students, I also use the second class period as a way to demonstrate the connection between entrepreneurship specifically by comparing the notion of entrepreneurial opportunity with the rhetorical concept of *kairos*. If the REK assignment asks students to focus on thinking like writers, the second heuristic, the Opportunity Checklist revision, helps them understand how, while doing so, they are also thinking like entrepreneurs.

Heuristic II: Connecting *Kairos* with Opportunity in Entrepreneurship

As mentioned in the introduction, Porter (2013) argues that rhetorical theory must be transferable. In this particular case, I would like students to be able to apply the theory learned in our class to other locations, not just of writing, but of thinking and decision making. Specifically, I use a second heuristic activity during this blog unit to connect their blog writing process to the types of strategic thinking students will use in entrepreneurship.

In the US, the rate of entrepreneurial activity is increasing (GEM, 2014) and, not surprisingly, the discipline of entrepreneurship is growing rapidly in higher educational institutions in the US and abroad (Myrah & Currie, 2006). In order to address this shift in business education, business communication courses need to acknowledge the connection between new entrepreneurial genres and more traditional business writing activities and theory, specifically, rhetorical theory in business communication.

Neck, Greene, and Brush (2014) call for an entrepreneurship curriculum that functions across classrooms, where reinforcement of entrepreneurial values permeates across disciplines. One way to do this in a business writing course is by focusing on the underlying rhetorical theory of all forms of business communication and demonstrating how foundational concepts of rhetoric inform, explain, and support writing in a changing entrepreneurial landscape.

Students at our institution are trained to think like entrepreneurs. In addition to creating social and economic value, their learning experience centers around "applying entrepreneurial thinking broadly" (Babson College). By demonstrating the similarities between the thought process of entrepreneurs and writers, I hope to reinforce both.

Neck et al. (2014) identify elements of play, empathy, creation, experimentation, and reflection as central to entrepreneurial thinking (and teaching). Students who may not identify as writers but feel well prepared in entrepreneurship may feel more comfortable with making rhetorical decisions when they see the similarities between these two ways of approaching a task. One way I encourage them toward this type of analysis is through the application of *kairos* to an entrepreneurship activity in which they borrow an invention activity from an entrepreneurship text in order to illustrate the way that rhetorical theory can be applied broadly.

In order to support this type of process thinking, entrepreneurship texts, such as *Teaching Entrepreneurship: A Practice-Based Approach* by Neck et al. (2014), provide activities aimed at helping students create, consider, and evaluate entrepreneurship ideas. If we consider entrepreneurship as a rhetorical act (the process of developing an argument in favor of a venture) the majority of activities included in Neck and company's text would fall into the traditional rhetorical canon of *invention*, for their purpose is to find and develop arguments in support of a particular idea.

In order to illustrate the nature of *kairos* and demonstrate the overlap of rhetorical thinking, I developed a heuristic based on an activity from *The Portable MBA in Entrepreneurship, 4th Edition* by Bygrave and Zacharakis (2015) called the Opportunity Checklist (see Appendix for full activity). As written, the Opportunity Screening Exercise asks students to evaluate a venture idea by considering the opportunity associated with a variety of categories related to customers. Students are presented with a characteristic of their target customer base, such as "Identifiable," and asked to choose between the Better Opportunity column's "Defined core customer" and the Weaker Opportunity column's "Undefined customer." They are asked to choose between the two and check the column that applies to their venture idea. The goal of the original activity is to evaluate the idea based on the number of metrics that fall under "Better Opportunity." According to Bygrave and Zacharakis (2015):

> We find the ideas that most often lead to successful businesses have two key characteristics: First, they are something that the entrepreneur is truly passionate about; second, the idea is a strong opportunity as measured on the opportunity checklist. To be sure of having a strong opportunity, entrepreneurs need a deep understanding of their customer, preferably knowing the customer by name.
>
> *(p. 115)*

Without specifically using traditional rhetorical terms, Bygrave and Zacharakis make an argument for early consideration of elements of *ethos* and *kairos* in individual entrepreneurship activities.

For the purpose of our class, I ask students to get into small groups and discuss and re-write the categories in terms of audience and a rhetorical system as it relates to their blog post preliminary topic. I asked students to reframe the activity as an evaluation of *kairos* and consider which of the metrics could also apply to a writing act. The question for students becomes, *how can we revise this checklist to serve our purpose of finding the best topic for our blog post?*

As we begin to make revisions to the checklist, students make some global changes first. They suggest changing "Customer" to "Audience" so that their new metrics were evaluating the audience of the assignment. Once we make this shift, students are surprised at how easily the chart can be used to evaluate the audience of a piece of writing with little revision.

The following is an example of the revisions one group made to the checklist during the most recent semester.

EXAMPLE REVISED OPPORTUNITY CHECKLIST

Metric on Original Opportunity Checklist	Revised Metric for Blog Post Checklist	Better Opportunity	Weaker Opportunity
Identifiable (customer)	Identifiable (audience)	Defined Core (audience) Clear who we are writing to	Undefined (audience) Unclear who the audience for this piece would be.
Demographics	Demographics	Clearly defined and focused (audience)	Fuzzy definition and unfocused (audience)
Window of Opportunity	Window of Opportunity (timeliness of writing)	Opening/Growing	Closing/Shrinking
Market Size	Audience Size	Large core group	Small, unclear group
Demand: Frequency	Potential Posting Frequency	Often and repeated: room for series of posts?	One-time post
Operating Expenses	Writing/ Researching Time and Relative Effort	Fixed and clear to author	Variable and potentially complicated
Competition: Number of Direct Competitors	Competition: Number of Direct Competitors (other writers)	Few: not many people writing blogs about this topic	Many: this topic has been written about extensively
Strength of Competitors	Strength of Competitors	Weak: no one has addressed this well yet	Strong: other writers are more qualified

As you can see from this example, major changes to the draft involve shifting consideration of "consumers" to "audience" and evaluating the opportunity of their potential topics from a perspective of *kairos*: timeliness of topic, relevance to audience, number and strength of competition, efficiency, and perceived reward of process (multiple posts).

Through this heuristic activity and subsequent discussion, students see that evaluating the opportunity of a venture requires a similar thought process to evaluating the opportunity of a rhetorical moment. Students are often surprised at the ease with which we re-configure elements of the original entrepreneurial heuristic to adapt it to a particular writing process. Students are able to highlight that a similar sort of thinking is required when considering how an idea is produced, evaluated, and made public.

After groups complete a revision of the Opportunity Checklist, students complete the revised checklist for each of their three preliminary topics, checking the boxes where appropriate and tallying their scores. The revised Opportunity Checklist heuristic helps students expand their focus on audience, speaker, and purpose and move toward an understanding of rhetorical systems as they imagine their changing, permeable network. In a blog post assignment, students are required to think beyond the traditional structure of the rhetorical situation to a more fluid context. For example, the nature of an internet blog post is that is a public writing act. Once a student rhetor hits post, the message is distributed. However, in digital writing, this message will continue with likes, comments, reposts, and reposts with counter-claims. Further, as this post is circulated, it may be used by another rhetor as part of their own message back across the interconnected rhetorical space and become part of a public rhetoric. This activity trains students to begin to look for the myriad opportunities in any given blog post. Once they have thoroughly vetted topics against the checklist, they choose one to begin the composing process for the final blog post assignment.

Conclusion

> To be effective, usable and useful, rhetoric theory must be prompt and push deeper thinking; it must be powerful in the respect that it enables you to see in a new way—to see events, texts, processes, positions, and people in a way that deepens your understanding and leads to more productive action. Rhetoric heuristics also need to be simple, memorable, and portable—transferable across a wide variety of situations and contexts.
>
> *(Porter, 2013, p. 140)*

Since the inclusion of these two heuristics in the blog unit, I've noticed significant changes in the blog post assignments. First, I've noticed a better-defined sense of topics at the point where students begin composing. Previously, students switched topics frequently, choosing a topic, writing for a bit, and then somewhat haphazardly choosing another topic. These two heuristics allow them to consider the viability of their topics before writing in several ways, and this translates to more defined topics when they begin writing. To this end, I have also noticed a higher quality of final posts overall. Students are choosing better topics, and this has resulted in a better final product.

Another observation is in the sophistication in how students talk about and consider *kairos*. Students seem better equipped to discuss the exigence of their topic more clearly. Specifically, I have seen students engage in dialog during peer review that focuses on the appropriateness of the post considering the broader conversation. In their final portfolio reflection, students are using terms like *kairos*, relevance, opportunity, timeliness, and appropriateness more frequently as they describe their writerly decisions.

Finally, I've noticed that students are able to provide overlap between entrepreneurship and rhetoric in a practical sense. Students seem to be able to see value in rhetorical theory for its ability to also describe and connect with the type of thinking entrepreneurs do. For graduate students, this connection is an important one. This unit gives them an opportunity to see the overlap between rhetorical theory—*kairos*—and entrepreneurship, providing them with a broad and profound understanding of how rhetorical theory informs communication and innovation practices. Seeing their writing process as a type of entrepreneurial thinking, students approach their topic and analysis of the audience with a new perspective.

References

Bacabac, F. (2015). Appropriating invention through concept maps in writing for multimedia and the web. *Business and Professional Communication Quarterly, 72*(2), 115–135. doi: 10.1177/2329490615576184.

Bitzer, L. (1968). The rhetorical situation. *Philosophy and Rhetoric, 1*, 1–14.

Blakeslee, A. M., & Savage, G. (2013). What do technical communicators needs to know about writing? In Johndan Johnson-Eilola and Stuart A. Selber (Eds.), *Solving problems in technical communication* (pp. 362–385). Chicago: University of Chicago Press.

Bygrave, W. D. (2011). The entrepreneurial process. In W. D. Bygrave and A. Zacharakis (Eds.), *The portable MBA in entrepreneurship*. Somerset, NJ: Wiley. doi: 10.1002/9781118256121. ch1

Bygrave, W. D., & Zacharakis, A. (2015). *The portable MBA in entrepreneurship*. Hoboken, NJ: Wiley. Retrieved from http://ebookcentral.proquest.com/lib/babson/detail. action?docID=2130972.

Cameron, M. (2012). "Economics with training wheels": Using blogs in teaching and assessing introductory economics. *The Journal of Economic Education, 43*(4), 394–407. doi: 10.1080/00220485.2012.714316.

Cooper, M.M. (1986). The ecology of writing. *College English, 48*(4), 364–375.

Crowley, S., & Hawhee, D. (2012). *Ancient rhetorics for contemporary students*. Boston, MA: Pearson.

Edbauer, J. (2005). Unframing models of public distribution: From rhetorical situation to rhetorical ecologies. *Rhetoric Society Quarterly, 35*(4), 5–24.

Ganim Barnes, N., & Pavao, S. (2017). The 2017 fortune 500 go visual and increase use of Instagram, Snapchat, and YouTube. *UMass Dartmouth Center for Marketing Research*. Retrieved from www.umassd.edu/cmr/socialmediaresearch/2017fortune500/#d. en.963986.

Global Entrepreneurship Monitor Consortium. (2014). *GEM Global Entrepreneurship Monitor – Global Reports*. Retrieved January 7, 2018 from www.gemconsortium.org/ report/49079

Kaufer, D., Gunawardena, A., Tan, A., & Cheek, A. (2011). Bringing social media to the writing classroom: Classroom salon. *Journal of Business and Technical Communication, 25*(3), 299–321. doi: 10.1177/1050651911400703.

Macduff, I. (2009). Using blogs as a teaching tool in negotiation. *Negotiation Journal, 25*(1), 107–124.

Macduff, I. (2012). Using blogs in teaching negotiation: A technical and intercultural postscript. *Negotiation Journal, 28*(2), 201–215.

Miller, C. R. (1994). Opportunity, opportunism, and progress: Kairos in the rhetoric of technology. *Argumentation, 8*(1), 81–96. doi: https://doi.org/10.1007/BF00710705.

Myrah, K., & Currie, R. (2006). Examining undergraduate entrepreneurship education. *Journal of Small Business & Entrepreneurship, 19*(3), 233–253.

Neck, H. M., Greene, P. G., & Brush, C. G. (2014). *Teaching entrepreneurship: A practice-based approach*. Northampton, MA: Edward Elgar.

Polunin, N., & Worthington, E. (1990). On the use and misuse of the term 'Ecosystem'. *Environmental Conservation, 17*(3), 274–274. doi: 10.1017/S0376892900032495.

Porter, J. (2013). How can rhetoric theory inform the practice of technical communication? In Johndan Johnson-Eilola & Stuart A. Selber (Eds.), *Solving problems in technical communication* (pp. 125–145). Chicago: The University of Chicago Press.

Rice, J. (2009). Networked exchanges, identity, writing. *Journal of Business and Technical Communication, 23*(3), 294–317. doi: 10.1177/1050651909333178.

Roth, D. (2015, July 9). *More than 1 million members are now publishing on LinkedIn* [Web blog post]. Retrieved from www.blog.linkedin.com/2015/07/09/1-million-linkedin-publishers.

Samuel, A. (2015, June 30). Have LinkedIn and Medium Killed the Old-Fashioned Blog? *Harvard Business Review*. Retrieved from https://hbr.org/2015/06/have-linkedin-and-medium-killed-the-old-fashioned-blog.

Smith, J. (2002). Time and qualitative time. In Phillip Sipiora & James S. Baumlin (Eds.), *Rhetoric and Kairos: Essays in history, theory, and praxis* (pp. 46–57). Albany, NY: SUNY Press.

Spartz, J., & Weber, R. (2015). Writing entrepreneurs: A survey of habit, skills, and genres. *Journal of Business and Technical Communication, 29*(4), 428–455.

Vanhoosier-Carey, G. (1997). Rhetoric by design: Using web development projects in the technical communication classroom. *Computers and Composition, 14*(3), 395–406.

Wardle, E. A., & Downs, D. (2014). *Writing about writing: A college reader*. Boston: Bedford/St. Martin's.

Appendix A—Reflective *Ethos* and *Kairos* Assignment

Reflective *Ethos* and *Kairos* Assignment

This invention (prewriting) assignment provides you with an opportunity to reflect on your credibility in a variety of areas and identify the relevance and timeliness of certain areas of your expertise.

For Case #3, you will be asked to create professional blog post, and the success of your blog will rely largely on two important factors: your ability to persuade your audience that you are a credible source on your topic and the relevant nature of the topic. Often activities like blogging—or cover letters and personal networking pitches—are difficult because we don't spend time systematically reflecting on our own expertise and developing a strategy for the writing occasion.

It is my hope that articulating your experiences and knowledge will help narrow down a relevant topic—and potential opportunity—for your blog.

I've asked you all to create a list of preliminary topics for your post. To help us narrow the list, I'd like you to answer the following question in paragraph form (complete sentences) providing as many concrete examples as possible.

As I mentioned in class, this is a writer-focused assignment, and you should try to quiet that editor in your head to allow yourself to more freely generate ideas (in other words, don't be afraid to generate some text).

Ethos (ethical appeal, credibility):

1. What would you consider to be your primary field of professional expertise? What is your experience (formSal and informal) in this field? What does this experience allow you to share with others?
2. What are your secondary areas of expertise? These may be interests or hobbies. What is your experience in these areas? What are you able to share with others?

3. Of the areas you've identified, which are you most comfortable writing about and why?

4. Of the areas you've identified, which are you most passionate about?
   Kairos (opportunity, relevance, appropriateness):

5. Considering the areas you listed above, which ones offer the best opportunity to write? Are any of these areas more relevant than others right now?

6. Consider your own professional goals (i.e., job/internship searching, promotion, changing field); would publishing on LinkedIn about one of these topics be appropriate and timely for your professional objectives?

7. Can you use this assignment to research or write about something useful in other areas of your professional lives? For example, could this assignment help you address a knowledge gap?

8. Look at your topics. Considering the word limit and platform for this assignment, eliminate any topics that aren't appropriate for a blog post.

Appendix B—Opportunity Checklist

Exhibit 3.11
Opportunity Checklist

DOWNLOADABLE CHECKLIST . . . USE EXHIBIT 3.11.DOCX FOR BOOK

Customer	Better Opportunities	Weaker Opportunities
Identifiable	PTA	STA
Demographics	Clearly defined and focused	Fuzzy definition and unfocused
Psychographics	Clearly defined and focused	Fuzzy definition and unfocused
Trends		
Macro market	Multiple and converging	Few and disparate
Target market	Multiple and converging	Few and disparate
Window of opportunity	Opening	Closing
Market structure	Emerging/Fragmented	Mature/Decline
Market size		
How many	PTA	STA
Demand	Greater than supply	Less than supply
Market growth		
Rate	20% or greater	Less than 20%
Price/Frequency/Value		
Price	GM > 40%	GM < 40%
Frequency	Often and repeated	One time
Value	Fully reflected in price	Penetration pricing
Operating expenses	Low and variable	Large and fixed
NI margin	>10%	<10%
Volume	Very high	Moderate

Customer	Better Opportunities	Weaker Opportunities
Distribution		
Where are you in value chain?	High margin, high power	Low margin, low power
Competition		
Market structure	Emerging	Mature
Number of direct competitors	Few	Many
Number of indirect competitors	Few	Many
Number of substitutes	Few	Many
Stealth competitors	Unlikely	Likely
Key Success Factors		
Relative position	Strong	Weak
Vendors		
Relative power	Weak	Strong
Gross margins they control in value chain	Low	High
Government		
Regulations	Low	High
Taxes	Low	High
Global Environment		
Customers	Interested and accessible	Not interested or accessible
Competition	Existing and strong	Nonexistent or weak
Vendors	Eager	Unavailable

Go through each category and mark whether your opportunity fits in the Better Opportunity or Weaker Opportunity column. The more marks in the Better Opportunity column, the better your chances at success. If you have more marks in the Weaker Opportunity column, your idea may not be an opportunity and you will face higher risk of failure. Think about ways you can change your opportunity or strategy to move some of the checkmarks to the Better Opportunity column. (Andrew Zacharakis (2010) from W.D. Bygrave & Andrew Zacharakis (Eds.), *The Portable MBA in Entrepreneurship*. Somerset, NJ: John Wiley & Sons.)

7

IT'S COMPLICATED

The White Paper as Exemplar within Complexes of Rhetorical Delivery

Matthew R. Sharp

According to Willerton (2012), white papers present information to help readers make a decision or solve a problem, but the primary purpose of the document is to build *ethos* for the author as a marketing strategy. By providing useful information to the reader, white paper authors—individuals or companies who have their own products or service to sell—demonstrate expertise in a particular subject matter or industry. The resulting *ethos* could eventually lead to a sale. A white paper, however, does not function alone. Other texts within an ecology of sales and business-related genres help move the potential client toward and through the final sale. This kind of coordination of multiple texts toward a common goal is a common practice within many industries and, therefore, needs to be reflected within the business communication classroom.

In order to do so, we must continue to expand the rhetorical canon of delivery to include rhetorical choices that go beyond simple choices of medium and visual design of a single publication. Rude (2004) suggests that we open up the canon of delivery "to accommodate related rhetorical acts over time" (p. 273) because some more comprehensive rhetorical exigencies require mediation by more than a single text or genre. Rude's focus was on the strategic use of reports by a non-profit organization to influence public policy, and she warned that her description of delivery within that context should not be conflated with a political or for-profit context. Concerned about the "suspicion of delivery as distortion" and "the hegemonic voice of business or government as usual," she emphasized her intention for reconceiving delivery in this way: encouraging "an increased sense of ethical responsibility for the publication and its uses" (Rude, 2004, p. 285). This chapter, however, is grounded in a belief that this same increased sense of responsibility for a publication's uses must extend beyond the nonprofit and public policy contexts and into the realm of business communication writ large. Not only are business communicators responsible, as Rude (2004) argues, for ensuring the ethical usage of the texts they produce, they must also take responsibility for how those texts coordinate with other texts and activities as they are published and circulated within systems of business activity. By expanding the canon of delivery to account for these considerations, we acknowledge the complexity of contemporary rhetorical exigencies and encourage business communication students to consider those complexities within our courses.

White papers, then, become one way to allow students to practice strategizing ways to deal with these complexities. Within an expanded sense of delivery, white papers function as one part of an ecology of business- and sales-related genres. This complex rhetorical situation is one of the advantages of teaching the white paper in a business communication classroom because it allows students to practice creating a document whose purpose is to perform a particular social action within a complex of related social actions. The white paper becomes a single move in a larger rhetorical strategy of multiple instances of delivery, and business communication students need experience in this kind of strategic and interweaving of multiple genres that all work together in a coordinated effort to accomplish a broader social action—the eventual sale of a product or service to a potential client.

Recovering Rhetorical Delivery

Throughout classical rhetoric, the rhetorical canon of delivery was treated as a necessary part of a rhetor's education. Even Aristotle (trans. 2007), who considered delivery a "vulgar matter" (Bk. III, Ch. 1, para. 5), acknowledged its necessity to the art of persuasion. In fact, many ancient rhetoricians considered delivery to be one of the more important aspects of rhetoric (Holland, 2016). Cicero (trans. 1970) claimed its primacy by saying it has "the sole and supreme power in oratory" (Bk. III, Ch. LVI). Without a strong delivery, even the most intelligent speaker could fail at persuading his audience, but with it, a speaker with much less intellect could impress the audience and succeed. Comprising considerations of both vocal quality and nonverbal gestures, the canon of delivery was, like memory, exclusively concerned with the performative aspect of a speech. Therefore, as the study and practice of rhetoric have evolved over the millennia and textual discourse replaced the spoken word, concern for what Brooke (2009) has called these "nearly vestigial canons" (p. 29) waned. In fact, Welch (1993) found that textbooks in the late twentieth century began to "truncate the five canons from five to three, so that invention, arrangement (form), and style repeatedly colonize the last two—memory and delivery—and then eradicate them" (p. 18).

Over the last few decades, however, rhetorical scholars have been working to reconceptualize the five canons of rhetoric to align more effectively with contemporary communication practices, theories, and technologies. Particular attention has been paid to the canon of delivery. In early attempts to revive delivery, this meant a focus on the affordances available to communicators through desktop publishing software, including concerns for typeface, layout, and even paper quality (Connors, 1993). As such, delivery was squarely a concern of *ethos*—a way to "affect readers' dispositions toward writers and their messages" (Connors, 1993, p. 66). Arguing for this revival, Welch (1993) claims that memory and delivery "do not wither with the growing dominance of writing; rather, they change form" (p. 19). As web technologies developed, those concerns transitioned from the page to the screen, and sound and image resurrected the performative aspect of delivery (Dragga, 1993; Handa, 2014). Delivery was equated during this revival with the choice of medium for a particular rhetorical act. The extra-textual, performative aspects of multimedia were seen as replacements for the human body in considerations of delivery: "the media forms stand as avatars in its stead, applying shape, color, and texture to the content of a given text" (McCorkle, 2012, p. 8).

Beyond considerations of medium, some scholars began to theorize delivery as pertaining to the material conditions of a text's production, distribution, and circulation. DeVoss and Porter (2006) claim that "the revolution is not just hypertext and it's not just the Internet and it's not just new media" (p. 180). Trimbur (2000) insists that we "see writing as it circulates through linked moments of production, distribution, exchange, and consumption" (p. 196). For Trimbur, delivery was wrapped up in "the material conditions of producing writing and getting it delivered where it needs to go" (Trimbur, 2000, p. 189). These material conditions affect the ways in which audiences interpret texts. Not only is a text affected by the decisions made during its production, it is also affected by how it is received by its audiences—the route(s) it takes and the contexts through which it travels to reach its destination.

Following Trimbur's concept of circulation as delivery, other scholars began seeing delivery as more than the performance of a text. DeVoss and Porter (2006) describe this new perspective as a paradigm shift "to an emergent and ill-understood view of writing as weaving digital media for distribution across networked spaces for various audiences engaged in different types of reading" (p. 179). In fact, most of the work to recover the canon of delivery in the twenty-first century has centered around its application to digital texts and how they circulate. McCorkle (2012) argues that this application of delivery to new media and its affordances is an historical pattern: the canon of delivery has always "helped to foster the cultural reception of emergent technologies of writing and communication by prescribing rules or by examining and privileging tendencies that cause old and new media forms to resemble one another" (p. 5). Following this historical pattern, Porter (2009) created new *topoi* of delivery in the digital age, including considerations for distribution, circulation, access and accessibility, interaction, and economics. And both Adsanatham, Garrett, and Matzke (2013) and Bourelle, Bourelle, and Jones (2015) applied conceptions of digital delivery to multimedia classroom projects in order to help their students more fully consider the ways in which their delivery choices would impact the audience. Ridolfo and DeVoss (2009) took it a step further and used delivery to ask questions about what they call rhetorical velocity—"a conscious rhetorical concern for distance, travel, speed, and time, pertaining specifically to theorizing instances of strategic appropriation by a third party" (p. velocity). While these theories of delivery acknowledge that texts (or the reception of them) may change over time due to the intricacies of publication and circulation, they lack a consideration of how texts interact with other texts as they're being delivered and after they've been delivered.

Complexes of Rhetorical Delivery

Rude (2004), on the other hand, offers a complex conception of delivery that takes aspects of publication and circulation into account as well as an understanding of delivery as "a series of strategic actions in which publications are crucial" (p. 276). She encourages the field to perceive the traditional rhetorical situation as "long-term, comprehensive, and complex" where a single exigence is not always resolved by a single text (Rude, 2004, p. 273). In fact, when an exigence is complex, she claims that "the work of rhetoric . . . requires vision beyond the single document" (Rude, 2004, p. 273). To achieve this vision, Rude (2004) adds a sense of time to the canon of delivery but a sense different from that of Trimbur (2000), DeVoss and Porter (2006), or Brooke (2009). Rude emphasizes the fact that change (the resolving of a complex exigence) can sometimes take years, and it often requires a message to be delivered repeatedly over multiple texts and other activities.

In Rude's (2004) study, she examined a report in which the Union of Concerned Scientists argued for the economic benefits of renewable energy. The report's argument, however, could not accomplish a change in policy on its own. It was part of a much larger strategy for change that included other reports and other genres (newsletters, emails, and press releases) as well as other types of nontextual activity, such as meetings and presentations. This kind of "web of interrelated and intentional actions moves an idea toward fruition and a plan toward implementation" (Rude, 2004, p. 286). Ridolfo (2012) claims that the strategic use of multiple texts across multiple media corresponds "to multiple discreet acts of delivery" (p. 7). But why can't the canon of delivery—a heuristic intended to guide a rhetor through the rhetorical resolution of an exigence—be large enough to accommodate consideration of multiple texts and other related activities?

The relationship between exigence and text is not necessarily one-to-one. Complex business goals are not necessarily accomplished in a single moment through a single text. More often, organizations coordinate multiple texts and activities to work toward their larger goals. Our theories of delivery need to be able to accommodate these complex rhetorical exigencies that require more than one text delivered in a finite time period. Rude (2004) thought the report from the UCS was "a tool of social action as well as a publication, and delivery is strategic action as well as visual design and medium" (p. 279). She believes the canons are flexible and adaptable enough to accommodate this expanded perception of delivery as complexes of multi-genre strategy, but in order to teach students how to navigate the requisite expansion of the rhetorical situation, we must understand how various texts, genres, and activities work together toward common goals.

Genre Ecologies

Rhetorical genre theory establishes the ways in which various artifacts work together to accomplish goals. Grounded in Miller's (1984) understanding of genres as typified responses to recurrent rhetorical situations, groups of genres become "typified rhetorical strategies" (Bawarshi, 2003, p. 17) and are often viewed through cultural-historical activity theory as mediational tools within activity systems. Russell (2009) calls research from this particular perspective writing, activity, and genre research. From the WAGR theoretical perspective, the basic activity system within a rhetorical study includes a subject using some text as a mediatory tool upon an object, individual, or group with a specific outcome in mind (Russell, 1995). It has a striking resemblance to the basic rhetorical triangle of writer, text, and audience, but it is reframed as a social action. Nardi, Whittaker, and Schwarz (2002) claim that "one of the strengths of activity theory is that it posits a sentient subject engaging in conscious actions attributable to specific objects" (p. 209). Sentient subjects are aware of their actions, and in acting they have specific goals in mind. To accomplish those goals, however, they must make use of mediatory tools, and more complex goals require more complex coordination of those tools. Spinuzzi (2001) calls this complex coordination of tools "compound mediation." Put simply, compound mediation reflects "the ways that workers coordinate sets of artifacts to help them get their jobs done" (Spinuzzi, 2001, p. 58).

Along the same line of thought, Devitt (2004) asserts that a single genre is rarely enough to accomplish all of an organization's goals, and she explains four ways in which collectives of genres have been theorized. A context of genres contains "all existing genres in a society or culture" (Devitt, 2004, p. 54). It is the largest collective of genres possible—held together by a comprehensive social unit of people who use them to mediate social activity. A repertoire of genres is slightly more specified: She defines it as the genres within a particular sphere of activity, such as the legal community. Even more specified is a genre system, which is a collective of genres that are clearly linked and governed by common users and a common purpose (Devitt, 2004). Bazerman (1995) defines genre systems as "interrelated genres that interact with each other in specific settings" (p. 98), and he emphasizes the structured nature of the relationships between genres within a genre system: "Only a limited range of genres may appropriately follow upon another in particular settings" (p. 98). A genre set, Devitt's (2004) fourth category, is a loosely defined collection of genres shared by a collective of individuals. Genre sets were first identified by Devitt (1991) in her study of tax accountants and intertextuality. Bawarshi and Reiff (2010) point out that they are a smaller collective of genres that are more bounded by the particular actions they enact; together, several genre sets form genre systems in order to allow "their users to enact complex social actions over time" (p. 88).

In their study of computer documentation systems, Spinuzzi and Zachry (2000) identified another way to describe collectives of genres—the genre ecology. According to Brooke (2009), ecologies are "vast, hybrid systems of intertwined elements" (p. 28). Genre ecologies include a variety of genres that are loosely related to each other and help groups of individuals to mediate complex activities (Wall, 2015). Spinuzzi and Zachry (2000) call them "clusters of communication artifacts and activities," which are "used to jointly mediate the activities that allow people to accomplish complex objectives" (pp. 171–172). What sets genre ecologies apart from the genre collectives explained by Devitt (2004) is an unpredictable and unstructured nature juxtaposed with a relatively stable appearance. Brooke (2009) explains that "ecologies can achieve a certain level of systematic stability or balance and may even appear stable from a long distance, but they are in constant flux" (p. 28). And, according to Luzón (2017), genre ecologies are contingent, decentralized, and relatively stable:

> Contingency refers to the opportunistic and spontaneous coordinations that people make among genres when trying to accomplish a task. Decentralization means that usability, design, and intention are distributed across the ecology of genres and that the interpretation and success of a genre depends on the genres that users connect with it, and on how these genres work together to mediate a given activity. Finally, relative stability refers to the fact that, although over time the interconnections between genres in an ecology tend to become conventional and consistent, ecologies are always dynamic, changeable, and flexible, with genres evolving or new genres being imported in order to respond to contingencies.
>
> *(pp. 446–447)*

Unlike genre contexts, repertoires, systems, and sets, genre ecologies recognize and account for the complexity of contemporary rhetorical situations that Rude (2004) describes. Genre contexts and repertoires are not quite particular enough to specific, complex goals of a single collective of users, and genre systems and sets are too structured and rule-governed to allow for the flexibility required by continually evolving, complex rhetorical situations. Within genre ecologies, different combinations of genres are available as mediatory tools for a rhetor's use, depending upon the particularities of a complex exigence (contingency). Individual genres themselves are the typified responses to recurrent aspects of these complex rhetorical situations, and certain combinations of genres may be more common than others (relative stability), but each complex exigence requires a unique collective of genres in order to achieve the rhetor's goals. That unique combination of genres act upon each other and the audience in unique and sometimes unexpected ways in order to achieve a unique effect (decentralization). In other words, even though a genre ecology may appear stable, it is always in flux because ecologies are always contingent on the particularities and goals of each situation.

Luzón's (2017) study of academic research blogs provides a useful illustration. Luzón found that the blogs are hybrid texts that make use of the affordances of new media to coordinate different genres in order to accomplish complex objectives. The blog posts within the study used a variety of genres—which Luzón categorized as publishing genres, conferencing genres, showcasing genres, and dissemination genres—to accomplish complex goals that support the research groups' social and work activity. Each post combined genres in unique ways in order to accomplish the purpose of the post. Luzón (2017) noted that

> there is not a fixed, stable relation between the purpose of a post and a set of genres. In each post the bloggers combine the genres and media that they consider appropriate to accomplish the purpose(s) of the post, which shows the contingency of genre ecologies: Different genres are coordinated opportunistically to achieve a specific purpose.
>
> *(p. 454)*

This opportunistic coordination of genres is central to the idea of a genre ecology because the collective use of genres within an ecology is much more flexible than the call-and-response structure of genre systems (Wall, 2015).

In a genre ecology, genres connect to other genres in specific ways, but those connections are more flexible and contingent upon the other genres in use and the context of a particular situation. One combination of genres may be a perfect fit within one context, but that same combination may not work within another context, even if the goals are the same. Within genre ecologies, "small changes can have unforeseen consequences that ripple far beyond their immediate implications" (Brooke, 2009, p. 28). Not only does the particular context affect the functioning of a genre, but the interactions with other genres within a collective affect how each genre functions (Devitt, 2004). Though this variability undeniably complicates our understanding of rhetorical situations, this complication is actually a strength of the genre ecology perspective and a reason why genre ecologies fit well within an expanded perception of delivery. The long-term, complex rhetorical situations that Rude (2004) encourages us to acknowledge require mediation by multiple genres. By acknowledging that complexity, organizations not only develop genres that respond to individual exigencies, but also entire genre ecologies of available genres, which can be combined opportunistically in response to unique, complex rhetorical situations. White papers are a perfect example of a genre that is often deployed opportunistically within an ecology of other business genres in order to accomplish a complex objective—closing a sale.

White Papers

White papers originated within the government sector. They were first used as a tool to explain government policy and provide a rationale for that policy. According to the consulting firm the Appum Group (n.d.), white papers were first adopted within the technology sector by the Manhattan Project in order to explain highly technical issues to nontechnical audiences. This particular usage of white papers expanded in the 1990s due to the significant increase of new technology and the distinct lack of easy-to-find and easy-to-understand documentation for that technology (Willerton, 2012).

Today, white papers are used within a variety of industries and are not limited to purely technical topics (McPherson, 2010). Stelzner (2007) places white papers in four categories: the technical white paper (describes how a technology works), the business benefits white paper (explains the business benefits of a particular solution), the hybrid white paper (explains both the business benefits and the technical aspects of a technology), and the government white paper (discusses the implications of government policy). Obviously, these categories allow for a broad variation in white paper topics. In fact, McPherson's (2010) dissertation study of 317 different white papers found that there seem to be "no limitations on the subject matter on which white papers may be written" (p. 150). White paper writer and consultant Gordon Graham (n.d.) goes so far as to claim that "anyone can call anything a white paper. And they do." From a WAGR perspective, Willerton (2012) interprets this flexibility as an indication that the genre of the white paper is not yet stabilized, which explains why textbook coverage of white papers is slim and varied (McPherson, 2010).

Despite this flexibility, the defining feature of a white paper seems to be a combination of its dual purpose and its method for achieving that purpose. Mackiewicz's (2012) discussion of a writing in the disciplines program in the College of Business at Auburn University explains this uniqueness:

> [A white paper] includes not only the genres of objective evaluation and recommendation reports but also marketing reports that proffer a company's product or service (e.g., developing and maintaining brand consistency across media channels) as the best solution to an industry problem (e.g., consumer confusion about company mission).
>
> *(p. 237)*

In fact, most contemporary definitions of white papers indicate that they are informative marketing documents that take the form of objective reports about a business problem. Campbell and Naidoo (2017) analyzed a corpus of 20 high-tech marketing white papers and found that many of them used rhetorical moves that support this definition. All 20 of the white papers analyzed introduced a business-related problem within the first portion of the white paper, and 19 of the 20 presented a specific solution to that problem in the second portion of the white paper. Next, a vast majority of the white papers (19 out of 20) prompted the reader to act in some way, and 15 of those implicitly or explicit prompted the reader to act on a specific solution to the problem, often by contacting the sponsoring company for more information about products and services. The fourth common move identified within Campbell and Naidoo's (2017) corpus of white papers was a move to establish the credibility of the white paper's author and/ or sponsoring organization by mentioning specific clients who had successfully applied the solution presented by the white paper, by listing the sources of the paper's research, and/or by directly providing information about the author or sponsoring organization. The final common rhetorical move of the white papers analyzed was to list legal considerations, such as copyright, permissions, or licensing information. These five common rhetorical moves illustrate that white papers attempt to provide readers with useful and credible information about a problem they face.

Their true rhetorical purpose, however, is to build the *ethos* of the author or sponsoring company (Willerton, 2007). Stelzner (2007) claims that the idea behind white papers is that if you give readers something of value, they'll give you their loyalty and business in return. The value of a white paper lies in its objective presentation of the best solution to a business or technological problem. Willerton (2008) interviewed engineering consultants about how they used white papers in their jobs and found that the consultants used them to "learn about new technologies and new applications of existing technologies" (p. 375). For the consultants, good white papers provided quick access to well-researched information and analysis, saving them from spending valuable (billable) time on conducting the research themselves. This use-value of white papers is why Stelzner (2007) believes white papers are effective marketing tools. Unlike traditional marketing materials, white papers are sought out by potential clients because of this use-value.

These previous studies show that white papers serve as authoritative information that help their readers make well-informed business decisions; therefore, the marketing purpose of a white paper necessarily must take a very "soft sell" approach (Stelzner, 2007; Willerton, 2012; Campbell & Naidoo, 2017). Willerton (2007) identifies a "tension" (p. 188) between the informational and persuasive purposes of white papers. Two of the engineering consultants in his study claimed that many white papers were "tainted" (Willerton, 2008, p. 376) by the sales pitch aspect of their dual purpose. Therefore, many readers approach white papers with skepticism (Willerton, 2007, 2008). They understand that in a market economy, knowledge is a commodity, and the knowledge gained from white papers comes at a cost. They expect vendors to present their product in the best possible light and make some effort to sell that product to them; that's the implied social contract of a white paper (Willerton, 2008). However, that social contract means that readers approach white papers "with their 'BS' detectors turned to maximum," as Graham noted in an interview with Willerton (2007). And that means any attempt at a "hard sell" strategy within a white paper will immediately put the reader on defense (Willerton, 2012). For white papers to be effective as a marketing genre, the focus of the document must remain on the objective analysis as a "soft sell" tactic—providing valuable information in exchange for increased credibility in the readers' eyes.

These readers include a range of individuals, from technical management staff to business executives—anyone who could contribute to the decision making process of adopting a new technology or purchasing a product or service from a vendor (Willerton, 2007). A white paper is a business-to-business marketing tool whose primary purpose is to generate sales leads to these prospective customers or clients (Willerton, 2007). Stelzner (2007) expands this description slightly by saying that white papers function to generate sales leads, demonstrate thought leadership in a particular industry, or help to close sales as a leave-behind after an initial sales call or presentation. Each of these purposes, however, relies upon the audience perceiving the author or sponsoring organization as a reliable source of information. Like other types of content marketing—which Wall (2015) defines as "a method of marketing a product or service by creating and distributing free informational or entertainment content" (p. 1)—white papers must be interesting and useful to their audiences on their own merits in order for them to be effective.

Also, like other types of content marketing, white papers, as soft-sell documents, are part of a larger strategy—an ecology of genres—to close the final sale. Other genres within the ecology could include blog posts, social media posts, email campaigns, newsletters, and press releases, among others (Wall, 2015). According to Willerton (2008), "white papers are just one information source among many"; they are "incomplete sources of information" (p. 380). Because audiences approach white papers with a bit of skepticism, they seek out additional information before making a purchase decision. In his interviews with engineering consultants, Willerton (2008) found that they would typically want to see additional documentation, attend field trials, or contact current customers before purchasing the technology discussed in a white paper. In other words, white papers rarely complete a sale by themselves. They can often be a springboard for a sale, but they are not often solely responsible for a sale. That's not their purpose. Their purpose is to generate leads. Along with other genres within a company's genre ecology, white papers work to "maintain an ongoing relationship where [prospective] customers are constantly in contact with the brand, increasing the probably that they will become customers" (Wall, 2015, p. 1). Each genre within the ecology accomplishes a different individual purpose. In the case of white papers, that purpose is to increase the company's credibility by showing them to have a particular expertise. Other genres may take a more hard-sell approach, and still other genres may take a more technical approach. In fact, Willerton (2007) found that the same white paper could be rewritten for multiple audiences—one with a more technical focus and one with a more business-benefits focus, to borrow from Stelzner's (2007) categories. The point is that white papers work with other documents within a company's genre ecology in order to accomplish the organization's complex objectives. New customers may be drawn in from any number of starting points, but each document, whether through calls to action or through links to other texts within the company's genre ecology, works to move a customer into what content marketers call "the buyer's funnel" (Wall, 2015, p. 80). For these ecologies to be effective, business communicators who write white papers must consider their interactions with these other genres as part of the development process. Expanding the canon of delivery to account for these considerations ensures that rhetorical theory reflects current workplace practice.

A reconceived canon of delivery, therefore, should include not only concerns for medium and visual presentation but also an understanding of how the white paper may be distributed—similar to Trimbur's (2000) circulation—and how it will interact with the other genres in a company's ecology as well as other texts that audiences may encounter within the industry's context. In terms of distribution, Willerton (2007) notes that white papers are often distributed through direct email campaigns from vendors, or they are shared among colleagues across formal and informal networks. Sharing happens through word of mouth, email, distribution lists, or white papers databases such as Bitpipe (www.bitpipe.com). They can function as a "leave-behind" print document after an in-person sales meeting or presentation (Willerton, 2007), or they can be downloaded to a mobile device (Eccolo Media, 2014). In any case, the planning and development of a white paper should include plans for the various ways it can be disseminated and used.

White Papers in the Business Communication Classroom

Perhaps this complexity of planning a white paper is one reason they are less prevalent in business communication courses than other genres. Willerton (2012), however, claims that white papers are prevalent enough in industry that they should be incorporated into business communication courses, and Mackiewicz (2012) similarly claims that the white paper is neglected by business communication courses, even though it is a particularly useful and prevalent genre. The Content Marketing Institute (2015) found that 71 percent of businesses surveyed used white papers as a business-to-business marketing tactic. And Eccolo Media (2014), a content development and strategy consultancy, found that white papers are the most frequently consumed type of vendor content, with 49 percent of respondents saying they used a white paper to evaluate a technology purchase decision within the last six months. The same survey found that white papers were also the most influential type of content during the purchasing process. Even though the genre continues to evolve, the white paper is clearly a prevalent and influential form of business-to-business marketing and communication; therefore, it should be more prevalent within business communication curricula.

As an assignment in a business communication course, the white paper has the potential to fulfill the pedagogical aims of one of the most commonly assigned projects—the formal report. The formal report is, historically, one of the most common assignments in business communication courses (Moshiri & Cardon, 2014). As Rude (1997) has noted, the report genre is a tool for organizational action. The purpose of a report is to document the process of problem-solving and recommend the best choice of action to solve a practical problem within the workplace (Rude, 1995). As such, report assignments require students to articulate a problem, conduct research, analyze that research in order to recommend a course of action for the audience, and communicate those findings in a rhetorically effective format (Vice & Carnes, 2001). Furthermore, those analytical and writing skills are complemented by subject knowledge within a particular business or industry (Roach, Tracy, & Durden, 2007). A white paper assignment would require students to use all of the same skills. Willerton (2012) discusses how the white paper would fit within different types of professional writing classes and recommends that it would fit particularly well within an upper-level, reports-focused class because of the similarities between the two genres. McPherson (2010) also recognizes several similarities between the report and white paper genres, although she resists classifying the white paper as a type of report because of the white paper's additional purposes beyond reporting or analyzing information. The similarities between the two genres include a research-based approach to analysis and argumentation as well as formatting conventions and common organizing elements such as section headings, lists, and front and back matter (Willerton, 2007; McPherson, 2010). While the white paper does have a marketing purpose beyond its appearance as an objective analysis of a business problem, its *ethos* and effectiveness stem from its usefulness to the reader as objective analysis, even within the social contract of a soft-sell marketing document.

That complex, dual purpose, however, can also be a strength of a white paper assignment in itself. The rhetorical situation of a white paper requires that it be simultaneously persuasive and objective (Willerton, 2007). This situation echoes one that students already practice in most business communication courses—the resume and/or cover letter (Moshiri & Cardon, 2014). The job search unit of many business communication courses emphasizes the need to be truthful while still highlighting students' strengths and minimizing their weaknesses (Willerton, 2007). White papers offer further practice in this kind of ethical yet persuasive business communication. Students must objectively and thoroughly analyze a business problem while simultaneously presenting a company's product or service in the best possible light. Regardless of industry or role, students will need experience in this type of complex rhetorical endeavor. After all, as sales icon Zig Ziglar (2009) said, "everyone is in sales."

Finally, and perhaps most importantly, white papers have the potential to allow students in business communication courses to practice an expanded conception of delivery. Rude (2004) asserts that it is a white paper writer's responsibility to consider the genre ecology within which the document will function:

> The writer is part of a collaborative team and may not be personally responsible for taking the document into the field, but the writer works with an understanding and vision of a publication within the web of related publications and activities.
>
> *(p. 286)*

Eyman (2007) claims that such an "understanding [of] the interactions of texts and contexts can yield a more comprehensive picture of interaction than the traditional approach of rhetorical invention, composition, and delivery" (pp. 208–209). White paper projects within business communication courses offer students the opportunity to envision these ecologies and contexts for themselves.

By doing so, students can more fully understand the relationships between different genres and the social actions that they accomplish. This kind of strategic planning of intersecting genres and activities "helps to develop our students into rhetoricians" who think beyond a single document and its accuracy (Rude, 2004, p. 284). Ding (2008) points out that teaching an entire activity system is more beneficial to students because no text exists in a vacuum:

> As no written product exists in isolation, to put the target genre in its actual activity system and to explicitly teach other components, rules, and expectations of that activity system can help novice writers to acquire discourse community knowledge, process knowledge, and rhetorical knowledge in addition to genre knowledge.
>
> *(p. 43)*

Seeing how this kind of genre interaction and opportunistic genre coordination works allows students to see how different genres are actually used within business contexts to accomplish particular goals and how those genres can work with a variety of other genres and activities in order to meet larger, more complicated goals.

As Willerton (2012) points out, a white paper assignment can fit into a variety of business or professional communication courses, but its fit depends on the objectives of the course and the preparation level of the students. White papers can teach many of the same skills as the formal report, but it does so within a more complex rhetorical situation. If students aren't quite prepared for that complexity, a white paper may be less effective than a simple report. The possibilities for a white paper assignment to teach students how to effectively function within and potentially even plan for complex genre ecologies, however, is promising.

A white paper assignment could be combined with other major projects or small assignments that allow students to practice other genres within the ecology of business or sales genres, depending on course learning objectives. Students could write sales or customer service letters, emails, brochures, documentation, or even web sites or social media plans that coordinate with the white papers they write. Instructors could choose the coordinating genres themselves, or the white paper could be part of a larger project where students decide from a list of potential genres to respond to their unique rhetorical situations. The project could be structured as an individual project or a collaborative project, and it could be based on a case study of a company and its product/service, a faux company of the student's own choosing, or even as a service-learning, client-based project, like Willerton's (2012) white paper assignment.

Regardless of the project's details, students must consider how white papers interact with other genres in order to fully practice an expanded concept of delivery that includes the strategy behind genre ecologies. Doing so could be as simple as writing a plan for an ecology to complement a white paper, something similar to the metageneric texts discussed by McNely (2017) or the genre ecology diagrams discussed by Spinuzzi and Zachry (2000). A more complex assignment would require students to not only think about how planned genres interact with the white paper within the genre ecology, but how other genres that may not be planned—such as white papers from other vendors—may interact with it. Ridolfo and DeVoss (2009) recommend thinking about the positive, neutral, and negative appropriations of a text and how those appropriations may be beneficial, neutral, or harmful "to the short- or long-term rhetorical objectives" (p. velocity) of the original work. Perhaps business communication students should consider these types of interactions with other texts in the genre ecologies of white papers. In any case, white papers have great potential to allow students in business communication courses to acknowledge the complexity of contemporary rhetorical exigencies and to practice strategizing ways to deal with these complexities.

Future research needs to be conducted in order to recommend best practices for white paper assignments that include strategies of expanded delivery. In general, few studies of white papers exist within the literature, but their prevalent use in practice has begun to inspire some study within technical communication, business communication, and marketing communication literature. Classroom studies of skill development could shed light on the best ways to encourage students to consider the effects of those possible interactions and how best to opportunistically make use of them. That research should also include more studies of white papers in use within business contexts. Campbell and Naidoo (2017) recommend that white papers should also be compared with other genres within their genre ecologies in order to determine how they are similar and where they differ.

Conclusion

By expanding the canon of delivery to include not only considerations for publication (medium and visual design) and circulation (context and reuse) but also considerations for the ways in which texts interact with other genres and activities within the genre ecologies and of business activity, we provide opportunities for business communication researchers and students to more fully visualize the ways that genres work together to perform complex social actions. In this expanded sense of delivery, the white paper is an ideal assignment within business communication courses. Its own complex rhetorical purposes echo the complexity of the activity system of business-to-business sales, and the opportunities to combine the white paper with any number of other business communication genres allow students to practice the strategy involved in planning these coordinated texts, genres, and activities.

References

Adsanatham, C., Garrett, B., & Matzke, A. (2013). Re-inventing digital delivery for multimodal composing: A theory and heuristic for composition pedagogy. *Computers and Composition, 30*(4), 315–331. doi: https://doi.org/10.1016/j.compcom.2013.10.004.

Appum Group. (n.d.). Origins of the white paper. Retrieved from http://web.archive.org/web/20050324040611

Aristotle. (2007). *On rhetoric: A theory of civic discourse* (Kennedy, G. A., Trans.) (2nd ed.). New York: Oxford University Press.

Bawarshi, A. (2003). *Genre & the invention of the writer: Reconsidering the place of invention in composition*. Logan, UT: Utah State University Press.

Bawarshi, A. S., & Reiff, M. J. (2010). *Genre: An introduction to history, theory, research, and pedagogy*. Fort Collins, CO: WAC Clearinghouse. Retrieved from http://wac.colostate.edu/books/bawarshi_reiff/.

Bazerman, C. (1995). Systems of genres and the enactment of social intentions. In A. Freedman & P. Medway (Eds.), *Genre and the new rhetoric* (pp. 79–104). London: Taylor & Francis.

Bourelle, A., Bourelle, T., & Jones, N. (2015). Multimodality in the technical communication classroom: Viewing classical rhetoric through a 21st century lens. *Technical Communication Quarterly, 24*(4), 306–327. doi: https://doi.org/10.1080/10572252.2015.1078847.

Brooke, C. G. (2009). *Lingua fracta: Towards a rhetoric of new media*. Cresskill, NJ: Hampton.

Campbell, K. S., & Naidoo, J. S. (2017). Rhetorical move structure in high-tech marketing white papers. *Journal of Business and Technical Communication, 31*(1), 94–118. doi: https://doi.org/10.1177/1050651916667532.

Cicero. (1970). *On oratory and orators* (Watson, J. S., Trans.). Carbondale, IL: Southern Illinois University Press.

Connors, R. J. (1993). Actio: A rhetoric of written delivery (iteration two). In J. F. Reynolds (Ed.), *Rhetorical memory and delivery: Classical concepts for contemporary composition and communication* (pp. 65–78). Hillsdale, NJ: Lawrence Erlbaum Associates.

Content Marketing Institute. (2015). *B2b content marketing: 2016 benchmarks, budgets, and trends—North America*. Retrieved from www.slideshare.net/CMI/b2b-content-marketing-2016-benchmarks-budgets-and-trends-north-america?ref=www.slideshare.net/CMI/slideshelf.

Devitt, A. J. (1991). Intertextuality in tax accounting. In C. Bazerman & J. Paradis (Eds.), *Textual dynamics of the professions: Historical and contemporary studies of writing in professional communities* (pp. 336–355). Madison, WI: University of Wisconsin Press. Retrieved from http://wac.colostate.edu/books/textual_dynamics/chapter14.pdf.

Devitt, A. J. (2004). *Writing genres*. Carbondale, IL: Southern Illinois University Press.

DeVoss, D. N., & Porter, J. E. (2006). Why Napster matters to writing: File sharing as a new ethic of digital delivery. *Computers and Composition, 23*(2), 178–210. doi: https://doi.org/10.1016/j.compcom.2006.02.001.

Ding, H. (2008). The use of cognitive and social apprenticeship to teach a disciplinary genre. *Written Communication, 25*(1), 3. Retrieved from http://wcx.sagepub.com/content/25/1/3.short.

Dragga, S. (1993). The ethics of delivery. In J. F. Reynolds (Ed.), *Rhetorical memory and delivery: Classical concepts for contemporary composition and communication* (pp. 79–96). Hillsdale, NJ: Lawrence Erlbaum Associates.

Eccolo Media. (2014). B2b technology content survey report. Retrieved from http://eccolomedia.com/eccolo-media-2014-b2b-technology-content-survey-report.pdf.

Eyman, D. (2007). *Digital rhetoric: Ecologies and economies of digital circulation*. Doctoral dissertation. Retrieved from ProQuest. (3282094).

Graham, G. (n.d.). The white paper FAQ. Retrieved from www.thatwhitepaperguy.com/white-paper-faq-frequently-asked-questions/.

Handa, C. (2014). *The multimediated rhetoric of the internet: Digital fusion*. New York: Routledge.

Holland, G. S. (2016). "Delivery, delivery, delivery": Accounting for performance in the rhetoric of Paul's letters. In S. E. Porter & B. R. Dyer (Eds.), *Paul and ancient rhetoric: Theory and practice in the Hellenistic context* (pp. 117–140). New York: Cambridge University Press.

Luzón, M. J. (2017). Connecting genres and languages in online scholarly communication: An analysis of research group blogs. *Written Communication, 34*(4), 441–471. doi: https://doi.org/10.1177/0741088317726298.

Mackiewicz, J. (2012). Relying on writing consultants: The design of a WID program for a college of business. *Journal of Business and Technical Communication, 26*(2), 229–258. doi: https://doi.org/10.1177/1050651911429924.

McCorkle, B. (2012). *Rhetorical delivery as technology discourse: A cross-historical study*. Carbondale, IL: Southern Illinois University Press.

McNely, B. (2017). Moments and metagenres: Coordinating complex, multigenre narratives. *Journal of Business and Technical Communication, 31*(4), 443–480. doi: https://doi.org/10.1177/1050651917713252.

McPherson, C. (2010). *Examining the gap between workplace white papers and their representation in technical communication textbooks*. Unpublished doctoral dissertation. Texas Tech University, Lubbock, TX.

Miller, C. R. (1984). Genre as social action. *Quarterly Journal of Speech, 70*(2), 151–167. doi: https://doi.org/10.1080/00335638409383686.

Moshiri, F., & Cardon, P. (2014). The state of business communication classes: A national survey. *Business and Professional Communication Quarterly, 77*(3), 312–329. doi: https://doi.org/10.1177/2329490614538489.

Nardi, B. A., Whittaker, S., & Schwarz, H. (2002). NetWORKers and their activity in intensional networks. *Computer Supported Cooperative Work, 11*, 205–242.

Porter, J. E. (2009). Recovering delivery for digital rhetoric. *Computers and Composition, 26*(4), 207–224. doi: https://doi.org/10.1016/j.compcom.2009.09.004.

Ridolfo, J. (2012). Rhetorical delivery as strategy: Rebuilding the fifth canon from practitioner stories. *Rhetoric Review, 31*(2), 117–129. doi: https://doi.org/10.1080/07350198.2012.652034.

Ridolfo, J., & DeVoss, D. N. (2009). Composing for recomposition: Rhetorical velocity and delivery. *Kairos: A Journal of Rhetoric, Technology, and Pedagogy, 13*(2). Retrieved from http://kairos.technorhetoric.net/13.2/topoi/ridolfo_devoss/intro.html.

Roach, J., Tracy, D., & Durden, K. (2007). Integrating business core knowledge through upper division report composition. *Business Communication Quarterly, 70*(4), 431–449. doi: https://doi.org/10.1177/1080569907309011.

Rude, C. D. (1995). The report for decision making. *Journal of Business and Technical Communication, 9*(2), 170–205. doi: https://doi.org/10.1177/1050651995009002002.

Rude, C. D. (1997). Environmental policy making and the report genre. *Technical Communication Quarterly, 6*(1), 77–90. doi: htts://doi.org/10.1207/s15427625tcq0601_5.

Rude, C. D. (2004). Toward an expanded concept of rhetorical delivery: The uses of reports in public policy debates. *Technical Communication Quarterly, 13*(3), 271–288. doi: https://doi.org/10.1207/s15427625tcq1303.

Russell, D. R. (1995). Activity theory and its implications for writing instruction. In J. Petraglia (Ed.), *Reconceiving writing, rethinking writing instruction* (pp. 51–77). Mahwah, NJ: Lawrence Erlbaum.

Russell, D. R. (2009). Uses of activity theory in written communication research. In A. Sannino, H. Daniels, & K. D. Gutiérrez (Eds.), *Learning and expanding with activity theory* (pp. 40–52). Cambridge: Cambridge University Press.

Spinuzzi, C. (2001). Software development as mediated activity: Applying three analytical frameworks for studying compound mediation. In M. J. Northrop & S. Tilley (Eds.), *SIGDOC '01: Proceedings of the 19th annual international conference on computer documentation* (pp. 58–67). New York: ACM Digital Library.

Spinuzzi, C., & Zachry, M. (2000). Genre ecologies: An open-system approach to understanding and constructing documentation. *ACM Journal of Computer Documentation, 24*(3), 169–181. Retrieved from http://portal.acm.org/citation.cfm?id=344646.

Stelzner, M. A. (2007). *Writing white papers: How to capture readers and keep them engaged.* Poway, CA: WhitePaperSource Publishing.

Trimbur, J. (2000). Composition and the circulation of writing. *College Composition and Communication, 52*(2), 188. doi: https://doi.org/10.2307/358493.

Vice, J. P., & Carnes, L. W. (2001). Developing communication and professional skills through analytical reports. *Business Communication Quarterly, 64*(1), 84–96.

Wall, M. A. (2015). *Click-through rhetoric: Genre and networks in content marketing.* Unpublished doctoral dissertation. University of Texas at Austin, Austin, TX.

Welch, K. E. (1993). Reconfiguring writing and delivery in secondary orality. In J. F. Reynolds (Ed.), *Rhetorical memory and delivery: Classical concepts for contemporary composition and communication* (pp. 17–30). Hillsdale, NJ: Lawrence Erlbaum Associates.

Willerton, R. (2007). Writing white papers in high-tech industries: Perspectives from the field. *Technical Communication, 54*(2), 187–200.

Willerton, R. (2008). Proceeding with caution: A case study of engineering professionals reading white papers. *Technical Communication, 55*(4), 370–382. doi: https://doi.org/10.4324/9780203846636.

Willerton, R. (2012). Teaching white papers through client projects. *Business Communication Quarterly, 76*(1), 105–113. doi: https://doi.org/10.1177/1080569912454713.

Ziglar, Z. (2009, May 11). Everyone sells. *Success.* Retrieved from www.success.com/article/everyone-sells.

8

EXPRESSING ACCOUNTABILITY AND ORGANIZATIONAL *ETHOS*

Business Dress as Visual Rhetoric

Valerie Creelman

Credibility or *ethos* as it relates to impression management, professionalism, and integrity informs many of the lessons business educators deliver in their classrooms, whether working with college freshmen, undergraduates, or more seasoned MBAs. How to establish, maintain, and enhance credibility shapes just about every aspect of our in-class discussions and the topics introduced there, from evidence-based argumentation and goodwill generation to professional presentation of oneself and one's work through effective impression management. Beyond our business communication classrooms, corporate mission statements, annual reports, CEO letters, building architecture, office interiors, and workplace attire represent a few of the many rhetorical *artifacts* by which organizations communicate their values, culture, beliefs, *ethos*, and identity to internal (employees) and external (clients, stakeholders, public) audiences. The rhetorical and communicative function of these texts in socializing employees and in managing public perception has been explored by rhetoricians and organizational discourse scholars alike (see, for example, Breeze, 2013; Cornelissen, 2017; DuBrin, 2011; Gagliardi, 1990; Hyland, 1998; Keyton, 2011). Other scholars have directed their attention to articulating the symbolic function of organizational dress and its influence on organizational dynamics, particularly in fostering employee legitimization and compliance (Joseph, 1986; Pratt & Rafaeli, 2001, Rafaeli & Pratt, 1993). Such studies have also examined how organizational dress can reflect and shape an organization's inner processes and social dynamics, offering insight into its social organization and relations (Pratt & Rafaeli, 1997, 2001; Rafaeli & Pratt, 1993). Exploring the communicative function of business clothing has likewise informed the research questions posed by business communication scholars examining the semiotics of business attire in the workplace and the various meanings it conveys to multiple audiences (Burgess-Wilkerson & Boyd Thomas, 2009; Cardon &

Okoro, 2009; DeKay, 2009; Kiddie, 2009). As a nonverbal form of communication in the workplace, employees' style of dress or attire represents a critical yet often overlooked element of an organization's communications strategy, not only in the shaping and expression of employees' identities within their organizations but also in managing clients' and stakeholders' impressions of an organization's corporate identity and culture. Using examples from the accounting industry as a touchstone for my discussion, I consider in this chapter the rhetorical function of business attire as the visual, aesthetic expression of organizational values and its influential role in the rhetorical process of establishing, maintaining, and enhancing an individual's *ethos* in the workplace.

Expressing Organizational *Ethos* Through Professional Codes of Conduct

Arthur Andersen and Enron, Lehman Brothers and Ernst & Young—these were just some of the long-standing accounting and financial services firms complicit in some of the most unforgettable accounting scandals to touch American financial history (Mulford & Comiskey, 2011; Norton, 2011; Toffler, 2003; see also "The 10 Worst," n.d.). Against this tarnished corporate landscape, the accounting industry worked tenaciously to regain public trust and confidence in their profession. To restore their public image, accounting firms responded to their external audience's uncertainty and skepticism by developing publicly accessible *Codes of Conduct*, a document genre intentionally designed to communicate their firms' values and expectations to their internal accounting employees and to assure external stakeholders and clients how compliance with those codes is maintained and monitored. Referencing the leadership message and core values expressed in KPMG International's inaugural 2005 *Global Code of Conduct: Performance with Integrity* as a departure point for my discussion, I begin this chapter by introducing this document as a rhetorical artifact responding to a specific crisis event in the accounting profession. I then proceed to trace how the core organizational values presented within it are embodied by the firm's employees. From there, using dress code practices within the accounting industry as a further reference point, I go on to discuss how business attire serves as both an influential, concrete visual expression of an organization's core values and a means to encode and convey its organizational *ethos*.

Drawing on Roland Barthes' *The Fashion System* (1990), J. Anthony Blair's (2004) work on the constitutive elements of visual arguments, and Pasquale Gagliardi's (2006) discussions of symbolic artifacts and the *aesthetic side* of corporate landscapes, my discussion offers business communication researchers and educators an accessible framework and vocabulary for exploring and discussing the communicative function of business attire. In doing so, this chapter traces how organizational dress acts as a form of visual rhetoric: visually presenting nonverbal messages about an organization and its employees that audiences or other organizational actors engage with in a dynamic and reciprocal way. With today's employers increasingly adopting a more flexible, casual approach to business attire as part of their recruitment strategies to attract and retain millennial employees (Fernandes, 2016), I then conclude this chapter by considering what the implications of this new workplace aesthetic means for business communication instructors as they broach the topic of business dress as part of their discussions of professional presence and nonverbal communication in the workplace.

Aesthetic Codes and Expression of Organizational Values

In describing what he terms the "aesthetic side" of organizational life, Pasquale Gagliardi (2006) explains how organizations are cultures with their own "symbolic systems of meaning," in which their identity, beliefs, norms, and values are expressed and encoded (p. 706). This system of meaning is conveyed across a variety of artifacts within a given corporate landscape (Gagliardi, 2006). For KPMG International, its 2005 *Global Code of Conduct: Performance with Integrity* was but one artifact by which it communicated to multiple audiences its core values, standards of ethical conduct, and systemic commitment to complying with those standards. More specifically, though, the document served to indoctrinate new and existing employees in *The KPMG Way*—its definition of "who we are, what we do, and how we do it" (p. 4)—and the standards of ethical behavior they are expected to uphold in their everyday business practices with each other and with KPMG's clients around the world. Within this document, the information presented follows an identifiable trajectory from the abstract to the concrete: from its general introduction of the intangible, abstract core values that define its organizational culture and belief system at the outset, to specific translation and explanation of how those ideals are to be concretely manifested in the everyday behaviors of its employees. We also witness within it a movement from the introduction of the abstract yet integral core value of *integrity* to pragmatic advice, prescripts, and direction on how to *perform* or act with integrity. Aptly sub-titled *Performance with Integrity*, the *Global Code*'s purpose is therefore designed to inform its member firms and their employees of its standards of ethical conduct and provide direction on how to comply with them in all aspects of their daily performance.

The rhetorical moves present in KPMG International's *Global Code*, from its definition of "who we are," in terms of its identifying system of values and beliefs, to "how we do it," in terms of a specific corporate ethic and a corresponding set of behaviors, reflect the way in which organizations try to translate their abstract "collective identity" or conception of themselves into identifiable concrete behaviors (Gagliardi, 2006, p. 710). This identity, Gagliardi further argues, is not only reflected in an organization's often imperceptible and ineffable "cultural code" (comprised of its beliefs, norms, and values) but also in its often more visible and palpable "aesthetic code" (2006, p. 706). "Every cultural system," he explains,

seems to have structural correspondences between its ontological or deon-
tological codes and its aesthetic codes, that is to say, between systems of
beliefs and of values, on the one hand, and specific patterns of relation/
combination between formal elements on the other.

(p. 709)

Gagliardi (2006) describes this translation or relation between "abstract sets of
'thinkable' beliefs and sensorially 'perceivable' concrete forms" as analogous to
the relation between *identity* and *style*: "Translating a particular conception of
ourselves into concrete behaviour," he explains,

> entails passing from an abstract definition of our *identity* to the adoption
> of a *style* . . . This problem is well known to those who are concerned
> with corporate identity, and who seek to translate particular conceptions of
> the collective self into subtle formal variants of elements—graphic, spatial,
> chromatic—that are sensorially perceptible.
>
> *(p. 710)*

The challenge Gagliardi describes here, of finding a way to translate a collective corporate *identity* into a recognizable *style* or way of being in the world,
to pass "from the conceptual abstract order to [the] formal concrete order" is, in
part, what KPMG seeks to achieve with its Code of Conduct. The process of
taking something as abstract as an accounting firm like KPMG's core value or
ethic of integrity and translating it into observable, concrete elements recognizable as the act or performance of integrity is the foremost challenge underlying
the organizational goals expressed in the "Leadership Message" that introduced
KPMG International's *Global Code of Conduct* to its multiple audiences in 2005.
In that Leadership Message, Mike Rake (2005), then Chairman of KPMG International, portrayed the accounting profession as under the intense glare of a public microscope. "Resulting scrutiny," he observed, "from governments, regulators,
business, and the media has placed our organization and our profession under the
spotlight as never before . . . and the accountability to regulators [has] never been
greater" (p. 1). After depicting the current corporate landscape in this way, Rake
(2005) then defined what KPMG's role is in responding to this public scrutiny.
"We believe," he explained, "in acting legally and ethically, and encouraging this
behaviour in the marketplace. We now have to *convince* a skeptical audience, however, and we have a mission to lead and explain" (p. 1, emphasis added). Moreover,
he reminded readers that KPMG's core value is *integrity* and that it underlies all
the principles delineated within the Code of Conduct. Of particular relevance to
my discussion here is how Rake's statements unwittingly characterized KPMG
and its member firms, employees, and partners as a corpus of rhetors collectively
responsible for *persuading* its "skeptical" audiences of their professionalism, credibility, and, of course, integrity. In doing so, he effectively configures KPMG and
its various constituents as engaged in the rhetorical act of persuasion and their

daily, observable behaviors as one of the rhetorical tools and recognizable formal elements by which they might demonstrate their commitment to their organization's core values.

As the introduction to KPMG Canada's (2005) *Canadian Code of Conduct* explicitly stated, "everything in this code is an expression of our commitment to *performance with integrity*" (p. 7). Here readers are reminded that the Code represents a *written* expression of that commitment. But as the statements and advice presented within it underscored, the daily expression or articulation of that commitment clearly rests with and is enacted by the firm's employees. Within the scope of this document, the responsibility for maintaining and protecting the firm's reputation lies squarely within the hands of its employees—a responsibility explicitly raised in the prefatory leadership messages. Through their everyday behaviors, actions, and practices, the firm's employees exhibit their commitment to these values and, in turn, the credibility of the firm they represent. Through the observable activities of its employees (their communications, practices, decisions, and appearance), the firm's various audiences will gauge and either accept or reject their claims of organizational integrity, credibility, trustworthiness, and professionalism. As the corporate actor performing within this landscape, the individual accountant's body is therefore configured as the performative site by which acceptable professional behavior and ethical conduct is enacted and monitored either by self or others. Interestingly, Deloitte's (2005) *Canadian Code of Conduct* makes that configuration even more explicit, telling its employees "You are Deloitte: you *embody* our values, principles, and service philosophy. It is your responsibility to ensure that your actions, words, and opinions, reflect well upon, and fairly represent, our firm" (p. 12, emphasis added). A firm's accountants thus become the living embodiment of the firm's organizational values and ethic.

This translation or assignment of the firm's core values onto the corpus of its accountants illustrates how within this "corporate landscape" (Gagliardi, 2006, p. 708) an employee's body also becomes one of a collection of artifacts that help concretize the firm's corporate values. "They too," Gagliardi asserts, "like material artifacts or inert nature, can be 'aestheticized,' thereby giving material form to a particular conception of an organization's identity and strategy" (p. 711). In describing the "embodied worker," Lynne Pettinger likewise confirms that within service industry cultures employees' bodies are often expected to perform the "aesthetic labour" of the corporate brands they represent (2004, p. 177). Auditing, for example, is a service industry, so professional auditors are acutely aware they have only one opportunity to make a positive first impression with a new or prospective client; therefore, attention to proper dress and business etiquette is part of the *aesthetic labour* their bodies perform on the job (Nichols, 2013). Indeed, as John T. Molloy once observed, "Impression is extremely important for accountants. Most clients have no way of knowing whether an accountant is effective or not. They're simply guessing at how good you are at accounting. So what you're selling is not expertise but the impression of your expertise" (1977, p. 111). In this way, the accountant's body becomes the concrete realization or "portable" symbol of the firm and its core values (Pratt & Rafaeli, 2001, p. 108). On this corporate stage, the accountants' bodies are the means by which integrity is performed, and the highly visible garments in which they are clothed—the tangible, material *style* of dress—becomes the costume by which the identity of the accountant and of the firm he or she represents is showcased. To enlist the dramaturgical terms Erving Goffman introduced to describe the performativity of impression management in everyday life and its components, the accountant as actor relies on the "expressive equipment" of his or her "personal front," of which appearance and, more specifically, clothing is one critical element (1959, pp. 22–24). As material object, the clothing becomes, as Roland Barthes conceptualized it, both the body's "substitute and its mask" (1990, p. 236); it can simultaneously reinforce an employee's commitment to the organization's values and its collective identity and cloak any identity that might differentiate an accountant from the firm. For example, to meet their professional objectives in the workplace, employees who self-identified as punk accommodated workplace expectations and dress norms by toning down aspects of their punk appearance (covering visible tattoos, removing facial piercings and/or earlobe plugs, and avoiding flamboyant hair color) or by subtly retaining more understated aspects of their punk identity such as wearing skateboard shoes with suits or work-appropriate jewelry bearing punk-inspired motifs (Sklar & DeLong, 2012).

As part of their analytical framework for studying organizational dress, Rafaeli and Pratt likewise propose that dress attributes can convey "central, distinctive, and enduring" organizational values (1993, p. 41) and symbolize those core values and beliefs (Pratt & Rafaeli, 1997, pp. 866–867; Trice & Beyer, 1993). To maintain and promote an image of conspicuous uniformity and consistency as part of its "One Firm" *ethos*, Arthur Andersen, for example, once dictated, during its early history, that its junior accountants wear the same style of suit and hat as part of creating a uniform image of the "Arthur Andersen Man" who would in turn uphold the "Arthur Andersen Way" (Toffler, 2003, pp. 25, 28–29). In the early 1990s, dark suits and white shirts were still the firm's official dress code. Not until January 2000 did the dress code depart from this standard and business casual first make its way into Arthur Andersen's offices (Toffler, p. 44). Within Rafaeli and Pratt's (1993) framework, such homogeneity in professional dress would not only symbolize the firm's commitment to offering consistent, reliable service to its clients, but also motivate junior accountants to comply with the "goals and standards of behaviour inherent to their role" as well as with the firm's organizational values. To adopt a dress style not in keeping with the cultural norm would signal an effort to "disidentify" with and an unwillingness to assimilate to the firm and its organizational values (Pratt & Rafaeli, 2001, pp. 106, 109; Munk, 1998, p. 64). In short, the professional attire of the accountant, whether implicitly or explicitly defined by an organization's culture, is one prominent *aesthetic code* through which an idealized image of the accountant and of the firm's collective identity and core organizational values can be embodied, encoded, and styled.

Professional Dress Codes and Organizational Values

Although not typically included in an accounting firm's Code of Conduct, the professional dress codes most accountants are expected to abide by during off-site visits with clients nonetheless represent another important way the accountant's body or appearance visually communicates or bolsters the written arguments of professionalism, accountability, and integrity expressed in Codes of Conduct. Those in charge of marketing and human resources at the top four accounting firms consistently report that in addition to professionalism, generally, a professional appearance, specifically, also conveys good judgment. As one human resources manager at PwC (formerly Price Waterhouse Cooper) stated, "Appropriate dress reflects good judgment and clients feel someone who has good judgment will give good advice" (as cited in Walker, 1993, p. 11). For KPMG, its employees' business attire is identified as an expression of the firm's professionalism and a critical part of how they present themselves to their clients. For its professional dress code, KPMG adopted a "Dress for the Occasion" policy whereby employees generally wear business casual but adjust the formality of their business attire according to their audience, purpose, and work environment. Their employees are therefore expected to "consider where they are going and who [*sic*.] they will be meeting." In this way, the level of formality in dress style is determined by context and audience in much the same way language formality is gauged by speech situation and audience. Ultimately, "the firm," as one KPMG spokesperson reported, "asks employees to consider whether or not they will be in contact with clients on a particular day and asks employees to dress accordingly, taking into account the client's own dress code" (as cited in Moore, 2016). PwC also endorses this flexible approach, expecting its employees to "use their judgment on what's appropriate to wear" (as cited in Moore, 2016). As Sue Horlin, its Australia-based human capital leader reported,

> It's not a 'dress up' or 'dress down' policy—all we are asking our people to do is to think about what they are doing each day, who [*sic*.] they are doing it with, and dress in a way that reflects that.
>
> *(as cited in Moore, 2016)*

For Grant Thornton Canada (2018), the intersection between the firm's credibility and its employees' appearance is explicitly addressed as part of the FAQs section on its company website. In response to a question about dress code, they wrote,

> Business casual, defined by clothing that is appropriate for meetings with clients, is the dress code we follow during normal business hours. We are a professional office and must remember that our image impacts our credibility with clients and potential clients. Depending on client engagements, regular business attire may at times be more appropriate than [business] casual.
>
> *("Careers")*

As Mark Sherfield, COO at BDO Grant Thornton, explained,

> Our guiding principle is to "dress for your diary [schedule], dress for the brand." While this recognizes that we don't always need to be in a formal "suit and tie," it acknowledges that our people are professional adults who can make the choices appropriate to their day.
>
> *(as cited in Moore, 2016)*

"At Deloitte," one spokesperson reported, "we trust our people to wear what is appropriate for the environment in which they are working" (as cited in Moore, 2016). As these statements amplify, an accounting firm's dress code and its employees' style of dress serve both as an extension and concrete expression of the values and beliefs expressed within their written codes of conduct. Their statements also identify the organizational dress of their accountants as extrinsic markers or signifiers of intrinsic characteristics (e.g., credibility, trustworthiness, competency, and/or professionalism) attributable to the wearer and, in turn, to the firm itself. Taken together, their statements therefore reveal a conscientious effort to manage or shape clients' impressions of and attitudes towards their organizations and its accountants by endorsing a style of business attire that shows, in its employees, the capacity to exercise good judgment.

Although a firm can enlist its organizational dress to shape and control its collective identity to outsiders, employees can likewise capitalize on their professional appearance to control and manage others' impressions. For some young professionals in the fields of finance, accounting, and law, the traditional business suit or professional attire is preferred to a business casual style because of its function as a "legitimizing emblem" (Joseph, 1986, p. 2; Rafaeli & Pratt, 1993, p. 50). For junior employees, more formal business attire helps bolster their self-confidence and convince supervisors and clients of their legitimacy and credibility. College students also associated dressing appropriately for work with experiencing a heightened sense of their work competency along with other positively regarded occupational attributes (Kwon, 1994a, 1994b). MBA students likewise reported feeling more competent, authoritative, and trustworthy when wearing formal business attire (Peluchette & Karl, 2007). Junior or visibly younger employees argue that as a corporate uniform, the traditional business suit helps relax or suspend corporate hierarchies, making them feel more like an equal when meeting with senior managers because of the visual "sameness" of their appearance in those social situations (Wen, 2000). For example, Bryan Avery, a millennial senior manager at a Seattle-based accounting firm, described still feeling "more comfortable in dress clothes when meeting with referral sources or clients, even if the clients tend to be laid back," but dressed business casual 75 percent of the time (Stiefel & Avery, 2016).

For visible minorities in the workplace, professional dress can contribute to a sense of solidarity and social equality among employees. While the absence of business suits can create a less stratified work environment, business casual policies can compromise the status of minority professionals. Not surprisingly, some junior and visible minority employees have a mixed attitude towards business casual days in their workplace, having reportedly been mistaken for service personnel and office couriers when wearing golf shirts and khakis (Wen, 2000). Compared with their European American counterparts, Hispanic and African Americans both indicated their preference for more formal business attire in workplace settings, seeing it as an important impression management tool for personal advancement in the workplace (Cardon & Okoro, 2009; Rucker, Anderson, & Kangas, 1999).

After the slump of the new economy in the 1990s, the backlash against casual dress policies sparked in 2001 reminds us that employees themselves are presciently aware of the rhetorical impact of formal business dress at socioeconomic levels, too. A notable movement away from casual dress to business suits was one of the key findings of a survey commissioned by the Men's Apparel Alliance in 2002. As then president of the Alliance, James Ammeen reported, "You're in a tough market, so if you want people to trust you, invest with you, you'd better look like a pretty serious person" (as cited in Temple, 2002). At the time of that survey, 19 percent of the companies re-instated more formal dress codes from 2001 to 2002. With many established professionals laid off or about to be so at the beginning of the 2007 economic downturn, and with a protracted recession imminent, a return to more formal dress practices immediately emerged. "When the economy gets tight," as Mark O'Connell, a professor at Toronto's Seneca College explained, "competition gets tougher for new jobs and for keeping current jobs, so levels of office dress rise across the board" (as cited in Kelly, 2009, p. L1). As these statements suggest, the professional business suit functions as a socio-political text, encoding and communicating employees' validity, equality, and competency in the workplace. Evident as a common theme is also the connection between formal business dress and the visual projection of an individual and an organization's legitimacy, credibility, and competency.

The Rhetorical Function of Business Attire in Establishing *Ethos*

Aristotle identified *ethos*, the personal character of the speaker, as a critical component in the rhetorical process of persuasion. "Persuasion," Aristotle (trans. 1954) explained, "is achieved by the speaker's personal character when the speech is so spoken as to make us think him credible" (Book I, Chapter 2, p. 25). That character, he argued, is comprised of "good sense, good moral character, and goodwill," and an individual perceived as possessing these qualities will inspire confidence in his audience and make a positive impression on them (Book II, Chapter 1, p. 91). For Aristotle that trust is achieved verbally: "by what the speaker says, not by what people think of this character before he begins to speak" (Book I, Chapter 2, p. 25). Aristotle's description does not, therefore, account for the persuasive role nonverbal elements can also have in establishing or maintaining individual *ethos*.

Taking rhetorical analysis beyond its traditionally logocentric roots, modern rhetoricians offer expanded definitions of rhetoric that broaden the objects of rhetorical analysis and encompass a range of previously excluded nonverbal forms of communication. Defining rhetoric as the "human use of symbols to communicate," Sonja Foss argues that rhetoric is not limited to spoken and written discourse but also includes "nondiscursive or nonverbal" symbols such as dress and architecture (2018, pp. 4–5, 2004). The suasory effects of visual images have motivated scholars such as Blair (2004) to define the constituent elements of visual rhetoric and to differentiate visual arguments from visual persuasion. To apply Blair's criteria, an accountant's business suit would not represent a visual argument, but instead a "visual rhetorical device" (p. 58), an accompanying backdrop designed to lend credibility to the accountant and the verbal messages he or she might espouse during meetings with colleagues and clients, thus contributing to the overall visual persuasion of the observer.

Erving Goffman's account of how people manage impressions in the performativity of everyday life accounts for the suasory effects of nonverbal forms of communication on the observer in daily social encounters. "Performance," as he defines it, "is all the activity of a given participant on a given occasion which serve to influence in any way any of the other participants" (p. 15). In his description of human communication, Goffman identifies individual expression as falling into two broad categories: "expressions given" and "expressions given off" (p. 4). The first category is concerned entirely with what individuals say, their verbal expressions. The second, however, is an infinitely more complex category comprised of nonverbal forms of expression such as appearance, manner, and gesture, which, Goffman argues, indelibly shape first impressions. For Goffman, clothing, facial expression, and gesture are some of the components comprising an individual's "expressive equipment" in managing their performance—the social front they present to the world. That performance is a persuasive act designed to influence observers and convince them that the performer possesses the attributes signaled by his appearance. As Goffman explains, "When an individual plays a part he implicitly requests his observers to take seriously the impression that is fostered before them. They are asked to believe that the character they see actually possesses the attributes he appears to possess" (p. 17). To be convincing, that performance and all its components must bear a congruence or unity that Goffman describes as a "coherence of front" (p. 24). Peluchette, Karl, and Rust (2006) describe the physical and mental effort involved in dressing appropriately and any "dissonance" individuals experience between what "they are expected to wear and what they would prefer to wear" as the "appearance labor" that goes into such performances (p. 50). Such *appearance labor* is especially evident in university and college students as they transition from full-time students to full-time employees and need to make wardrobe decisions and purchases that reflect this new identity (Kang, Sklar, & Johnson, 2011).

Goffman's definition of performance, its influence on observers, and its multimodal aspect bears important relevance to organizations as they manage the various elements of their employees' performances. When we re-consider the organizational values promoted in KPMG International's *Global Code* in articulating the behaviors that contribute to the *Performance of Integrity*, we can appreciate how the "aesthetic side" of organizational life Gagliardi describes serves a critical role in helping to manifest in concrete form organizational values and *ethos* that define its organizational culture. As Goffman's emphasis on unity asserts, though, for an organization or firm's "performance" to be persuasive, there must be congruence between the impression an organization as an institution aspires to project and the impression its individual employees as organizational representatives project. In other words, all aspects of an accountant's activities, from their behavior to their physical appearance, in their daily social encounters with clients and stakeholders, must create a unified impression in projecting the firm's corporate identity and brand.

The connection between business dress as an expression or aesthetic encoding of an individual's credibility or *ethos* I've highlighted throughout this chapter helps crystallize then how business clothing is a visual statement, a symbolic type of utterance or message from which people elicit informational visual elements and create meaning in their efforts to understand and assign meaning to the individuals they engage with and to which they respond accordingly. As Pratt and Rafaeli contend, the observable attributes of professional dress (e.g., color, fabric, and style) are "meaning-laden symbols" that trigger an array of learned associations in the observer that are attributed not only to the wearer but also to the organization (1993, p. 37). An employee's clothing is therefore one of a cluster of symbolic systems fashioned by an organization's culture from which its value systems can be read or interpreted. This symbolic element is captured in what Barthes (1990) identified as a garment's "vestimentary code," the elaborate signifying system by which its meaning is encoded and deciphered. In mapping the rhetoric of the fashion system, he asserts that clothing not only bears its own "poetics" (p. 225) but that an individual garment can carry its own "rhetorical connotation" (p. 234), some of which, like the business suit, become ossified over time.

As a visual rhetorical device, the accountant's traditional business suit signifies or connotes a visual message about the employee's *ethos* and that of the firm he or she represents. However, the viewer's participation in that interpretive process also reminds us that whatever meaning or message such professional attire has is created reciprocally via the observer's understanding of and aesthetic response to what that clothing item means within a particular organizational culture, and within a culture as a whole, and all the learned associations attributed to the meaning-making symbols within it. This reciprocal, collaborative shaping of meaning and message about the wearer's identity reminds us also that researchers investigating the communicative element of workplace clothing may need to resist applying traditional communication models. For scholars exploring the communicative elements of clothing and fashion, fashion theorists like Malcolm Barnard (2007) take a cautionary approach, warning that clothing and fashion are a different type of communication, one that resists and transcends existing telegraphic models of communication that represent the communicative process as the tidy transfer of information and meaning from sender to receiver. "Meaning," Barnard argues, "is constructed in the interaction between an individual's values and beliefs (which they hold as a member of a culture) and the item of a visual culture" (p. 175). Any meaning that is created, he argues, is a shared meaning created through a collaborative understanding of what those visual fashion items mean to the viewer and the values, beliefs, and attitudes held by that individual within a specific cultural environment. The way in which Barnard positions viewers as the ones making sense of the fashion statements they encounter, or attributing meaning to the visual items of fashion they're presented with, corresponds with how McCroskey (2017) positions the receiver, or audience, of another's communication as the one who determines the source's *ethos* based on the visual and verbal messages received.

Reading the Rhetorical Situation: Implications for Educators and Employers

In *Generation Me*, Jean Twenge (2006) advised employers that the millennial generation of students presently populating our classrooms will value flexible schedules and workplace independence and will, not surprisingly, "respond well to a casual dress code" (p. 218). More than a decade later, Twenge's advice has fully materialized in the more relaxed business dress practices the Big Four accounting firms have adopted to reflect their re-designed work environments and to attract and retain a new millennial generation of accountants. In June 2017, EY Canada (formerly Ernst & Young) announced the unveiling of its new "reimagined workplace" in downtown Toronto. Defining its new modern aesthetic are floor-to-ceiling windows, sit-to-stand desks, and workspaces "designed to be flexible, fluid, and focused on *how* people work best" and to support creativity, collaboration, and learning ("New EY Tower," 2017). Ushering in this new aesthetic are also changes EY made to its existing dress code in 2017 when it added jeans to its list of acceptable business clothing, a change in keeping with the more flexible "Dress for Your Day" approach (see Figure 8.1) PwC Canada had already introduced the year before in June 2016 when promoting "Flexibility" (from Flex days to Flexitime) as a vital part of its work culture (PwC Canada, 2018).

Comfort is the new trend in office wear (Binkley, 2016), and when Steve Jobs made Levi's 501s and a black turtleneck his uniform, "power jeans" entered the boardroom and established a new aesthetic, primarily in more creative industries like media and marketing (Binkley, 2009). Traditionally more conservative, accounting, law, and financial service firms have been slow to adopt this trend, but with a new generation of employees who value comfort and self-expression in their clothing, we see a gradual movement away from standard business attire within these industries (Binkley, 2008a; Binkley, 2008b). As EY Canada and other accounting firms shape their brand and work space, we see a new aesthetic

 **PwC Canada** ✅
@PwC_Canada

 (Follow) ⌄

We're #PwCProud of our new
#dressforyourday guidelines! Starting today,
wearing denim isn't just for Fridays!

3:31 PM - 17 Jun 2016

FIGURE 8.1   Screenshot of PwC Canada Tweet

emerging as part of this new brand culture within the accounting industry, but these changes are introduced on a cautionary note. On the "Business appropriate attire" section of its website, EY prefaces its list of what (and what not) to wear with the following statement:

> We encourage our people to dress comfortably and in a way that reflects personal style, while also making sure we look like experienced, knowledgeable business advisors that we are. While a professional image cannot substitute for performance, a less than professional image can detract from the way we are perceived. In the eyes of our clients and the business community, *you* are EY. Our brand—and your brand—is in your hands!
>
> *(EY, 2017)*

In explaining its "Flexible Dress" code, PwC Canada (2018) tells its current and prospective employees, "We trust you to choose the clothes to wear to work that best represent yourself and the PwC Brand. It's about being yourself and being comfortable throughout the work week as part of our flexible dress code called #DressForYourDay." Critical to both messages presented here is how the firm and its accountants are configured as partners in brand management, that is, in maintaining the integrity and professionalism of the brand. Therefore, for EY not just anything goes: jeans must be well fitted and in good condition; jeans with holes, distressed appearance, or excessive embellishment are not permitted. While athleisure wear is likewise making an unwelcome appearance into some workplace office environments (Teitell, 2015), leggings and athletic attire remain on the "not this" list of EY and other Big Four accounting firms.

In promoting and preserving its brand, KPMG also recognizes their brand is in the hands of its junior employees and isn't leaving anything to chance, using its resources to fully educate and orient its new hires by investing heavily in how they dress. In 2014, KPMG U.S. attracted the attention of the *Wall Street Journal* when 1,200 of its summer interns each received a $200 gift card to either the Men's Warehouse or Banana Republic as part of its welcome dinner and fashion show presentation featuring recruiters modeling office style dos and don'ts. Accessories were also included as welcome gifts: men received silk ties and women a piece of work-appropriate jewelry. According to Kathy Schaum, its national campus recruiting director in the U.S., KPMG spends approximately $400,000 annually on gift cards, since they recruit roughly 2,000 interns a year (Korn, 2014). Because almost 90 percent of its interns will later become full-time firm employees, KPMG U.S. regards this approach as a sound investment and a supportive way to communicate to its new interns in a non-confrontational, positive way acceptable business attire and hopefully avoid awkward conversations, unwanted reprimands, and mutual embarrassment later. To further help university students bridge the transition from campus life to corporate life at their firm, KPMG U.S. developed KPMG Campus, a dedicated section on its website designed to help students develop a personal brand in keeping with the firm's brand culture. The "Dress for Success" section of its Branding U platform states, "How you dress is important when Branding U. Here are a few points from KPMG U.S. to help you navigate through the sometimes confusing business casual dress" (KPMG Campus, 2018; KPMG Canada Careers, 2016). KPMG Canada's recruiters and talent attraction specialists also prove an invaluable resource during recruitment season in helping students understand its brand culture, guiding them on how to "Dress for Success" (see Figure 8.2) and make a positive first impression at networking events.

The current advice being offered by accounting practitioners on how best to navigate the new "Dress for the Occasion" or "Dress for Your Day" dress code practices is consistent in advising new hires to assess whom they're meeting with, where they're meeting them, and what they're meeting about (Burns Perryman, 2012; Fortune et al., 1995; Gutierrez & Freese, 1999; Stiefel & Avery, 2016). Translated into rhetorical terms, what employers are effectively prompting new hires to do is to make an informed decision about what to wear based on reading and evaluating the three key elements of any rhetorical situation: namely, audience, purpose, and context. Are new recruits fully equipped to do so? Not necessarily:

KPMG Canada Careers ✓
@KPMGCareersCA

(Follow) ⌄

Decrypting company dress code policies is not always easy. Learn how to best do so with this advice from @Erik_KPMG.

Dressing for success

Erik Reed, KPMG Talent Attraction Specialist, Regions East

February 2016

2:10 PM - 8 Jul 2016

FIGURE 8.2   Screenshot of KPMG Canada Tweet

partly motivating KPMG U.S.'s in-house fashion show and gift card giveaway were questions and uncertainties previous interns had voiced about its business casual dress code. As well, internal evidence revealed that new interns weren't always reading the rhetorical situations they encountered correctly and that they needed guidance in this area. Some new interns were dressing, as Kathy Schaum described it, "not in a way we would have preferred" (as cited in Korn, 2014).

All of which raises the question: How can we better prepare students to read these rhetorical situations correctly in the context of our business communication courses?

As business communication instructors, we are well positioned to guide students on how to read these rhetorical situations on the job and to navigate these more flexible but also more nuanced dress code practices that now define the modern workplace. As a starting point, the lessons we presently teach our students about how to analyze the rhetorical situation for every written document and oral presentation they prepare are just as relevant and as applicable here. Guiding that analysis are the familiar critical thinking questions: Who is your audience? What is your purpose? What is the context? Undergraduate students with little real-world work experience communicating in formal business environments may not always appreciate the importance of rhetorical analysis in planning their messages, but discussing this process in relation to what future employers are expecting of them in terms of dressing appropriately at work might have greater relevance for them as they contemplate future job prospects. Although we are not likely to distribute generous gift cards to popular clothing retailers to make our pedagogical point, there's still much we can do to support our students in understanding these new "Dress for the Occasion" directives shaping the aesthetic and work practices of today's corporate cultures.

Simply raising their awareness of these new dress practices is itself an important first step. As part of the job search module, many of us already discuss with students how to build their personal brand through networking and developing their resumes, cover messages, and LinkedIn profiles. A natural extension of that discussion is to highlight these new dress code practices as they research the corporate culture of the employers they're targeting and prepare for that initial job interview. To initiate that discussion, instructors could begin by incorporating any one of the following activities into their course modules:

1. Ask students to offer their own opinions of what they think a "Dress for Your Day or Occasion" policy means and what they would do to ensure they understood what that practice means. Here, have them consider what strategies they might use (from consulting with a supervisor or researching the client) to ensure they didn't misread or misinterpret the rhetorical situation and risk compromising their or their employer's credibility.

2. As an in-class group activity, have students create their own dress code for an accounting firm and have them identify what clothing items and accessories should or should not appear on this list. Then have them compare their lists with those available on some of the actual accounting firm websites mentioned in this chapter or for their targeted employer. Have students note what items they have listed that do or do not appear on the firm's lists, or clothing items or accessories they might have questions about. This would be a good opportunity to discuss work-appropriate accessories and how visible tattoos or piercings may detract from an overall professional appearance.

3.　Have students visit a firm's site like PwC Canada's where flexibility is fully endorsed and have them report back the various styles of clothing and business-appropriate accessories they see junior employees like themselves wearing. See if they notice differences in how employees are depicted across different firms' sites and what that might indicate about each firm's brand culture.

4.　Part of this new flexibility means accounting firm employees are now working remotely from home or other off-site locations more often than not. To do so, they are using collaborative tools like Google Hangouts, a platform that supports video meetings, chat, and instant messaging, among other features. As PwC Canada (2018) reports on its website, they have "Gone Google" to support a collaborative work environment ("Careers"). The new EY@ Work office design also features virtual collaboration rooms, so employees can work with colleagues and clients located throughout North America and around the world ("New EY Tower," 2017). Discuss with students what steps they would take to present a polished appearance when preparing for video meetings with clients or colleagues, especially with those located in different countries where business casual may not be the cultural norm. This could also be a good opportunity to discuss how some companies have developed dress code guidelines for employees' online avatars to ensure a professional presence is also maintained when conducting meetings in virtual business settings (see, for example, Betts, 2009).

5.　Finally, since most firms report they are client-focused and that dress practices should reflect the client's dress code, present students with diverse types of workplace scenarios they're likely to encounter that differ in terms of context (e.g., on-site vs. off-site meetings; urban office vs. rural, agricultural, or mining environments); audience (e.g., familiar colleague vs. a new client or a new team member in a different international location); purpose or type of meeting; and level of formality required.

Beyond these suggested activities, instructors can also consult the useful guidelines and recommended activities Kiddie (2009) and McPherson (1997) provided as part of their respective discussions for helping students navigate casual business wear dress policies within different corporate environments.

Concluding Remarks

In 2009, Sam DeKay reported that most business communication books "offer only a cursory exploration of the topic of business attire," usually in the context of employment interview preparation and then primarily as a "preliminary to serious communication" rather than a form of communication itself (p. 349). A decade later, his assessment remains mostly true. Our most widely used business communication textbooks predominantly address the topic of business attire or professional presence in chapters discussing how to prepare for the job interview or deliver a business presentation. Others discuss the impact of physical appearance within their chapters on interpersonal or nonverbal communication. All ultimately convey the message to "Dress for Success," to make a positive first impression at the job interview. However, including some mention of what steps students can take to navigate today's more flexible dress code practices will help ensure our students enjoy long-term career success. By knowing how to dress appropriately on the job for various business encounters with colleagues and clients, our students will be well positioned to sustain the positive first impression they initially made at their job interviews and earn themselves a favorable performance review.

More recent audits of course content within the business communication curriculum indicate that teaching business presentations and employment communications related to the job search continue to be major topics covered in our business communication courses (Moshiri & Cardon, 2014; Truss, 2009). Interpersonal communication, of which nonverbal communication is an integral part, is also reportedly gaining greater attention within our course curricula (Moshiri & Cardon, 2014). All these course modules serve as logical places in which to introduce and discuss with students the changes in corporate culture today and the ensuing impact it is having on what businesses and their clients are expecting of millennials in terms of presenting and maintaining a professional appearance. Among his findings, Truss (2009) also discovered that topics related to discussing or analyzing communication theories received "minimal coverage" (p. 402), suggesting that "instructors place a heavier emphasis on praxis than on theory" (p. 409). Citing Du-Babcock (2006) and Littlejohn (2007)'s respective arguments about the value of teaching students the theories that inform business communication praxis, Truss reminds us that students gain a richer understanding of the concepts they practice if they understand some of the theory that informs them. In the workplace, Generation Y frequently wants to know *why* they're being asked to complete a task and *why* it's important (Espinoza, Ukleja, & Rusch, 2010; Lancaster & Stillman, 2010; Twenge, 2014). While our classroom time is often limited, we should at the very least remind students that the same rhetorical analysis that guides their critical decision making in preparing written and oral messages for our courses will likewise serve them well in conducting the *appearance labor* they will need to perform as part of their personal branding and impression management strategies at work. By training them to read these rhetorical situations correctly, we also prepare them to manage the highly visible, nonverbal messages their workplace clothing and overall appearance will convey to others about their professionalism, competency, and *ethos*.

References

Aristotle. (1954). *Rhetoric* (Rhys Roberts, W., Trans.). New York, NY: Modern Library.
Barnard, M. (Ed.). (2007). Fashion statements: Communication and culture. In *Fashion theory: A reader* (pp. 170–181). New York, NY: Routledge.
Barthes, R. (1990). *The fashion system* (Ward, M., & Howard, R., Trans.). Berkeley, CA: University of California Press.

Betts, M. (2009, November 2). Employee avatars will need dress codes. *Computerworld*, p. 8.

Binkley, C. (2008a, January 31). Law without suits: New hires flout tradition: Young attorneys' casual attire draws criticism at big firms; A crackdown on Ugg boots. *The Wall Street Journal*. Retrieved from www.wsj.com/articles/SB120175142140831193.

Binkley, C. (2008b, November 13). What sneakers say about your soul—Young workers rebel against standard business attire; The significance of Chuck Taylors. *The Wall Street Journal*. Retrieved from www.wsj.com/articles/SB122654186690223299.

Binkley, C. (2009, November 6). The relentless rise of power jeans. *The Wall Street Journal*. Retrieved from www.wsj.com/articles/SB100014240527487035746045745014631048730016.

Binkley, C. (2016, September 18). The new trend in office wear: Comfort. *The Wall Street Journal*. Retrieved from www.wsj.com/articles/the-new-trend-in-office-wear-comfort-1474251001.

Blair, J. A. (2004). The rhetoric of visual arguments. In C. A. Hill & M. Helmers (Eds.), *Defining visual rhetorics* (pp. 41–61). Mahwah, NJ: Lawrence Erlbaum.

Breeze, R. (2013). *Corporate discourse*. London, United Kingdom: Bloomsbury.

Burgess-Wilkerson, B., & Boyd Thomas, J. (2009). Lessons from *Ugly Betty*: Business attire as a conformity strategy. *Business Communication Quarterly*, *72*(3), 365–368.

Burns Perryman, E. (2012). Fashion & finance: Dos and don'ts for new recruits. Retrieved from www.accountingtoday.com/opinion/fashion-amp-finance-dos-and-donts-for-new-recruits.

Cardon, P. W., & Okoro, E. A. (2009). Professional characteristics communicated by formal versus casual workplace attire. *Business Communication Quarterly*, *72*(3), 355–360.

Cornelissen, J. P. (2017). *Corporate communication: A guide to theory and practice* (5th ed.). Thousand Oaks, CA: Sage.

Davis, F. (1992). Do clothes speak? What makes them fashion? In *Fashion, culture, and identity* (pp. 3–18). Chicago, IL: University of Chicago Press.

DeKay, S. (2009). The communicative functions of business attire. [Editorial]. *Business Communication Quarterly*, *72*(3), 349–350.

Deloitte Canada. (2005). *Code of conduct: Personal accountability, recognizing the power of one.* [Corporate document]. Canada.

Du-Babcock, B. (2006). Teaching business communication: Past, present, and future. *Journal of Business Communication*, *43*, 253–264.

DuBrin, A. J. (2011). *Impression management in the workplace: Research, theory, and practice*. New York, NY: Routledge.

Espinoza, C., Ukleja, M., & Rusch, C. (2010). *Managing the millennials: Discover the core competencies for managing today's workforce*. Hoboken, NJ: Wiley.

EY. (2017). Business appropriate attire. [Corporate document.] Retrieved from http://rsvp.ey.com/CSG3/2017/1702/1702-2201687/FSO_Portal/Content/Business%20appropriate%201-pager_2016.pdf.

Fernandes, D. (2016, January 19). MassMutual's relaxed dress policy aims to appeal to millennials. *The Boston Globe*. Retrieved from www.bostonglobe.com/business/2016/01/19/massmutual-more-relaxing-dress-policy/q4EKNkKpySJCAkbpnUuxTJ/story.html.

Fortune, M., Francis, B. C., Gallegra, P., Miller, R. J., Stemler, G. J., & Whitman, K. M. (1995). Focus on: Dress code. *Journal of Accountancy*, *179*(5), 39–42.

Foss, S. K. (2004). Framing the study of visual rhetoric: Toward a transformation of rhetorical theory. In C. A. Hill & M. Helmers (Eds.), *Defining visual rhetorics* (pp. 303–313). Mahwah, NJ: Lawrence Erlbaum.

Foss, S. K. (2018). *Rhetorical criticism: Exploration & practice*. (5th ed.). Long Grove, IL: Waveland Press.

Gagliardi, P. (Ed.). (1990). *Symbols and artifacts: Views of the corporate landscape*. Berlin, Germany: Walter de Gruyter.

Gagliardi, P. (2006). Exploring the aesthetic side of organizational life. In S. R. Clegg, C. Hardy et al. (Eds.), *The SAGE handbook of organization studies* (2nd ed., pp. 701–724). Thousand Oaks, CA: Sage.

Goffman, E. (1959). *The presentation of self in everyday life*. New York, NY: Anchor Books.

Grant Thornton Canada. (2018). Careers: Students and recent graduates. FAQs. Retrieved from www.grantthornton.ca/en/Careers/students-and-recent-graduates/faqs/.

Gutierrez, T., & Freese, R. (1999, April). Dress-down days. *CPA Journal, 69*(4), 32.

Hyland, K. (1998). Exploring corporate rhetoric: Metadiscourse in the CEO's letter. *The Journal of Business Communication, 35*(2), 224–245.

Joseph, N. (1986). *Uniforms and nonuniforms: Communication through clothing*. New York, NY: Greenwood Press.

Kang, M., Sklar, M., & Johnson, K. K. P. (2011). Men at work: Using dress to create and communicate identities. *Journal of Fashion Marketing and Management, 15*, 412–427.

Kelly, D. (2009, November 14). Despite tough times, bespoke suits make the cut. *The Globe and Mail*, pp. L1–L4.

Keyton, J. (2011). *Communication & organizational culture: A key to understanding work experiences* (2nd ed.). Los Angeles, CA: Sage.

Kiddie, T. (2009). Recent trends in business casual attire and their effects on student job seekers. *Business Communication Quarterly, 72*(3), 350–354.

Korn, M. (2014, June 18). Where interns learn how to dress. *The Wall Street Journal*. Retrieved from https://blogs.wsj.com/atwork/2014/06/18/what-interns-should-wear-to-work/.

KPMG Campus. (2018). Tools for you: Branding U. Retrieved from www.kpmgcampus.com/tools-for-you#branding-u.

KPMG Canada. (2005). *Canadian code of conduct: Performance with integrity* [Corporate document]. Toronto, Canada: Author.

KPMG Canada Careers. (2016, July 8). Decrypting company dress code policies is not always easy. Learn how best do so with this advice from @Erik_KPMG [Tweet]. Retrieved from https://twitter.com/@KPMGCareersCA.

KPMG International. (2005). *Global code of conduct: Performance with integrity* [Corporate document]. Retrieved from https://home.kpmg.com/content/dam/kpmg/pdf/2016/07/global-code- of-conduct.pdf.

Kwon, Y. (1994a). Feeling toward one's clothing and self-perception of emotion, sociability, and work competency. *Journal of Social Behavior and Personality, 9*(1), 129–139.

Kwon, Y. (1994b). The influence of appropriateness of dress and gender on the self-perception of occupational tributes. *Clothing and Textiles Research Journal, 12*(3), 33–39.

Lancaster, L. C., & Stillman, D. (2010). *The M-factor: How the millennial generation is rocking the workplace*. New York, NY: HarperBusiness.

Littlejohn, S. (2007). *Theories of human communication*. Florence, KY: Wadsworth.

McCroskey, J. C. (2017). Ethos: A dominant factor in rhetorical communication. In *An introduction to rhetorical communication: A western rhetorical perspective* (9th ed., pp. 62–82). New York, NY: Routledge.

McPherson, W. (1997). "Dressing down" in the business communication curriculum. *Business Communication Quarterly, 60*(1), 134–146.

Molloy, J. T. (1977). *The woman's dress for success book*. Chicago, IL: Follett Publishing.

Moore, S. (2016, June 22). Dress code policies in the accountancy profession. Retrieved from https://economia.icaew.com/features/june-2016/dress-code-policies-in-accountancy-firms.

Moshiri, F., & Cardon, P. (2014). The state of business communication classes: A national survey. *Business and Professional Communication Quarterly, 77*(3), 312–329.

Mulford, C.W., & Comiskey, E. E. (2011). Creative accounting and accounting scandals in the USA. In M. J. Jones (Ed.) *Creative accounting, fraud and international accounting scandals* (pp. 407–424). West Sussex, England: Wiley.

Munk, N. (1998, March 3). The new organization man. *Fortune*, 63–74.

New EY Tower brings firm's purpose to life. (2017, June 27). Retrieved from www. newswire.ca/news-releases/new-ey-tower-brings-firms-purpose-to-life-631088003. html.

Nichols, R. (2013, April 17). Auditors must make a positive first impression. Retrieved from www.accountingweb.com/aa/auditing/auditors-must-make-a-positive-first impression.

Norton, S. D. (2011). Bank failures and accounting during the financial crisis of 2008–2009. In M. J. Jones (Ed.) *Creative accounting, fraud and international accounting scandals* (pp. 425–452). West Sussex, England: Wiley.

Peluchette, J., & Karl, K. (2007). The impact of workplace attire on employee self-perceptions. *Human Resource Development Quarterly*, *18*, 345–360.

Peluchette, J., Karl, K., & Rust, K. (2006). Dressing to impress: Beliefs and attitudes regarding workplace attire. *Journal of Business and Psychology*, *21*, 45–63.

Pettinger, L. (2004). Brand culture and branded workers: Service work and aesthetic labour in fashion retail. *Consumption, Markets & Culture*, 7(2), 165–184.

Pratt, M. G., & Rafaeli, A. (1997). Organizational dress as a symbol of multilayered social identities. *Academy of Management Journal*, *40*, 862–898.

Pratt, M. G., & Rafaeli, A. (2001). Symbols as a language of organizational relationships. *Research and Organizational Behaviour*, *23*, 93–132.

PwC Canada. (2016, June 17). We're #PwC Proud of our new #dressforyourday guidelines! Starting today, wearing denim isn't just for Fridays! [Tweet]. Retrieved from https://twitter.com/@PwC_Canada.

PwC Canada. (2018). Careers: Campus recruiting. Retrieved from www.pwc.com/ca/en/careers/campus-recruiting/why-pwc.html#flexibility.

Rafaeli, A., & Pratt, M. G. (1993). Tailored meanings: On the meaning and impact of organizational dress. *Academy of Management Review*, *18*(1), 32–50.

Rake, M. (2005). Leadership message. In *KPMG International Global code of conduct: Performance with integrity* [Corporate document]. Retrieved from https://home.kpmg.com/content/dam/kpmg/pdf/2016/07/global-code- of-conduct.pdf.

Rucker, M., Anderson, E., & Kangas, E. (1999). Clothing, power and the workplace. In K. Johnson & S. Lennon (Eds.), *Appearance and power: Dress, body, culture* (pp. 59–77). New York, NY: Berg.

Russ, T. L. (2009). The status of the business communication course at U.S. colleges and universities. *Business Communication Quarterly*, *72*(4), 395–403.

Sklar, M., & DeLong, M. (2012). Punk dress in the workplace: Aesthetic expression and accommodation. *Clothing and Textiles Research Journal*, *30*(4), 285–299.

Stiefel, D., & Avery, B. (2016, October). Generational viewpoints: Dress for success. *Accounting Today*, *30*(10), 48.

Teitell, B. (2015, October 30). Yoga pants count as "business casual" now? *The Boston Globe*. Retrieved from www.bostonglobe.com/lifestyle/2015/10/30/yoga-pants-they-count-business-casual-now/S4TgdTqY5K8fIxXks0hrdP/story.html.

Temple, J. (2002, February 22). Old economy makes a comeback; so does its traditional uniform. *San Francisco Business Times*. Retrieved from www.bizjournals.com/sanfran cisco/stories/2002/02/25/story5.html.

The 10 worst corporate accounting scandals of all time. (n.d.) [Infographic]. Retrieved from www.accounting-degree.org/scandals/.

Toffler Ley, B. (2003). *Final accounting*. New York, NY: Broadway Books.

Trice, H., & Beyer, J. (1993). *The cultures of work organizations*. Englewood Cliffs, NJ: Prentice Hall.

Twenge, J. M. (2006). *Generation me: Why today's young Americans are more confident, assertive, entitled—and more miserable than ever before*. New York, NY: Free Press.

Twenge, J. M. (2014). *Generation me: Why today's young Americans are more confident, assertive, entitled—and more miserable than ever before. Revised and updated*. New York, NY: Atria.

Walker, T. (1993, November). No suits, no ties, no service. *CA Magazine*, 11.

Wen, P. (2000, July 28). Office casual-dress policies spark confusion, even a backlash. *Knight Ridder/Tribune Business News*. Retrieved from www.highbeam.com/doc/1G1-63758013.html.

9

THEORIZING THE ROLE OF BIG DATA VISUALIZATION

Moving Visuals from Delivery to Invention

Dale Cyphert

Data visualization entered the business curriculum with the widespread adoption of spreadsheets in the late 1970s, gaining additional attention when PowerPoint became an expected feature of business presentations (Cyphert, 2007). Visual design basics, typically with some attention to the ethical use of data, now comprise a standard chapter in undergraduate business communication textbooks. Pedagogical treatment of visual communication has evolved with each introduction of new tools (Brumberger, 2007; Cyphert, 2004, 2007), moving instruction from a focus on spacing, fonts, and tables into computer-generated graphics, hyperlinks, image quality, and, most recently, attention to formatting for mobile viewing. With the dawn of Big Data, business communication seems poised to adapt yet again, but this chapter suggests the possibility of significant disruptions in the curriculum.

The implications for business communication instruction would involve more than simply updating the requisite chapter on data visualization. Pedagogy necessarily adapts to evolving rhetorical norms as they reflect the slow progression of culture across philosophical eons (Black, 1980; Ehninger, 1968). But now and then a major advance in communication technology challenges rhetorical norms to the point of shifting the rhetorical paradigm (Cyphert, 2010). Literacy, the printing press, and electronic media famously generated cultural resistance (Eisenstein, 1979; Gronbeck, Farrell, & Soukup, 1991; Havelock, 1968; Jamieson, 1998; Lentz, 1989; McLuhan, 1964; Ong, 1967; Postman, 1985). Recent advances in computer-generated graphics and online communication have garnered similar criticism for the dangers they pose to acceptable and effective public discourse (Funkhouser, 1937; Jarvenpaa & Dickson, 1988; Pennings, 2014; Vogel, Dickson, & Lehman, 1986; Yates, 1985). The pedagogical challenge involves recognizing the difference. Should we warn students against the temptations of a technology that violates the rules of acceptable discourse, or is this a time that requires our participation in a shifting paradigm?

Three phenomena point toward Big Data visualization as a symptom of rhetorical revolution. Critics warn that Big Data poses economic, philosophical, and social threats to Western norms of reasoned discourse, while data visualization tools demonstrably require rhetorical competencies not previously understood as an element of visual communication. Meanwhile, those utilizing Big Data in public discourse reflect a new understanding of how data visualization functions in the construction of rhetorical appeals. The new tools do not merely offer improvements in the visual *delivery* of information; they bring the visual manipulation of data into the realm of *invention*.

Big Data, Data Visualization, and Visual Analytics

As pragmatic, resource-rich early adopters, business users have historically capitalized on new technologies. Merchants leveraged written bills of lading, printing presses, television cameras, and blogging platforms as they emerged—and were typically criticized for violating the discourse rules of the day. That familiar dynamic appears again in the arguments over Big Data. Described by data scientists as one of the most significant advances in the history of computing (Ekbia et al., 2014), social critics predict these same tools will lead to the destruction of clear thinking, reasoned discourse, and moral behavior (boyd & Crawford, 2012; Ekbia et al., 2014; Gregg, 2015). Meanwhile, business communication instructors explore visualization tools adopted by our students' prospective employers, turning our classrooms into laboratories of rhetorical change.

Our pedagogical response should begin with an examination of the thing that lies on our laboratory bench. Big Data has been called mere business hype: a "mythology" created to market "Big Data solutions" that falsely implies significant changes in research simply because the datasets increase in size (Crawford, Miltner, & Gray, 2014, p. 1664). Admittedly, as a defining term *Big Data* offers minimal utility, with *Big* variously used to describe the vast amounts of data being generated and collected, the exploding capacity of computing power that allows its analysis, and the point at which human cognition must relate differently to the information load (Ekbia et al., 2014). Human interaction with data lies within the domain of rhetoric, and we find that in this cognitive domain, size does not properly describe the most important characteristic. The key factor involves the size of the data being communicated relative to the totality of data (Mayer-Schönberger & Cukier, 2013). Advances in computing power allow the manipulation of such massive datasets that analysis can now encompass *all* the data without the filtering, segregation, or biases inherent in selecting suitable samples for study. As Rob Kitchin (2013) puts it, *Big* means $n =$ all, with implications for epistemological presumptions that support traditional appeals to *logos*.

A more salient term for many instructors, *data visualization*, describes a longstanding element of the business communication curriculum, emerging in the late sixties as graphical displays of data. Instructors have already begun to explore the demands for new data visualization skills (Brumberger, 2015; Cyphert, 2017), and new software offers interesting options for animation, dynamic data connections, and interactive design. Having seen software advances previously, an instructor might sensibly assume that "the 'old stuff' still applies" to visualization of data, however Big it might be. Choices have expanded beyond pie charts, graphs, and tables to include interactive and geospatial tools and additional color and pattern choices, but the goal remains to clearly, professionally communicate the data "in a visually interesting way" (Amy Igou, personal communication, 17 Jan 2017). One expert user stresses that even when data becomes more available or more important or visualization tools change, the art of "communicating data" remains "at once analytical, articulate, and creative" (B. Jones, 2014, p. ix), and gives advice to begin with attention to the situation, the message goals, and audience needs—goals consistent with any business communication instructor's course.

A third key term, *visual analytics*, seems to best capture the revolutionary nature of the Big Data technology. Descriptions of peta-, tera- or exabytes of data as millions of videos uploaded to YouTube each second or zillions of library books worth of information seem abstract and difficult to comprehend in practical terms—because they are. When data can no longer be "visualized in its totality," human understanding depends on visualization tools (Anderson, 2008 para 4), the heuristics, simplifications, abstractions, and glosses that allow us to see a forest as something more than a mind-numbing expanse of unique trees. The technological capacity to analyze huge datasets depends on "creative approaches to *visualizing* data" as the human ability to perceive and interpret patterns becomes "integral to the process of creating knowledge" (Shaw, 2014 para 3). This form of reasoning taps into tacit cognitive processes inherent in visual perception (Thomas & Cook, 2005), and represents a departure from the explicit argumentation valorized in Western rhetoric as acceptable public discourse. Visual analysis moves the communication task beyond clearly delivering numeric or graphical information; now the display of data has moved into the realm of invention, where data display requires the insightful, creative, and persuasive manipulation of data to reach, explain, and defend conclusions.

Moving Instruction From Delivery to Invention

From both practical and theoretical perspectives, business communication instruction traditionally frames data visualization as a mode of delivery. Especially at the undergraduate level, instruction focuses on the creation of clear, effective, professionally performed messages to convey content drawn from functional business courses within the curriculum. Management coursework might address strategic, persuasive, or leadership message construction (Cyphert et al., 2016), but textbooks designed for the general undergraduate business communication course still focus on written (and increasingly oral) delivery that meets traditional standards: clear, correct, concise, courteous, character, coherent, and complete (Hagge,

1989). Graphic and visual modes of communication have been subsumed into the framework, with the instructional goal of creating equally clear, complete, and concise visual support for written or orally delivered messages.

Updating visual technology might seem trivial, but from ancient times, visual communication has played a contested rhetorical role (Finnegan & Kang, 2004). While obviously effective, the emotional, psychological, and physiological appeals were considered subsidiary to the rational appeals of verbal argument (Kenney, 2002). Not until the 1970s did theorists address the "whole buzzing, blooming, impossibly complex" array of rhetorical processes beyond verbal discourse (Booth, 1971, p. 95), and not until the end of the twentieth century did visual rhetoric begin to emerge as an area of scholarship (Hill & Helmers, 2004). Even so, theorists initially framed visuals as tools of memory and delivery (Kenney, 2002; Medhurst & DeSousa, 1981) or stylistic devices (McQuarrie & Mick, 1996). While images could enhance the delivery of an argument by evoking memories and emotions (Osborn, 1986; Edwards & Winkler, 1997), establishing associations (Blair, 2004) or identification (Olson, 1983; Osborn, 1986), or clarifying information (Osborn, 1986; Foss, 1994), their "illustrative and decorative" (Hill & Helmers, 2004, p. 2) role remained separate from the "verbal discourse, debate, argument, and thoughtful reflection" (p. 3) of critical discourse.

A few contemporary theorists have suggested that visual processes can play a role in invention, the process of generating or adapting ideas to make a convincing case. Persuasive effect can arise from the ordering and framing of images (Lake & Pickering, 1998; Lancioni, 1996), and Charles Kostelnick (2004) points out that designing visuals so that readers can comprehend and retain information necessarily involves cognitive processes. Others continue to dismiss visual arguments as merely enthymematic, however, susceptible to ambiguity, limited to just one or two simple premises, and lacking any dialectic capacity (Blair, 2004). Finnegan and Kang warn that such interpretations reflect "dominant linguistic/rational norms" (2004, p. 396) that understand rhetorical effectiveness only in terms of what can be done with words. A fully realized theory of visual rhetoric must account for how it persuades, not merely how it enhances verbal persuasiveness.

Big Data challenges the dominant paradigm on two counts. First, the tools that permit visual analytics exploit important realms of human reasoning that lie outside the boundaries of *logos*, verbal reasoning—and outside the logocentric parameters of reasoning as it was understood by the ancients. Visual analysis does not construct verbal claims and argument; implicit cognitive processes discern patterns, recognize relationships, and apprehend concepts directly from visual perception. The user might choose to translate those insights into verbal claims and arguments, but more effective persuasion results from showing those same visuals to an audience with the expectation that their implicit cognitive reasoning will reach the same conclusion. Such a display of personal insight might be perfectly acceptable *poetics*, the aesthetic and emotional realm of drama, literature, and poetry, but lies outside the realm of acceptable rhetorical discourse.

Secondly, Big Data embraces analytical methods that defy the scientific method's traditional tests of reasoning and evidence. Western philosophy understands science as a deductive process of causal logic designed to uncover the truth inherent in an objective reality, generally referred to as objective rationalism. Scholars build predictive theories from empirical evidence and known relationships, develop hypotheses that can be tested with further data, and systematically prove or disprove the theory. The process depends on carefully collecting representative, objectively verifiable data and rejects individual outcomes, emotional response, personal narrative, aesthetic preference, and divine inspiration as equally subjective, unacceptable forms of evidence. The computer-generated algorithms of Big Data analysis, on the other hand, capitalize on the "abundance, exhaustivity and variety, timeliness and dynamism, messiness, and uncertainty, [and] high relationality" (Kitchin, 2014, p. 2) of the entirety of available information. Massive processing power can uncover correlations independently of predictive theory or causal explanation.

These challenges have elicited critique across all three rhetorical dimensions, a sure sign that norms have been violated (Cyphert, 2001). Any new communication technology can drive major social and cultural change. As users learn new skills or the mode introduces a new relationship between referent and message, a new technology "has the capacity to influence, often quite profoundly, the nature and qualify of the lives of those who use it" (Silverstone, 1991, p. 151). When those changes pose a challenge to the customary ways in which public discourse is conducted, they necessarily challenge the community's assumptions about who holds sufficient status, acceptable mental capacity, or procedural skill to appropriately and effectively participate in the rhetorical community (Cyphert, 2010).

Digital media scholars were among the first to sound the Big Data alarm (boyd & Crawford, 2012; Fuchs, 2017; Gitelman, 2013; Lupton, 2015), focusing primarily on the legal and ethical concerns surrounding the surreptitious capture of data from unsuspecting and nonconsensual users in the context of social media. Discussion ranges, however, across a multitude of academic, legal, business, and political venues around fundamental issues of epistemology, technology, methodology, and aesthetics (Ekbia et al., 2014). Business users, in particular, have been singled out, presumed evil by some for their capitalist motivation (Fuchs, 2017) or because they monopolize data resources (boyd & Crawford, 2012; Ekbia et al., 2014; Richards & King, 2013), but many have pointed more broadly toward cultural and social effects of Big Data that raise the specter of "changes in the way society governs itself" to rival those introduced by the invention of the printing press (Mayer-Schönberger & Cukier, 2013, p. 184).

Threats to a Moral Public Sphere: Big Data as a Technical Gatekeeper

One dimension of rhetorical norms involves the status, discursive, and demographic markers that signal legitimate participation in public discourse. Every rhetorical community exhibits norms of citizenship: rules about the appropriate personal characteristics or social status that warrant citizenship (Cyphert, 2001). Moral claims for inclusion, from women, for instance, demanding the right to vote, offer an explicit challenge to the rhetorical order. The technical aspects of Big Data present a subtler challenge, but one that appears to authentically threaten presumptions of *who* ought to participate in public decision making.

Because the huge resources needed to store and analyze such large amounts of data "are predominantly in the hands of powerful intermediary institutions, not ordinary people" (Richards & King, 2013, p. 44), critics assume the worst. Those who champion the tools and insights of Big Data are accused of touting a "utopian vision" of what technology can do, without attending to the "gap between these visions and socioeconomic and cultural realities" or the political strife caused by that gap (Ekbia et al., 2014, p. 1527). Critics warn that governments and corporations will benefit from the "individuals being mined, analyzed, and sorted" with "our democracy diminished" as a result (Richards & King, 2013, p. 45).

Egalitarian democracy presumes the value of equal access to the public sphere, and Big Data tools seem to afford unequal access and power to corporate interests. Even with sufficient controls to prevent abuses, however, Big Data creates fundamental shifts in the valuation of data, with significant rhetorical effects. The information value of a huge dataset is not inherent in their collection and storage, but dynamically dependent on their *interpretation* in context. Meaningfulness, an inherently cultural construct (Gitelman, 2013), requires "multiple social agents" (Helles & Jensen, 2013) and depends entirely on the context in which the data were gathered (boyd & Crawford, 2012). Free access to Big Data has no value without the technical expertise and social capital to glean meaning from it. The key gatekeeper role thus shifts from those who hold information toward those able to use data.

A key facet of the "Big Data mindset" involves recognizing and acting on the value of data (Mayer-Schönberger & Cukier, 2013, p. 124): noticing it, digitally recording it and ultimately connecting or using it to create value will drive businesses and economies. Ubiquitousdigital data gathering shifts value from data collection, such as a utility company's expensive human meter reading, to the analysis of automatically collected real-time data, accruing value from the implementation of dynamic pricing and usage incentives (Ernst & Young Foundation, 2015). However, the entity that owns the data might have no ability or interest in using it, creating an entirely new information value chain (Mayer-Schönberger & Cukier, 2013). The new gatekeeper becomes the entrepreneurial entity that finds a way to monetize the value of *interpreted* data for use in public discussion.

When value is understood to be inherent in the data, social and political structures protect the public by ensuring the integrity of data it receives. That might include full disclosure to force the release of data, but also involves vetting processes to guarantee its accuracy. Critics have resisted what appears to be a crumbling of these protections. Data, once "obscure and difficult to manage," can be released to anyone able to purchase the computing technology, "regardless of their training" (boyd & Crawford, 2012). The machines' algorithms simply bypass the "traditional gatekeepers of knowledge in the state, the universities, and the market," who spent long years of training to learn to gather and properly interpret accurate, valuable data, and thus put civilization at risk when computer users can create policy without the "regulating force of philosophy" (Berry, 2011, p. 8).

Managers and officials, once secure in their ability to control decisions by virtue of the data they controlled, are finding their status threatened by "statisticians, and database managers and machine learning people" who can "extract wisdom from it" (Hal Varian, Google's chief economist, quoted in Mayer-Schönberger & Cukier, 2013, p. 125). The holders, curators, and evaluators of information find themselves losing their gatekeeping power and status to the computer-assisted creators of useful, evocative, or timely information displays. The moral relationships of public discussion shift, valuing the contributions of those who can analyze data over those whose claim on value rests in their ownership of data.

Threats to Rational Thought: Big Data as the End of Theory

Epistemological norms govern the foundational rules of what might be reasonably discussed, as well as the ways a rational audience should reach a valid conclusion (Cyphert, 2001). Feminist, postmodern, and cross-cultural challenges to the logocentrism of Western rhetorical norms have led to greater appreciation for diverse ways of knowing as well as the limits of objective rationalism, but Big Data calls for more than an adjustment in *what* must be known to form a conclusion. The very possibility of reaching rational conclusions appears to be under attack.

Chris Anderson (2008), editor of *Wired* magazine, prompted a firestorm of protest when he proclaimed Big Data as the end of theory, describing Google's predictive success as evidence the scientific method is obsolete. With enough data and processing power, the diagnostic tools of science—building models, developing hypotheses, and testing theory—no longer provide value, he claimed, saying that now "correlation is enough" to create knowledge (para 13). Critics responded that reliance on Big Data thus demolished "instrumental reason" (Fuchs, 2017, p. 54) by replacing public discourse with decision algorithms. The prospect that a computer might automatically mine data, detect patterns, and implement the results scares observers (Kitchin, 2014), especially those who appreciate the "older forms of intellectual craft" (boyd & Crawford, 2012, p. 666) that Western philosophy developed to replace the primitive empiricism of the ancient world.

Challenges to Western rationalism trace to the quantum collapse of certain reality (Kline, 1980; Prigogine, 1997) and complexity (Capra, 1997; Wolfram, 2002), along with neurobiological understanding of implicit cognition (Reber, 1993; Sun, 2001). Across the sciences, massive computing power has allowed a shift from "causal explanations to predictive modeling and simulation" (Ekbia et al., 2014, p. 1530), moving science from "conditions of scarce data and weak computation"

(Kitchin, 2014, p. 6) requiring deductive methods to create "abstract and reductionist constructions" of knowledge based on partial information, toward a process to investigate "dynamic, fine-grained" information "approaching 'reality' itself" (Chandler, 2015, p. 836).

A second aspect of traditional scientific methods involves statistical sampling and analysis that allow the testing of a theory with just a small set of data—an important tool when data was scarce and expensive to store. Those methods work, however, on the assumption that the sample mirrors a largely homogeneous whole. Big Data explodes the limits of these methods in the technological capacity to examine every instance in relation to every other instance. Rather than focus on the data that offers the most accurate picture of a generalized theory, science can now examine variety. No piece of data need be excluded or rejected from the sample because it is different from the aggregated average or norm (Chandler, 2015). In pragmatic terms, science can now learn from variation, contradictions, anomalies, and outliers (Mayer-Schönberger & Cukier, 2013) and investigate a world that "is complex, not bound by generic laws and rules but by feedback loops and changes through iterative and complex relational processes" (Chandler, 2015, p. 850). Big Data clearly threatens established epistemological norms inherent in our rhetorical traditions but fosters new ways of investigating and thinking that seem to offer far more promise in an era of data plenty.

Threats to Public Decorum: Big Data as Return of the Poetic

Norms of public engagement govern the performances of public decision making (Cyphert, 2001), a realm that has absorbed enormous disruption over the past hundred years. Notions of *how* communities might legitimately reach agreement have embraced visuality of a media era, activism of the sixties, and infinite circulation in a digital public sphere. Big Data appropriates and magnifies all three, perhaps to the point of bypassing human participation entirely.

Much of the discussion surrounding Big Data concerns the visual display of results generated by an algorithm, with considerable debate over the way human cognition might apprehend or interpret the results (Ekbia et al., 2014). With the introduction of film and television, visual methods of communication have been condemned for their degradation of public discourse (Jamieson, 1998; McLuhan, 1964; Postman, 1985), and "a return of the unconscious" (Silverstone, 1991, p. 156) that undid everything literacy had done to move human civilization "away from its unreflexive, unconscious, primitive state" of orality (Silverstone, 1991, p. 156). Computer generated graphics elicited equal concern (DeSanctis, 1984; Tufte, 2003), and Big Data's visual analytics draw fire on the basis that visual design rules calling for simplification, clarity, or beauty might lead to oversimplification, specious reasoning, or misleading aesthetics (Ekbia et al., 2014). Critics worry that decision makers will succumb to their "visually elegant and intuitive" dashboards, which "can tempt managers to forget about the all-important nuances of data-driven decision making" (Shapiro, 2017, para 4).

These critics echo long-standing rhetorical norms that have been traced to Plato's arguments against the poets, banned in his *Republic* (1952 (c360 B.C.)) so their intuitive, implicit inducements could not contaminate public discourse. Plato's charges against the poets did not center on their aesthetics, which were acceptable as theatric entertainment, but on their capacity for engaging the public with an undemanding, unconscious, formulaic discourse that loosed in the audience a shared emotional experience (Havelock, 1968). Rhetorical theory since has acknowledged the existence of *pathos*, but has not strayed far from Plato's characterization as a dark horse that must be controlled, with significant effort, to reach wisdom (1956, p. 246a-b). The visual analytics central to Big Data might go farther than simply violating that rhetorical norm; computing power might have finally harnessed visuals' inherent rhetorical power to evoke and create implicitly shared knowledge.

Plato's aim was to disallow the emotionally aroused mob any place in public decision making (Havelock, 1968), and legitimate discourse would instead rely on the individual citizen to develop and discuss his own independently derived conclusions. The explicit comparisons of the dialectic became the only reliable path toward truth, and rhetorical ideals mimicked logic, as best they could, with a public discourse of individuals presenting claims and counter-claims until a reasoned decision could be made. The age of media threatened to replace articulated discourse with mass audiences' interpretive participation (McLuhan, 1964) and a "participatory mystique" that fostered a communal sense (Ong, 1982, p. 136). Some Big Data critics similarly worry about social contamination, concerned that an individual human mind cannot comprehend its results without the mediation of "trans-disciplinary work, technological infrastructures, statistical analyses, and visualization techniques" (Ekbia et al., 2014, p. 1527), a process that introduces layers of selection, ordering, interpretation, and distribution that promise to substantively change the way we analyze data.

Besides their heavy reliance on visual forms of communication, Big Data technologies foster the sharing of those visuals, both during the collaborative process of analyzing data and in the expectation that audiences will continue to participate in its interpretation and sharing. The phenomena calls forth concern that such "translational work" involves interpretation and reinterpretation that necessarily "renders the accuracy of the claims problematic" (Ekbia et al., 2014, p. 1532) Any pretense of explicit, intentional, instrumental rhetoric seems to have crumbled with a technology that fosters a distributed, tacit, use of heuristics to generate an extended collective response.

Furthermore, a major value of data tools such as a digital dashboard involve the audience's capacity to share not only in the interpretation of the mediated, visual message but also in the analysis of the underlying data. No longer a receiver or even a co-creator of the communication experience, the audience receives a message embedded in tools that allow revision and reinterpretation of the data content. When the transmission multiplies in the digital world of email chains and retweets, any presumptive norms of intellectual authorship seemingly vanish in a gallery of infinitely interpretive mirrors.

The almost inevitable sharing of visual images has led some theorists of visual rhetoric to focus on social circulation as the primary rhetorical process, in contrast to the traditional understanding of communication as the persuasive transmission of ideas from rhetor to audience (Finnegan & Kang, 2004). Meanwhile, contemporary research in social psychology (Surowiecki, 2004), distributed cognition (Cole, 1996), and learning organizations (Senge, 1994) has amply illustrated robust processes of collective decision making that fail to conform to the traditional norms of Western public discourse. The charge that Big Data violates norms of reasoned discussion seems valid; these tools demonstrate the degree to which our ancient theories delegitimized robust rhetorical processes simply because they did not yet understand their methods of inducement.

Implications for Business Communication Pedagogy

Major shifts in rhetorical practice present a changing environment that necessarily calls for pedagogical adjustments. The technical requirements of any new software present classroom and resource challenges, as do evolving employer practices and work expectations. When the technology challenges rhetorical norms, as Big Data clearly does, we can expect significant—perhaps even disruptive—changes. As the function of visual communication shifts from illustrative aids in the delivery of a clear message toward the inventional realm of analysis and knowledge creation, we can anticipate changes across instructional focus, skill requirements, and curricular organization.

Instructional Focus

Those teaching data analytics often describe the field in terms of descriptive, prescriptive, and predictive analytics (Sharda, Delen, & Turban, 2018). The first category seems rather obviously relevant to the instructional focus of business communication, although all three present challenges to traditional distinctions between data analysis and its visual display. Descriptive analytics involves making sense of the computer-generated data, visually manipulating the output to create clear, insightful displays to facilitate decision making. Students might be taught a simple three-stage method of analysis, first prioritizing the data in some way (e.g., by size, quantity, or distance from a point). Next, differences or patterns are rendered using color, size, shape, and shading, and finally changes are examined over time to develop conclusions about rate, growth, or variation (Shasidar Kaparthi, personal communication, 20 Jan 2017).

A typical data visualization textbook (B. Jones, 2014) approaches the topic within a highly rhetorical framework that reflects principles taught in business communication courses. Jones' instructions for Tableau, the most common software for general business use (Marr, 2017), reinforce familiar guidelines for graphical clarity, reducing ambiguity and avoiding misinterpretation (or misrepresentation).

In no sense does the software that harnesses Big Data seem to challenge the productive rhetorical norms of data display. Yet, sophisticated rhetorical choices must also be made in preparing the data for display, constructing interactive displays, and communicating the nuances of Big Data results.

Tableau users appreciate the seamless capacity for a single analyst to evaluate the data available to answer a business question, import publicly available data that might be a suitable proxy, develop an "exploratory dashboard" to gain "insights" into the data, and then create a final display to foster the audience's ability to explore the data relationships that demonstrate the analyst's discoveries (B. Jones, 2014, p. 275). This exciting scenario involves several tasks, however, that seem far removed from those typically associated with the creation of charts and graphs in a business communication course.

The current data display assignment more typically starts with a dataset that represents the statistical results that *answer* a business question. Those results might have been generated in Excel from sales or operations data, or even as SSPS results from a marketing research project. The business communication student transforms that data, typically in Word or PowerPoint, as a communicative graphical display. Even allowing for more integrated, problem-based instructional activities, the necessary steps of blending data sources, scrubbing and reconciling the structures to evaluate the data, defining and locating acceptable proxies for missing data, and engaging in the creative work of developing "insights" are not part of the data display process as we generally understand it.

The interactive presumptions of data dashboards, the dominate output format, further involve deciding what amount and type of interaction a targeted audience should have with the data display. The software demands choices of framing elements (descriptive text, key performance indicators, metrics, multiple annotations) and interactive elements (filters, sheet actions), as well as the potential for direct access to other resources (URL links, multimedia, reference links, notations). The rhetorical task is more akin to designing the entire book, not merely preparing the graphical content of a single page. Ben Jones (2014) compares the preparation of a chart or table to the ingredients of a full meal that is the dashboard.

Finally, Big Data's algorithmic results shift the responsibility for creating a plausible causal narrative from those who developed a theoretically sound hypothesis onto those who must convincingly report the machine's results. To begin, the display must clarify whether the data comes from the entire population or represents just a sample (B. Jones, 2014). Given those important distinctions, "variation and uncertainty really matter" and confidence in proportions "can have a huge impact on the conclusions and decisions that follow" (B. Jones, 2014, p. 123). Having to explain how the data was cleaned and analyzed forces a more thoughtful presentation—not just of the results, but also in the development of those results.

The instructional scope in an era of Big Data shifts from attention to the physical characteristics of the visual *product* to the rhetorical *processes* involved in constructing a visual message. Cara Finnegan (2004) has noted the implications of moving theoretical attention beyond the product, a rhetorical artifact that relies on something beyond words for its effect, toward exploration of the ways in which image functions in public discourse. But, as Sonja Foss (2004) points out, those theories remain concerned with the responses of lay viewers who lack technical expertise in the production of images. The technical and analytical requirements of Big Data point us to consider a third perspective: visual rhetoric as the *process* by which visual representation brings forth an idea.

An obvious instructional response might be to tap the writing analogs of drafting, revising, editing, and production, but the sheer speed of implicit cognition and the anticipation of multifaceted, co-creative interactions with an audience suggest that effective Big Data visualization might depend on a very different inventional process, perhaps more akin to the creative processes of graphic arts, film, or political theater. We can be sure, however, that Big Data will exacerbate the challenge for students who focus on technology tools and struggle with developing rhetorical competence. New technology platforms seem, on the surface, to call for more technical focus, but the complexities of Big Data suggest an opposite driver toward more complex and complete rhetorical instruction.

Skill Expectations

The most salient issue for business communication instruction might be whether Big Data places new rhetorical expectations on those who use the new tools. The well-designed chart or table, whether used in a presentation slide or a dashboard, can make the difference "between being ignored and achieving your objective" (B. Jones, 2014, p. 270), but visual design with Big Data tools calls for a more involved creative process. Ben Jones (2014) describes building a dashboard as a process involving drafting and revising, and he advises finding a peer editor to "play with it" to determine whether the dashboard is working as desired (p. 271). Data visualization calls for more than the technically adept construction of a visual illustration to support verbal communication, but a process comparable to writing or speechmaking in the "creative thought" and "diligent drafting" required (p. 239).

Descriptive analytics require skills beyond those of graphic design. First, dashboard construction allows communicators to select from an array of internal and external datasets. The goal is not merely to display the results of analysis but to choose data input that will allow the software to perform analysis. Users must guard against inappropriate data sources (Crawford et al., 2014) or careless reliance on a software's source defaults (Shapiro, 2017). Then, effective data display requires that the user understand the level of precision possible and expected from the data (B. Jones, 2014) and guard against the human propensity to see specious causal relationships (Mayer-Schönberger & Cukier, 2013). The distinguishing functionality of dashboard software lies in a user's ability to "simultaneously query the data and view the results" (B. Jones, 2014, p. 15).

Working with the entire dataset—and without a previous analysis that might have developed a hypothesis to guide the manipulation of the data—the task of data display now involves "the data discovery process (finding insights in data) as well as the data communication process (creating explanatory graphics, exploratory dashboards, and data storytelling)" (B. Jones, 2014, pp. 15–16). As with the inventional process of locating arguments that will persuade a given audience, data visualization calls on intuition, empathy, and creativity to make sophisticated judgments about what the data means for the business. Big Data display includes perceiving relationships and patterns that might answer a business question and presenting that insight as a plausible narrative to others (Shoztic, Bible, Nelson, & Stein, 2016).

As the business purpose moves from descriptive analytics to prescriptive analytics, the skill requirements grow increasingly sophisticated. While the business task involves a straightforward calculation of optimized processes, the rhetorical parameters of reporting results can become complex. For example, a geospatial analysis of locations, fuel use, driver time, and so on, might aim to optimize the routes for a trucking company. The results, displayed as a dashboard, would then guide management decisions regarding business development, fleet operations, human resources, and so on. Dashboard design reflects "a set of priorities and assumptions about what's important" (Shapiro, 2017 para 5) to the business, however, and the questions cannot be answered only in terms of design clarity or aesthetics. If visual cues regarding priorities, level of relevant detail, refresh rates, or data interactions do not align with business priorities, the results might be communicated in a useless or even damaging way.

Teaching students to anticipate an audience's perspective and potential questions has always been an important but difficult concept, perhaps even a threshold concept that must be understood before a student can grasp later concepts (Pope-Ruark, 2011), and Big Data's integration of analysis and display increases both technical and rhetorical complexity. The goal of "giving users the ability to interrogate the data to find hidden insights" (B. Jones, 2014, p. 228) requires not just an understanding of the display content, but also an anticipation of the users' contexts and functional uses of the content in context, and the degree of interpretive effort that context will call forth in the audience.

The strongest social and philosophical critique of Big Data lies in the arena of predictive analytics, which uses mathematical, statistical, and computational algorithms to locate correlations and relationship patterns within the data. The results, consisting typically of correlations or relationship patterns, need not be visual, but visual display offers interpretive assistance. Strings of statistical results showing petabytes of infinitely interrelated data points remain largely incomprehensible, and visualization tools were developed specifically to provide an "easy" way to "quickly" view, compare, and combine data for "sophisticated analysis" (B. Jones, 2014, p. ix). Much of the concern lies with that interpretive ease, which allows data visualization to "augment or overrule human judgment" (Mayer-Schönberger & Cukier, 2013, p. 141).

Examples abound of specious correlations, but advocates can point to an equal number of situations where "it may be more advantageous to eschew *why* in favor of *what*" (Mayer-Schönberger & Cukier, 2013, p. 190). The tools of Big Data challenge rhetorical norms of human judgment, but pragmatic results provide evidence that traditional epistemologies were "more appropriate for a small-data world where one never has enough information, or the right information, and thus has to rely on intuition and experience to guide one's way" (Mayer-Schönberger & Cukier, 2013, p. 142). The inherently verbal Western norms of rational judgment might well be violated, but demonstrably effective results create the need for a new rhetoric to guide a visual form of reasoning that will "let the data speak" (Mayer-Schönberger & Cukier, 2013, p. 141) in effective and appropriate ways.

At this point, the challenges to the business communication curriculum might be most clear. As teachers of delivery skills, we work within the boundaries of traditional rhetorical understanding. As visual display moves toward the realm of invention, however, instruction necessarily moves into the realm of testing, bending, and even creating new rhetorical conventions. Ancient theorists recognized certain rules of invention, which called on a culture's *topoi* to construct appeals that could be reliably effective within definable cultural parameters. Those heuristics remain useful, but the rules themselves have evolved—and occasionally shattered—over the past few thousand years. Eloquence, after all, arises when the generic rhetoric of the day cannot adequately express emergent understandings shared by an audience. The communication of predictive results pushes the curriculum beyond the teaching the design rules of the community into the realm of inventing eloquent messages that speak to the emergent values of a Big Data world.

Curricular Implications

Beyond the greater rhetorical sophistication called for within a business communication course, the larger curricular effects of Big Data promise major impacts. Users have recognized that the complex sequence of sophisticated data visualization tasks (Liu, Cui, Wu, & Liu, 2014, p. 1373) requires clarity about the desired business impact (Li, Kassengaliyeva, & Perkins, 2016) as well as deep contextual knowledge about the industry, business strategy, and data sources (Kerr, Hausman, Gad, & Javen, 2013; Kitchin, 2014). Employers also distinguish between analytics specialists, who might earn a statistics or systems degree to focus on the delivery of data, and the general business graduate who must effectively function as an "analytics consumer" in order to add value (Ernst & Young Foundation, 2015). A specialist might build the dashboard tools, but every professional will need "knowledge of how the underlying data was generated, a deep understanding of the business context, and exceptional critical thinking skills" in order to use the dashboard effectively (Shapiro, 2017, para 4).

A typical recommendation suggests that business students learn with "real-world" datasets and case studies (Shoztic et al., 2016). Such instruction would involve significant shifts across the entire business curriculum, however, where the full range of skills involved in data visualization are currently taught in separate courses. Data collection methods, typically taught in a marketing or research course, must integrate with statistical analysis, generally a separate statistics or business analysis course. Context knowledge derives from numerous courses, which might not be integrated in a business strategy or project course until the students' senior year. Technical design issues might be taught only to information systems majors, while audience analysis and narrative principles appear in the business communication course.

Taken together, the incorporation of *Big Data* visualization into the business curriculum clearly calls for much more than developing a new instructional unit in the communication course. Content knowledge, along with the *topoi* and argumentation norms of the business function, must be available to the student, along with technical skills for using (and perhaps building or sharing) a dashboard, as well as the communication skills needed to create a persuasive interpretive narrative. Further, the business communication curriculum functions within a network of courses, majors, and programs that must all adapt to Big Data's impact on job responsibilities and expectations. Whether we respond from within the current course configuration or initiate change across the curriculum, traditional distinctions between invention of the business content and its instrumental delivery have been made obsolete.

Predictions for Business Communication Performance

As the era of Big Data evolves, new rhetorical appeals, techniques, and performances will emerge. Ultimately, normative expectations will arise as *topoi*, genre, and rules of decorum develop over time. Definitive predictions cannot yet be made, but we might predict a few characteristics by observing the pioneers. Several Tableau dashboard exemplars (Tableau, n.d.) offer clues, as does a highly regarded presentation from the late Hans Rosling, a distinguished professor of international health whose presentations have been widely praised as "the best stats you've ever seen" (TED Conferences LLP, n.d.), earning him worldwide fame as "the man in whose hands data sings" (McVeigh, 2017). These early indicators support the inventional role of technology-enhanced visual communication, and offer hints that traditional distinctions among *logos*, *pathos*, and *ethos* might warrant significant revision.

The Primacy of Logos: The Data Speaks

Whether used to build a dashboard, distribute as a slide, or create the substance of a presentation, Big Data technologies function as both content creators and communication tools. An electronic visual typically displays multiple data points with minimal labeling, and touching any data point will often result in a pop-up or link to additional detail. The visual, distributed electronically, either alone or as part of report or presentation, allows a viewer to further explore and often manipulate the data. Similarly, Rosling's presentation[1] (Coleman, 2015) consists of a demonstration of economic, demographic, health, crime, and environmental data gathered around the world since 1800, millions of data points that a visitor to his website ("Data in Gapminder World," n.d.) can slice and dice in any conceivable way.

A dashboard implicitly presents the manipulation of data as the primary tool of managerial decision making, and Rosling explicitly emphasizes the primacy of *logos*, proclaiming, "I'm a scientist; I deal in facts" (1:07); he enfolds his evidence in a promise that his persuasive task will be "easy" because he can work "from my huge database" (0:38). Rosling expects his audience to perceive Big Data as better data, confident that his audience values data-driven decision making. Just as the electronic displays lack any explicit claims about the evidentiary value of the data, Rosling presents data without any explanatory theory, explicit claim-warrant structure, or value argument to support making decisions based on empirical data.

An increasing reliance on data for managerial decision making can be traced to a post-WWII explosion of operations research and management science, later encouraged by the tools of spreadsheet software and computer-generated graphics. Big Data tools extend the trend with easy access to more data and simplification of its convincing display. The rhetorical departure is not in the appeal to bigger or better displays, but in the absence of any verbal argument structure to complete the appeal to *logos*. The epistemological contrast between explicit verbal argument and implicit visual argument discussed above emerges in these presentations as the lack of space or time devoted to the development of an explicit verbal argument in an appeal that lets the data speak for itself.

This abandonment of explicit claim and warrant allows what might be the more significant effect of Big Data: the shift from arguments of generalization toward arguments of variability. The computing power allows Big Data tools to locate patterns and relationships across the entire dataset, freeing the rhetor from any obligation to establish the generalizable validity of sampled data. Instead, the rhetor can draw on correlations, variations, and diverse perspectives to build an argument. Dashboard tools offer a wide range of graphic options, but the most compelling offer an array of data color coded to differentiate by some characteristic. A mosaic of colored tiles, for example, provides a time series of news articles colored to represent the various topics covered (C. Jones, n.d.). Rather than make an argument about general trends or most common types of new articles, the graphic invites the viewer to discern patterns in the variations.

Similarly, rather than offer a general rule to "define" poverty, Rosling explains that "everyone has their own idea" (5:03), demonstrating with eight video clips of individuals around the world saying, "I'm poor," followed by descriptions, which range widely from "We only eat once a day" to "we don't know if we can go to university" (5:11). He pointedly avoids making a generalization about poverty to demonstrate both variety of experience and variety across nations. The focus on variety allows Rosling to build an argument with video and photos of specific families in Malawi, Burundi, India, Zimbabwe, Nigeria, and Papua New Guinea to "really understand that they want to build a new house" (16:25).

Dashboard data arrays allow the viewer to drill down through increasingly smaller segments, sometimes as far as individual data points. Rosling's performance similarly parses worldwide data by nation, income level, and life circumstance to reach unique stories of individual people. Such arguments reject aggregation as a form of proof, embracing instead the idiosyncratic, and the visual form allows an audience to become convinced by the authenticity of personal experience. Rhetoric in a Big Data age does not call on its massive size to inundate an audience with multiple examples of a point. Instead, it persuades by inviting an audience to examine the *logos* of individual experience.

The Repurposing of Pathos: Aesthetic Warrants

The Platonic suppression of emotional appeals as effective but unworthy for use in reasoned discourse evolved into a general presumption that artistic forms lay outside the proper domain of rhetorical discourse. Contemporary theorists have recognized their historical integration (Branham, 1980; Bryant, 1953; Walker, 2000), but the subsequent rehabilitation of literature, photography, and performance as rhetorical artifacts nevertheless perpetuates the dichotomy between rational truth and aesthetic effect (Reeves & Stoneman, 2014). With Big Data's visual analytics, rhetorical performances have begun to demonstrate the integration of data and display as visual analytics and refute the ancient but arbitrary distinction between a visual argument's epistemological content and pleasurable effect.

Rosling offered his statistics to make persuasive points about world health and economic conditions, describing his methods (Rosling, 2009) as just a better way to present statistical information. Nevertheless, TED marketing stressed the presentation's aesthetic value, motivating nearly 12 million viewers to watch a 20-minute speech on economic statistics with the promise of a presentation delivered "with the drama and urgency of a sportscaster" ("The best stats you've ever seen," 2006). Similarly, developers of Big Data tools consistently warn against the dangers of allowing elegant aesthetics to mislead or distract audiences from the rational data message (Ekbia et al., 2014; Shapiro, 2017), yet arresting design characterizes the exemplars (Tableau, n.d.)

A fully developed theory of visual rhetoric remains on the horizon, but Big Data performances demonstrate the constructive, inventional potential of aesthetic rhetoric to locate and establish truth within a responding audience (Reeves & Stoneman, 2014). Returning to the ancient understanding of truth (*aletheia*) as the uncovering of knowledge, an aesthetic appeal does not simply evoke emotional response. Instead, the visual presentation of patterns and relationships fosters implicit understanding of otherwise unknowable truths. Because Big Data's visual analytics lies outside the realm of explicit logic, its tools necessarily capitalize on the argumentative warrants of aesthetic performance. Visuals perform the inventional function of bringing forth the unsayable to establish a claim about the world.

Rosling, for example, performs a dynamic relationship between its citizens' life expectancy and a nation's per capita GDP. He barely sketches any causal relationship and instead lets the visual display of the data function as both argument and evidence. The strikingly simple data displays, comprised of brightly colored bouncing circles, demonstrate geographical contrasts, changing conditions, and economic and health relationships across the past two hundred years. The speaker, offering entertaining commentary, becomes a verbal aid to the visual. Human beings believe what they see with their own eyes, and the aesthetics of the data elicit sustained attention and an intuitive grasp of the knowledge displayed.

Arresting visual graphics are equally important in data dashboards, although their tactile nature seems to capitalize as well on an aesthetic of participation. Query and display tools tempt a user to play the game, and warrants emerge from the viewers' manipulation of the data. An interactive display of color terms (Luminoso, n.d.), for example, provides an irresistible display of colors and patterns that invites implicit understanding of language, perception, and gender. As contemporary theories of visual rhetoric and aesthetics converge on a recognition of knowledge-producing methods that lie beyond verbal argument (Finnegan & Kang, 2004; Reeves & Stoneman, 2014), Big Data presentations demonstrate the inventional power of *pathos*.

The Mediation of Ethos: Proof in the Interaction

Contemporary audiences widely engage with political, civic, and business speakers by way of YouTube and TED Talks, where they have come to expect enthusiasm, storytelling, visuals, and connection (Kedrowicz & Taylor, 2016). The online venues typically feature a huge screen behind the speaker, which increasingly displays dynamic, interactive data visualizations. Similarly, as Big Data analysis tools make their way onto the desktops of business executives, politicians, and lobbyists, the expectations of documents and presentations of every kind increasingly call for interactive displays of dynamic data. A competent and credible Big Data rhetor cannot merely claim expertise and affinity with the audience; *ethos* derives as well from an ongoing relationship among rhetor, data, and audience.

The visual salience of Big Data provides new tactics for traditional claims of competence. The trend toward a highly entertaining style featuring dynamic storytelling, a known effect of the "fast-surfing" digital era (Kedrowicz & Taylor, 2016, p. 356), shows in Rosling's enthusiastic performance. Impishly dancing around the data, Rosling engages in literal hand waving, seeming to guide the bubbles of national GDP across the screen of time. Referring only vaguely to himself as a "scientist" (1:07) and later as a "professor" (6:00), Rosling offers no credentials. Nor does he mention the sources of his data. Data journalist David McCandless (2010) describes Big Data visualization as "a form of knowledge compression . . . a way of squeezing an enormous amount of information and understanding into a small space" (13:49). Here, the compression allows Rosling to collapse the verbal cues of competence into a visual *ethos* argument: no credentials, no citations, no proclamations of credibility—just big, bright, beautiful, convincing data.

The more significant Big Data impact appears in the *ethos* claims of relationship with an audience. Downplaying his own academic or ownership connections to the data, Rosling focuses instead on engaging the audience in their own relationships with the data. The relationship begins, again, with a visual claim. Contemporary *ethos* claims to transparency and honesty rely on the trope of an interactive town hall or listening tour audience to allow the Q&A session that is already ubiquitous in business presentations (Neher & Heidewald, 2015), and Rosling capitalizes on the audience's presence with a transparent display that allows the camera to show him through the data. He verbally reinforces that implicit relationship claim with an explicit invitation for the audience to use the data for their own purposes, engaging them in a quiz, complete with quiz-show graphics (2:44), and utilizing the Big Data dashboard image to drill down on a data point in response to the audience's implied query. Extending the live audience trope as a demonstration of the speaker's willingness to respond with authenticity, Big Data's interactive dashboards further expand the tools of *kairos* to include offering data in the manner that allows an audience to find "just what she needs—the information, the pattern, or the anomaly—at that moment she needs it" (Bodie, n.d., p. 9).

This relational *ethos* extends across the mediated rhetorical landscape. Electronic media, especially internet communication, have dramatically changed the nature of public discourse. Every audience includes "a broader audience of people both in real time, through live-streaming video, and after the fact" (Kedrowicz & Taylor, 2016, p. 370), such that digital delivery necessarily includes elements of accessibility, distribution, and ownership as well as attention to digitally created identity and interaction (Porter, 2009). Rosling's presentation, a typical example, was broadcast on BBC Two on three different occasions. Then, multiple short clips appeared on both the BBC website and YouTube, where viewership has now reached nearly 100,000, and the full performance remains permanently available at the Gapminder website.

That website, like the dashboard links that increasingly accompany Big Data presentations, demonstrates the fully interactive relationships in public circulation of a message that marks this next era of *ethos* claims. Along with the video, the Gapminder website provides access to the most current version of the source databases and interactive Big Data query and display tools that facilitate the audience's ongoing relationship with the data. Just using video playback controls, comment boxes, and social media tools, today's "virtual audiences respond in ways that demonstrate their co-ownership of a presentation" with replication, remixing, and reformatting (Kedrowicz & Taylor, 2016, p. 369). The sharing of Big Data provides the audience with an additional capacity to reanalyze the data, joining the rhetor in a permanently dynamic relationship with the data. In an era of endless knowledge creation and recreation with the audience, a rhetor's *ethos* no longer resides within, but in the character of an ongoing relationships among presenter, audience, and data.

Normative Resistance or Rhetorical Revolution

Those who teach rhetoric necessarily guard the boundaries of reason and decorum and serve as gatekeepers who ensure a citizenry able to engage in responsible civic discourse. Our classrooms might explore communication methods, modes, and goals as they emerge, but we aim to incorporate new techniques into accepted rhetorical practice. New genre might emerge, and audience expectations might change, but our instructional job requires that we incorporate change within the normative paradigm. New forms of evidence might allow the creative invention of new appeals, while styles of delivery might change over time, but we expect to work within an ancient and robust understanding of rhetoric.

The age of Big Data seems to promise a fundamental challenge to ancient premises. Utilizing a technology that allows both rhetor and audience to engage implicit cognitive processes unknown to ancient theorists, Big Data visualization cannot be expected to fit easily within their logocentric norms of reasoning. Coupled with the visuality of our hypermediated rhetorical era, Big Data tools also explode the norms of performance and audience relationship. The observation that visual display has shifted from the canon of delivery to the canon of invention only scratches the surface of what might be an authentic revolution in Western rhetoric. Our instructional role will include a responsibility to create knowledge about its nature.

Note

1 Quotations from the presentation are provided with times from this uploaded version.

Works Cited

Anderson, C. (2008). The end of theory: The data deluge makes the scientific method obsolete. *Wired*. Retrieved from www.wired.com/2008/06/pb-theory/.

Berry, D. M. (2011). The computational turn: Thinking about the digital humanities. *Culture Machine*, *12*(online), 1–22.

The best stats you've ever seen. (2006). *TED*. Retrieved from www.ted.com/talks/hans_rosling_shows_the_best_stats_you_ve_ever_seen.

Black, E. (1980). The mutability of rhetoric. In E. E. White (Ed.), *Rhetoric in transition: Studies in the nature and uses of rhetoric* (pp. 71–83). University Park, PA: The Pennsylvania State University Press.

Blair, J. A. (2004). The rhetoric of visual arguments. In C. A. Hill & M. Helmers (Eds.), *Defining visual rhetorics* (pp. 41–61). Mahwah, NJ: Lawrence Erlbaum.

Bodie, M. (n.d.). *Rhetoric in tech and context: Big data in the college, culture, and classroom.* Academia. Retrieved from www.academia.edu/14761131/Rhetoric_in_Tech_and_Context_Big_Data_in_the_College_Culture_and_Classroom.

Booth, W. C. (1971). The scope of rhetoric today. In L. F. Bitzer & E. Black (Eds.), *The prospect of rhetoric: Report of the national development project* (pp. 93–114). Englewood Cliffs, NJ: Prentice-Hall.

boyd, d., & Crawford, K. (2012). Critical questions for big data: Provocations for a cultural, technological, and scholarly phenomenon. *Information, Communication & Society, 15*(5), 662–679.

Branham, R. J. (1980). Ineffability, creativity, and communication competence. *Communication Quarterly, 28*(3), 11–21.

Brumberger, E. R. (2007). Making the strange familiar: A pedagogical exploration of visual thinking. *Journal of Business and Technical Communication, 21*(4), 376–401.

Brumberger, E. R. (2015). *Professional communication competencies for today's workplace: An analysis of job postings.* Paper presented at the 80th Annual International Conference of the Association for Business Communication, Seattle, WA.

Bryant, D. C. (1953). Rhetoric: Its functions and its scope. *The Quarterly Journal of Speech, 39*, 401–424.

Capra, F. (1997). *The web of life: A new scientific understanding of living systems.* New York: Anchor Books, Doubleday.

Chandler, D. (2015). A world without causation: Big data and the coming of age of posthumanism. *Millennium: Journal of International Studies, 43*(3), 833–581.

Cole, M. (1996). *Cultural psychology: A once and future discipline.* Cambridge, MA: Belknap Press of Harvard University Press.

Coleman, D. (Writer). (2015). Don't panic—How to end poverty in 15 years [television broadcast]. In D. Hillman (Producer), *This world.* United Kingdom: BBC TWO.

Crawford, K., Miltner, K., & Gray, M. L. (2014). Critiquing big data: Politics, ethics, epistemology. *International Journal of Communication, 8*, 1663–1672.

Cyphert, D. (2001). Ideology, knowledge and text: Pulling at the knot in Ariadne's thread. *Quarterly Journal of Speech, 87*(4), 378–395.

Cyphert, D. (2004). The problem of PowerPoint: Visual aid or visual rhetoric? *Business Communication Quarterly, 67*(1), 80–84.

Cyphert, D. (2007). Presentation technology in the age of electronic eloquence: From visual aid to visual rhetoric. *Communication Education, 56*(2), 168–192.

Cyphert, D. (2010). Obscene, mundane, and frivolous technologies: Maintaining the boundaries of decorum. *Explorations in Media Ecology, 9*(1), 21–36.

Cyphert, D. (2017). *Big data visualization: What do our students need to know?* Paper presented at the Annual International Conference of the Association for Business Communication, Dublin.

Cyphert, D., Dodge, E. N., Holke-Farnam, C., Hillyer, K. N., Iyer, K., Lee, W. M. E., & Rosol, S. (2016). *Defining Employer Expectations: Communication Activities, Behaviors, and Events in the 21st Century Business Environment.* Paper presented at the 81st Annual Conference of the Association for Business Communication, Albuquerque, NM.

Data in Gapminder world. (n.d.). *Gapminder.* Retrieved from www.gapminder.org/data/.

DeSanctis, G. (1984). Computer graphics as decision aids: Directions for research. *Decision Sciences, 15*(1), 463–487.

Edwards, J. L., & Winkler, C. K. (1997). Representative form and the visual ideograph: The Iwo Jima image in editorial cartoons. *Quarterly Journal of Speech, 83*(3), 289–310.

Ehninger, D. (1968). On systems of rhetoric. *Philosophy and Rhetoric, 1,* 327–339.

Eisenstein, E. (1979). *The printing press as an agent of change.* Cambridge: Oxford University Press.

Ekbia, H., Mattloll, M., Kouper, I., Arave, G., Ghazinejad, A., Bowman, T., . . . Sugimoto, C. R. (2014). Big data, bigger dilemmas: A critical review. *Journal of the Association for Information Science and Technology, 66*(8), 1523–1545.

Ernst & Young Foundation. (2015). *Analytics mindset: Analytics and the implications for accounting departments.* Paper presented at the Ernst & Young Academic Resource Center Colloquium, Dallas, TX.

Finnegan, C. A. (2004). Doing rhetorical history of the visual: The photograph and the archive. In C. A. Hill & M. Helmers (Eds.), *Defining Visual Rhetorics* (pp. 195–214). Mahwah, NJ: Lawrence Erlbaum.

Finnegan, C. A., & Kang, J. (2004). "Sighting" the public: Iconoclasm and public sphere theory. *Quarterly Journal of Speech, 90*(4), 377–402.

Foss, S. K. (1994). A rhetorical schema for the evaluation of visual imagery. *Communication Studies, 43*(3–4), 213–224.

Foss, S. K. (2004). Framing the study of visual rhetoric. In C. A. Hill & M. Helmers (Eds.), *Defining Visual Rhetorics* (pp. 303–313). Mahwah, NJ: Lawrence Erlbaum.

Fuchs, C. (2017). *Social media: A critical introduction* (2nd ed.). Los Angeles, CA: Sage.

Funkhouser, H. G. (1937). *Historical development of the graphical representation of statistical data.* Belgium: Bruges.

Gitelman, L. (Ed.). (2013). *Raw data is an oxymoron.* Cambridge, MA: MIT Press.

Gregg, M. (2015). Inside the data spectacle. *Television and News Media, 16*(1), 37–51.

Gronbeck, B. E., Farrell, T. J., & Soukup, P. A. (Eds.). (1991). *Media, consciousness, and culture.* Newbury Park, CA: Sage.

Hagge, J. (1989). The spurious paternity of business communication principles. *The Journal of Business Communication, 26*(1), 33–55.

Havelock, E. A. (1968). *Preface to Plato.* Cambridge, MA: Harvard University Press.

Helles, R., & Jensen, K. B. (2013). Making data—big data and beyond: Introduction to the special issue. *First Monday, 18*(10).

Hill, C. A., & Helmers, M. (2004). Introduction. In C. A. Hill & M. Helmers (Eds.), *Defining Visual Rhetorics* (pp. 1–23). Mahwah, NJ: Lawrence Erlbaum.

Jamieson, K. H. (1998). *Eloquence in an electronic age: The transformation of political speechmaking.* New York: Oxford University Press.

Jarvenpaa, S. L., & Dickson, G. W. (1988). Graphics and managerial decision making; Research based guidelines. *Communications of the ACM, 31*(6), 764–774.

Jones, B. (2014). *Communicating data with Tableau: Designing, developing, and delivering data visualizations.* Sebastopol, CA: O'Reilly Media.

Jones, C. (n.d.). 2016 summer recap: A visualization of the noteworthy news from memorial day to labor day. Retrieved from www.tableau.com/solutions/gallery/news-recap-summer-2016.

Kedrowicz, A. A., & Taylor, J. L. (2016). Shifting rhetorical norms and electronic eloquence: TED talks as formal presentations. *Journal of Business and Technical Communication, 30*(3), 352–377.

Kenney, K. (2002). Building visual communication theory by borrowing from rhetoric. *Journal of Visual Literacy, 22*(1), 53–80.

Kerr, K., Hausman, B. L., Gad, S., & Javen, W. (2013). *Visualization and rhetoric: Key concerns for utilizing big data in humanities research*. Paper presented at the IEEE International Conference on Big Data, Silicon Valley, CA.

Kitchin, R. (2013). Big data and human geography: Opportunities, challenges and risks. *Dialogues in Human Geography, 3*(3), 262–267.

Kitchin, R. (2014, April–June). Big data, new epistemological and paradigm shifts. *Big Data and Society*, pp. 1–12.

Kline, M. (1980). *Mathematics, the loss of certainty*. New York: Oxford University Press.

Kostelnick, C. (2004). Melting-pot ideology, modernist aesthetics, and the emergence of graphical conventions: The statistical atlas as of the United States, 1874–1925. In C. A. Hill & M. Helmers (Eds.), *Defining visual rhetorics* (pp. 215–242). Mahwah, NJ: Lawrence Erlbaum.

Lake, R. A., & Pickering, B. A. (1998). Argumentation, the visual, and the possibility of refutation: An exploration. *Argumentation, 12*, 79–93.

Lancioni, J. (1996). The rhetoric of the frame revisioning archival photographs in *The Civil War*. *Western Journal of Communication, 60*, 397–414.

Lentz, T. (1989). *Orality and literacy in Hellenic Greece*. Carbondale, IL: Southern Illinois University.

Li, M., Kassengaliyeva, M., & Perkins, R. (2016). Better questions to ask your data scientists. *Harvard Business Review*. Retrieved from https://hbr.org/2016/11/better-questions-to-ask-your-data-scientists.

Liu, S., Cui, W., Wu, Y., & Liu, M. (2014). A survey on information visualization: Recent advances and challenges. *Visual Computer, 30*, 1373–1393.

Luminoso. (n.d.). *Visualizing the XKCD color survey*. Retrieved from https://colors.luminoso.com/.

Lupton, D. (2015). *Digital sociology*. London: Routledge.

Marr, B. (2017, 20 July). The 7 best data visualization tools in 2017. Forbes Tech [blog post]. Retrieved from www.forbes.com/sites/bernardmarr/2017/07/20/the-7-best-data-visualization-tools-in-2017/#d2ab5a96c30e.

Mayer-Schönberger, V., & Cukier, K. (2013). *Big data: A revolution that will transform how we live, work, and think*. Boston: Houghton Mifflin Harcourt.

McCandless, D. (2010). *The beauty of data visualization*. Retrieved from www.ted.com/talks/david_mccandless_the_beauty_of_data_visualization.

McLuhan, M. (1964). *Understanding media: The extensions of man*. New York: Mentor, New American Library.

McQuarrie, E. F., & Mick, D. G. (1996). Figures of rhetoric in advertising language. *Journal of Consumer Research, 22*, 424–437.

McVeigh, K. (2017, 8 February). Hans Rosling, statistician and development champion, dies aged 68. *The Guardian*. Retrieved from www.theguardian.com/global-development/2017/feb/07/hans-rosling-obituary.

Medhurst, M. J., & DeSousa, M. A. (1981). Political cartoons as rhetorical form: A taxonomy of graphic discourse. *Communication Monographs, 48*, 197–237.

Neher, D., & Heidewald, J. (2015). *Business curriculum practices survey 2015: Placing skills and curriculum in context*. Paper presented at the 80th Annual International Conference of the Association for Business Communication, Seattle, WA.

Olson, L. C. (1983). Portraits in praise of a people: A rhetorical analysis of Norman Rockwell's icons in Franklin D. Roosevelt's "Four Freedoms" campaign. *Quarterly Journal of Speech, 69*, 15–24.

Ong, W. J. (1967). *The presence of the word*. New Haven: Yale University Press.

Ong, W. J. (1982). *Orality and literacy: The technologizing of the word*. London: Methuen & Co, Ltd.

Osborn, M. (1986). Rhetorical depiction. In H. W. Simons & A. A. Aghazian (Eds.), *Form, genre, and the study of political discourse* (pp. 79–107). Columbia, SC: University of South Carolina Press.

Pennings, A. J. (2014). Lotus spreadsheets—The killer app of the Reagan revolution—Part I. Writings on Digital Strategies, ICT Economics, and Global Communications [blog post]. Retrieved from http://apennings.com/how-it-came-to-rule-the-world/spreadsheets-the-killer-app-of-the-reagan-revolution-part-1/

Plato. (1952 [c.360 BC]). *The republic* (Vol. 7). Chicago: Encylopaedia Britannica, Inc.

Plato. (1956). *Phaedrus* (Helmbold, W. G., Trans.). New York: Palgrave Macmillan.

Pope-Ruark, R. (2011). Know thy audience: Helping students engage in a threshold concept using audience-based pedagogy. *International Journal for the Scholarship of Teaching and Learning, 5*(1), Article 6. doi: 10.20429/ijsotl.2011.050106.

Porter, J. E. (2009). Recovering delivery for digital rhetoric. *Computers and Composition, 26,* 207–224.

Postman, N. (1985). *Amusing ourselves to death: Public discourse in the age of show business.* New York: Viking.

Prigogine, I. (1997). *The end of certainty: Time, chaos and the new laws of nature.* New York: Free Press.

Reber, A. S. (1993). *Implicit learning and tacit knowledge.* New York: Oxford University Press.

Reeves, J., & Stoneman, E. (2014). Heidegger and the aesthetics of rhetoric. *Philosophy and Rhetoric, 47*(2).

Richards, N. M., & King, J. H. (2013). Three paradoxes of big data. *Stanford Law Review Online, 66*(41).

Rosling, H. (2009). *TED and Reddit's 10 questions / Interviewer: Reddit users.* Gapminder. Retrieved from www.gapminder.org/videos/ted-and-reddits-10-questions-to-hans-rosling/.

Senge, P. M. (1994). *The fifth discipline: The art and practice of the learning organization.* New York: Doubleday.

Shapiro, J. (2017). 3 ways data dashboards can mislead you. *Harvard Business Review.* Retrieved from https://hbr.org/2017/01/3-ways-data-dashboards-can-mislead-you.

Sharda, R., Delen, D., & Turban, E. (2018). *Business intelligence, analytics, and data science: A managerial perspective* (4th ed.). New York: Pearson.

Shaw, J. (2014, March–April). Why "big data" is a big deal: Information science promises to change the world. *Harvard Magazine.* Retrieved from https://harvardmagazine.com/2014/03/why-big-data-is-a-big-deal.

Shoztic, K., Bible, W., Nelson, E., & Stein, S. (2016). Developing tomorrow's auditor. *Financial Executive,* 40–44.

Silverstone, R. (1991). Television, rhetoric, and the return of the unconscious in secondary oral culture. In B. E. Gronbeck, T. J. Farrell, & P. A. Soukup (Eds.), *Media, consciousness, and culture: Explorations of Walter Ong's thought* (pp. 147–159). Newbury Park: Sage.

Sun, R. (2001). *Duality of the mind: A bottom-up approach toward cognition.* London: Psychology Press.

Surowiecki, J. (2004). *The wisdom of crowds.* New York: Doubleday.

Tableau. (n.d.). Tableau viz gallery. Retrieved from www.tableau.com/solutions/gallery.

TED Conferences, LLC. (n.d.). Hans Rosling at TED2006: The best stats you've ever seen. Retrieved from www.ted.com/talks/hans_rosling_shows_the_best_stats_you_ve_ever_seen.

Thomas, J. J., & Cook, K. A. (Eds.). (2005). *Illuminating the path: The research and development agenda for visual analytics.* Richland, WA: Pacific Northwest National Laboratory.

Tufte, E. R. (2003). *The cognitive style of PowerPoint*. Cheshire, CT: Graphics Press LLC.

Vogel, D. R., Dickson, G. W., & Lehman, J. A. (1986). *Persuasion and the role of visual presentation support: The UM/3M study*. Management Information Systems Research Center Working Paper Series (MISRC-WP-86–11). Minneapolis, MN.

Walker, J. (2000). *Rhetoric and poetics in antiquity*. Oxford: Oxford University Press.

Wolfram, S. (2002). *A new kind of science*. Champaign, IL: Wolfram Media Inc.

Yates, J. (1985). Graphs as a managerial tool: A case study of Du Pont's use of graphs in the early twentieth century. *International Journal of Business Communication, 22*(1), 5–33.

10

"IT FELT LIKE SOMETHING THE WORLD NEEDED TO SEE"

Organizational Social Media and the Collective Memory

Ashley Patriarca

Introduction

It's a cliché at this point that the internet never forgets—or, at least, that social media never wants us to forget anything. Consider, for example, the daily, ritualized public expressions of memory that appear on Facebook. It's your 5-year "friendiversary," or your parent's birthday. Two years ago, you took a picture of a pet who's no longer with you, or you went on vacation with a loved one. Or, perhaps, you stumble upon the memorialized profile of a high school classmate. Each of these reminders of a past time, or a past life, supplement or extend our individual memories of these and other events. Further, these invoke the *Rhetorica ad Herrenium*'s advice to young rhetors that they develop "backgrounds" and "images" of key items to serve as memory aids. Recent scholars have explored this tendency towards memorializing individual experiences (e.g., Richardson & Hessey, 2009; Carroll & Landry, 2010).

Despite this scholarly focus on how social media impacts individual memory, little work has been done on the effects of social media on *organizational memory*, or the information and knowledge created throughout a business or organization's lifespan (Walsh & Rivera Ungson, 1991). In this chapter, I address the ways in which social media serves as the collective memory for/of businesses and organizations, using United Airlines as a primary case study. Further, I explore methods by which instructors can use the rhetorical canon of memory to prepare students for working as social media communicators within businesses and organizations.

Organizational Memory

Organizational memory has been part of organizational communication research for more than 25 years, following the publication of Walsh and Rivera Ungson's

(1991) foundational exploration of the concept. In their work, Walsh and Rivera Ungson define organizational memory as similar to individual memory in that the organization has elements that collect, process, interpret, and retain information for future use by the organization (much as an individual's mind would with personal memories). This vision of organizational memory relies on anthropomorphizing organizations into near-human (or at least cyborg) figures that think, remember, and learn. In its earliest formulations, organizational memory is developed internally by an organization, although it may be shaped by the organization's interactions with both internal and external stakeholders (Walsh & Rivera Ungson, 1991). Unlike human memory, then, organizational memory is necessarily collective, though singular in voice.

Organizational memory is also reified through internal- and external-facing official documents, such as policies, websites, newsletters, and emails (Anteby & Molnar, 2012). Coverage of the organization through newspapers, television news, and other media also shape and reinforce organizational memory (Walsh & Rivera Ungson, 1991). These classic characteristics mean that an organization's memory of itself is necessarily somewhat slow to change, given that official organizational documents can take some time to develop and publish. Moreover, organizations in general are slow to change (Hannan & Freeman, 1984), even with daily media updates via newspaper or television. Most organizations receive little to no regular media coverage, meaning that those organizations' memories are formed solely via internal (though potentially external-facing) documents. This lack of external feedback has historically given those organizations even greater control over their collective memory. If events or details are omitted from internal documents, it's almost as though they never existed.

More recently, researchers have sought to understand the links between organizational storytelling and memory, arguing that the primary method by which organizational memory is preserved and communicated is through informal and formal storytelling (Ackerman & Halverson, 2000). Bird (2007) notes that a women's networking group within a large corporation used narratives to develop a collective, though partial, memory for the organization for which they worked. Narratives and storytelling continue to play an important role in organizational memory; however, the number of people who are able to tell stories for and about organizations has increased, and the stories they tell are not always approved by the organizations themselves.

Organizational Memory in the Time of Social Media

With the advent of social media, the foundational concepts of organizational memory become more complicated. Like individual memory, organizational memory has become increasingly fragmented and outsourced to our devices. Building on Vannevar Bush's memex concept, as well as the work of technical communication scholars such as Clay Spinuzzi, Bill Hart-Davidson, and Derek

Van Ittersum (2009) calls this outsourcing of memory to devices, software, and other repositories "distributed memory." Van Ittersum argues that this distribution of memory is *necessary* to modern work practices; many of the complicated analytical tasks that professional writers complete on a regular basis simply couldn't be completed without being able to shift from a draft housed in a word processing application to an internet browser to search for the answer to a key question about that draft and back again. I argue that social media further expands this idea of distributed memory, which Van Ittersum limits primarily to professional writers. Not only is social media used by organizations and their employees to create and establish organizational memory, it is used by private individuals—potential stakeholders in those organizations—to contribute to and interrupt the previously monolithic concept of organizational memory.

One way in which social media complicates organizational memory is through the relative permanence of posts. Facebook, Twitter, and their ilk *seem* ephemeral, with posts moving quickly through a timeline, only to be buried under more recent posts or those that the site's algorithms deem more relevant; in the case of Snapchat, a photo-sharing platform, posts literally disappear within seconds unless the viewer saves a screenshot. Despite this apparent transience, the joke about the internet never forgetting has some measure of truth. Recent Twitter posts are searchable from the site itself, while older posts are more easily found using specific keywords, including the organization's account name, with a search engine. More, all tweets from 2010 to 2017 were archived by the Library of Congress, lending a permanence to those texts; however, as of January 1, 2018, the Library of Congress began archiving only selected, notable tweets (Wamsley, 2017). In addition, Facebook's On This Day feature promotes older personal posts, meaning that the memory of any commentary an individual made about an organization is reinforced year after year.

Another way in which social media interrupts organizational memory is by redefining who can contribute to that memory. In earlier decades, the number of people who could establish or maintain organizational memory was limited to individuals within that organization and journalists who covered the organization for their publications. On social media, customers and other stakeholders can write publicly to and about organizations. The collective voices of thousands or even millions of stakeholders can create a public uproar that firmly alters the organization's memory of itself—as well as its immediate public reputation.

This collective public uproar can fuel and be fueled in turn by news media, both traditional and online. Television and print media still publicize organizational crises when they occur; however, they typically do so via summarizing the collective public response to an organization, rather than highlighting a volume of individual responses. In contrast, online news aggregators such as *Buzzfeed* and the *Huffington Post* embed public posts within articles, allowing their readers to view the original posts in their entirety, rather than through the filtered commentary of a journalist or blogger. Both of these approaches bring additional public attention to a crisis, which can encourage more social media users to join online conversations about the organization.

What effects do these social media affordances have for organizational memory? Let us consider several recent experiences of United Airlines. In March 2017, a passenger named Shannon Watts tweeted that a United gate agent prevented two teenage girls wearing leggings from boarding a flight from Denver to Minneapolis and forced a 10-year-old girl wearing leggings to change into a dress (Watts, 2017). Watts, who also had public notoriety as founder of the nonprofit organization Moms Demand Action, directly addressed the company in her tweet, demanding a response. By the time the flight landed in Minneapolis, public outrage had been sparked, with thousands of comments on the original post (Stack, 2017). Because Watts cited the company in her original post, these comments were also directed at United's Twitter account.[1] Given the rapid criticism, United sought to respond quickly; unfortunately, their first response was to cite company policies that required pass travelers[2] to wear business casual and that permitted gate agents the right to turn passengers away if those passengers were inappropriately dressed (United Airlines, n.d., cited in Stack, 2017). In this response, the company appeared to be using organizational memories of previously successful strategies to address crises regarding dress code policies; however, this approach failed because the response was too dogmatic. The company could not explain the rationale for the policies; thus, customers continued to fear they might be removed from their own flights. The collective, networked characteristic of social media ensured that the airline's tepid responses were analyzed, criticized, and mocked.

When a second crisis occurred for United just two weeks later in April 2017, the public collective memory of the company had already been shaped: United relied on policy but couldn't explain the rationales behind that policy. This crisis involved a customer, Dr. David Dao, being removed from his flight; however, his removal involved security officers physically dragging Dao from his seat on the plane, seriously injuring him as a result. Two other passengers filmed Dao's removal and posted their videos to social media, where those videos went viral; one of these passengers, Tyler Bridges, told the *New York Times* that he felt the video was "something the world needed to see" (Victor & Stevens, 2017). In his statement, Bridges acknowledges the power of social media users to publicize and memorialize events that an organization would clearly rather have everyone forget. United's response to this second crisis was also less than effective. Initial company responses attempted to scapegoat Dao for the violence inflicted upon him, with spokespeople saying that flight attendants had asked Dao several times to deboard the plane before security became involved. In addition, then-company CEO Oscar Munoz apologized for "reaccommodating" passengers (Victor & Stevens, 2017). Social media users again roasted the company for its responses and what several users and journalists called "Orwellian language" (Hiltzik, 2017). Social media users also cited the Denver incident as a precursor to this one, arguing that two crises in less than a month signaled serious problems with the organization. Because social media also lends itself to humor, users frequently incorporated humorous memes within their critiques. For example, user Jamison Foser posted the following, which received more than 3,000 retweets and nearly 5,000 likes on Twitter: "UNITED: Leggings are a breach of decorum. ALSO UNITED: We will beat you and drag you from the plane if we want your seat for our employee" (Foser, 2017). This public pushback against the language of traditional crisis communication created tangible results for the company. Two days after the video of the incident went viral, United's stock dropped $1.4 billion (Shen, 2017). On the same day that the stock dropped, Munoz followed his initial statement with a deeper apology and a promise to review the company's overbooking policy (Munoz, 2017). Within three weeks, the company settled with Dao for an undisclosed amount (Maza, 2017).

Following the settlement with Dao, the company seemed to return to its standard operating procedure and hoped social media users would forgive and forget. Indeed, the company seemed to settle into a quiet period for several months. In March 2018, though, two more crises re-ignited the public organizational memory of United Airlines. In the first and more horrifying 2018 incident, a flight attendant required a passenger to place her dog and its carrier into the overhead compartment; unsurprisingly, the dog died as a result of this treatment (Almasy & Jones, 2018). This incident doesn't seem to have been isolated, either; of the 24 animals who died while on flights with US-based airlines, 18 deaths occurred on United flights (Office of Aviation Enforcement and Proceedings, 2018). One day after the dog's death, United again found itself at the center of controversy when it mistakenly sent another dog to Tokyo rather than Kansas (Bishop, 2018).

Social media users again immediately responded to these two crises. One Twitter user, herself an airline management specialist, noted "Another scandal for United Airlines after the tragic loss and mishandling of Pets during air travel. Almost one year after airport officers forcibly dragging a United passenger down an airplane aisle" (Hoogervorst, 2018). Most, however, were even more blunt in their critiques of the airline, questioning how the company is able to remain in business: "How is @united airlines 1) always in some sort of scandal and 2) still in business. Always in the news for harming people and killing beloved pets. Will never fly this awful airline #BoycottUnitedAirlines"[3] (Van Marel, 2018). The massive, rapid social media response again pushed the company to respond. In the week following the first 2018 incident, United announced that it would suspend its pet transportation program (Smith, 2018).

United's case demonstrates the challenge of social media for the company's organizational memory. Although the company can attempt to shape its own narrative, to craft the public memory of itself, and to encourage stakeholders to forget negative memories, any situation that brings the company into the news reminds stakeholders of the company's previous behavior. Within news media, journalists add brief summaries of previous controversies to the ends of their articles or television segments. Social media users refer to those controversies, adding links to news coverage for users who may not remember them.

This newer organizational memory, which is shaped by social media and exemplified here by United Airlines, necessarily includes details that an organization would prefer to omit. Replies, retweets, and screenshots that can reappear even if an organization deletes a post all become part of the information that shape not just the public collective memory of an organization, but also the organization's own internal collective memory. Each of these four crises will remain part of the collective organizational memory of United for years, if not decades, shaping the company's policies and social media responses. In addition, they will shape customer and shareholder responses to each official document the company publishes.

The Rhetorical Canon of Memory

If research into organizational memory cannot adequately address the challenges organizations may face with the advent of social media, what will? Here, a return to classical rhetoric may benefit scholars, practitioners, and teachers of business communication. Memory is a vital concept in classical rhetoric, serving as one of its five canons alongside invention, arrangement, style, and delivery. However, the concept became somewhat derided over the years as a rote activity with no clear impact on a writing-based rhetorical practice. Only recently has memory regained some of the importance it originally bore. In this section, I examine the treatment of memory by Aristotle, Cicero, Longinus, and Quintilian and suggest ways in which it might provide a useful framework for considering social media's effects on organizational memory.

In *On Memory and Reminiscence*, Aristotle begins by establishing the constraints of memory: We cannot have a memory of the future, nor can we understand a memory within the present moment. Memory, thus, only refers to our recollections of past events (Part 1). He asks whether what we remember is the actual event, or physical detail, or whether it is a faint impression that bears little or no relation to that objective truth. In this argument, Aristotle seems almost disappointed that memory must necessarily be fallible. In contrast, Quintilian does not perceive these impressions as flaws; rather, they enrich an individual's understanding of their own past. In this view, the memory of a place is not limited to the physical qualities of a place; it is also composed of the individual's memories of the events occurring there, as well as the emotions associated with those events (Book XI, Chapter 2).

The importance of memory is reflected in the practice needed to support it. The writer of the *Rhetorica ad Herennium*, popularly believed to be Cicero, writes that memory can be a natural facility, but it is one that can also be improved by practice (Pseudo-Cicero, Book 3, Chapters 16–24). Quintilian agrees, arguing that memory is the foundation for all other skills in oratory; that the rhetorician cannot recall and respond to an opponent without recalling that opponent's speech, nor can the rhetorician create an effective argument without relying on an extensive store of memorized knowledge (Book XI, Chapter 2). Both Aristotle (Part 1) and Cicero (I. v. 17–19) urge rhetoricians to use mnemonic practices to improve their memory. The *Rhetorica* writer elaborates on this reference, encouraging rhetoricians to develop a system of images and associations to prompt the memory. This method seems to be the basis for much of the derision surrounding memory; later scholars viewed history and law as information that is safest to entrust to written, permanent, presumably infallible documents.

For these earliest classical rhetoricians, however, the act of committing detail to writing was a crutch for a rhetorician. The memory is sharpest, they argued, when the mind must rely solely on itself. As writing became increasingly accepted for rhetoricians, it shifted from a practice that competed with a speaker's memory to one that complemented the memories of readers. For Longinus, who taught in the third century A.D., writing that remains within the individual's or the public's memory is writing that is sublime (Longinus, Book VII, p. 10). Thus, a reader's memory of a piece of writing in effect proves the quality of that writing. However, a reader's memory of writing can be complicated by what is being written about. Longinus also notes that the memory of failures is far more likely to remain than that of successes (Book XXXIII, p. 45), suggesting that a piece of writing focusing on an individual's failure may be memorable, even if it is not otherwise of high quality. We can see this tension reflected in the current tendency of social media to highlight organizational crises. A social media user can post text that accuses an organization of failure, whether that accusation is supported with evidence or not. Whether that post is well-written or not doesn't matter; what matters is the circulation of the post. Social media posts that focus on the positive aspects of an organization rarely circulate at the levels of negative critique, with their origin frequently assumed to be from the company itself.

Social media, which makes its texts widely available and accessible across place and time, upends some of these classical perspectives on memory. While individuals may not hold within themselves a physical memory of events, they can access the details of those events directly with a simple search on a computer or mobile device or indirectly by seeing it referenced in a social media platform timeline. This distributed memory practice lends itself particularly well to assignments in the business communication classroom, which I address in the next section.

Rhetorical Concepts of Organizational Memory and Social Media in the Business Communication Classroom

The business communication classroom has, to a certain extent, embraced concepts of classical rhetoric. As early as 1985, scholars noted parallels between successful business communication and Aristotelian rhetoric (Kallendorf & Kallendorf, 1985); this work, which was published in the journals of the Association for

Business Communication (one of the largest organizations focused on the teaching of business communication), argues that successful writers in business contexts rely on concepts from classical rhetoric far more than they may realize. Although they do not directly address the effects of these findings for business communication pedagogy, they offered the field a starting point for this discussion. Building on the work of Kallendorf and Kallendorf, researchers have explored the ways in which business speakers develop and present *ethos* (Beason, 1991; Cyphert, 2010), how fundraising letters incorporate *pathos* (Myers, 2007), and deliberative rhetoric as a method for responding to a crisis (Johnson & Sellnow, 1995), among other topics. Further, business communication textbooks include sections on invention, style, delivery, and arrangement, which, if they do not actively reference classical notions of those four canons, are clearly and deeply based in their key concepts.

However, the field has not been as quick to emphasize the canon of memory, which was so important to the classical rhetoricians. Like technical communication and composition, business communication has until recently viewed the canon of memory as rote memorization, with little to offer modern students. This reluctance puts it somewhat at odds with organizational memory research, which has viewed memory as worth exploration, although researchers in this trajectory have also typically viewed memory as rote in the sense of relegating it to the in-house technology used to preserve organizational knowledge.

Despite the historical disdain for memory, recent scholarly reclamations of memory within the field have made the canon ripe for a fuller pedagogical reclamation. This section offers suggestions for incorporating the rhetorical canon of memory into the business communication classroom. These suggestions emerge from my own (and, in several cases, other scholars') pedagogy, as well as professional best practices, and can be adapted for students at both undergraduate and graduate levels.

Memory as Reflection

The most common way to approach the rhetorical canon of memory in the business communication classroom is to develop assignments that ask students to reflect on and assess their choices; this choice has become an increasingly popular one in both composition and technical communication classrooms within the past 20 years (Ryan, 2004; Bourelle, Bourelle, & Jones, 2015). In this use, memory becomes a method of knowledge transfer from course to course (or from course to profession, or from course to public life). In my own business communication classrooms, memory-as-reflection is emphasized following students' collaborative projects. These projects span the final month or so of the semester and incorporate multiple assignments, including a project plan, a business plan, and a pitch presentation. As students complete the final elements of the project, students write a brief, informal reflection that asks them to

- recall specific details about their group's collaborative experiences;
- analyze how they felt about those experiences;
- evaluate how those details and feelings affected the group's process and final deliverables;
- determine if there were other paths they could have taken as a group, and;
- decide what lessons they could take into the next collaborative writing project, whether that project is in another classroom or in the workplace.

This short writing assignment, which is heavily based on the work of Gibbs (1988), also encourages students to develop two skills highly valued by the Association to Advance Collegiate Schools of Business (AACSB): their ability to work in diverse work environments and their ability to reflect (AACSB, 2017, p. 35). Anecdotally, this type of reflection seems to work: Students who come to this class and project with prior collaborative experience in my classes frequently refer to that previous experience as having shaped the current experience. Further, students who go from this course to another course in our university's Business and Technical Writing minor refer specifically to the reflection as shaping their collaborative experiences. This assignment, however, does not explicitly incorporate organizational *social media* research, although it certainly addresses an individual's memory of the temporary organization formed by a collaborative group.

Analysis of Organizational Memory on Social Media

If we shift our emphasis on memory from the students' individual memories to the collective memory of the organizations for which they may someday write, this canon becomes even more pertinent to business communication pedagogy. In an undergraduate business communication classroom, a project focused on organizational memory and social media might begin by analyzing what organizations choose to publish (or memorialize) on their social media platforms, as well as stakeholder responses to those posts. Taken together, these posts and responses—including any organizational reactions to the stakeholder responses—take a snapshot of the organization's collective memory of that moment.

One trajectory for this project could ask students to trace and analyze a recent, although not current, crisis for an organization. This potential trajectory reflects Aristotle's insistence that we cannot understand memory within a present moment, only in our recollections of the past. Moreover, it acknowledges Longinus' assertion that negative events are far more likely to be memorable for individuals; on an organizational level, it would make sense that a crisis could generate a longer-lasting effect on the collective memory of that organization.

One possibility for this assignment would have students researching the November 2017 social media discussions of Papa John's pizza. On November 1, 2017, company founder and then-CEO John Schnatter criticized NFL players who had taken a knee during the US national anthem in protest of institutional violence against black men (Taylor, 2017a). In response to Schnatter's critique, which had been issued as a public statement to company shareholders, neo-Nazi website *Daily Stormer* published a post calling Papa John's pizza the "official pizza of the alt-right" a day later (as cited in Maza, 2017). Though the pizza company publicly disavowed the *Daily Stormer* endorsement on November 14, 2017 (Porter, 2017), many members of the public viewed the company's comments as coming too little, too late. For the nearly two weeks separating Schnatter's initial comments from the final statement, individuals on Twitter, Facebook, and other social media platforms blasted the company, including responses to the company's regular social media posts, with comments describing the company and its products as racist or neo-Nazi.[4] In response to the public outcry, Schnatter announced he would step down as CEO of the company he founded in mid-December 2017 (Taylor, 2017b). Schnatter's departure was not the only effect of the *Daily Stormer* debacle. The company's October-to-December sales were down 3.9 percent compared to the previous year, and in February 2018, the Papa John's company and the NFL ended their national corporate sponsor relationship (Rovell, 2018).

The Papa John's crisis illustrates the ways in which social media has altered collective memory for organizations. It's hard to imagine that a large, publicly traded company would welcome an association with neo-Nazis via public posts that are easily shared (and shared again and again). Yet the company was decidedly slow to respond to this association in an era that requires rapid response. Instead, they continued to publish celebratory posts about their products for nearly two weeks, a tone-deaf and untimely response according to the responses from many social media users. This response left a communications vacuum, one in which social media users contributed their own increasingly negative public takes on an incident that the company would rather they forget. As a result, the company experienced immediate and continuing negative effects. More, this incident will likely re-emerge as part of the collective memory of the company when it returns to the news cycle, perhaps even as soon as its replacement as sponsor is announced for the next NFL season.

To complete an assignment focused on the Papa John's crisis, students could locate the *Daily Stormer*'s original post, social media users' posts and responses to Papa John's posts, the company's tweets and responses to the incident, and media coverage of the crisis. To keep the assignment manageable for both students and instructors, instructors may wish to set either a recommended timeframe or a limit on the number of posts a student must analyze. As students write their analysis, they should be able to assess the effectiveness of the company's response on social media, including assessing the *kairos* or timeliness of the response, the audience awareness, and the appropriateness of the writing style. More, they should be able to trace the reception of the organization's response within secondary media such as newspapers and websites. Each of these elements contribute to the collective memory of an organization, making them key data points for analysis.

Because students would analyze a recent, but not current, event, they can also identify the ways in which the response would affect public memories of the organization. This effect could be measured in several ways: (1) researching whether social media users continue to refer to the incident in their references to the company, (2) researching whether traditional news accounts refer to the incident, and/or (3) researching whether relatively permanent, public, online third-party sites such as Wikipedia refer to the incident in their coverage of the company. However, as noted in the Papa John's example, these references may not appear until the company returns to the news or social media spotlight.

This Analysis of Organizational Memory assignment provides several benefits for a business communication classroom. First, it encourages students to understand and reflect on current professional practice regarding business communication on social media. This process provides important pedagogical scaffolding for assignments that require students to create or maintain organizational social media accounts. Second, it reminds students that the act of writing for an organization is not an isolated activity; the structure of social media encourages feedback from not just the text's intended audience, but also connections of those intended audience members and individuals completely unconnected to the original audience. Thus, the crafting of this business communication must account for the certainty that unintended audiences will view and respond to the text. Finally, it also addresses AACSB standards that require students to develop ethical knowledge and reasoning, analytical thinking ability, and written communication skills (AACSB, 2017, pp. 34–35).

Developing Organizational Memory on Social Media

As students become adept at analyzing the ways in which organizational memory is constructed on social media, they can move into developing more active production of organizational memory. This production activity can occur via multiple assignments, though here I will focus on two: writing a social media strategy and running a social media account for a client organization.

Assignment Option 1: Social Media Strategy

The first of these production-based assignments, the social media strategy, is a document that guides an organization's social media coordinators as they create content and respond to stakeholders. In professional organizations, it is generally developed by social media coordinators in collaboration with public relations specialists, content creators, and social media analysts, as well as other organizational leaders. Given that focus on collaboration, the social media strategy assignment provides an excellent opportunity for collaboration among students. Ideally, this collaborative student team will include students from different majors to reflect the variety of skillsets represented in the workplace equivalent. This assignment is also an opportunity for service-learning or client-based work, if instructors have established relationships with departments across campus, nonprofits, or small businesses in the community.

Once the members of each social media strategy team have met each other and selected or met the group's client, the research begins. Students collectively research the client's intended audience(s), purpose for social media, and organizational culture, among other details;[5] once complete, this research guides the development of the social media strategy. This initial process matches current best practices for social media strategies, as discussed in both trade publications and organizational public relations sites (e.g., Foster, 2015; University of Minnesota, 2016). It also reflects the need to understand an organization's rhetorical situation before creating communication on its behalf.

As students begin drafting the social media strategy, they must consider several key areas: (1) platform choice, (2) content creation, and (3) guidelines for responses to stakeholders. Decisions they make in each area should, again, emerge from the research they conducted in the first stage of this project and have long-lasting effects on the collective memory of the organization.

Platform Choice

The selection of social media platform(s) is crucial for any organization. For example, some organizations do very well on Instagram, which emphasizes the visual aspects of social media, while others may struggle with the platform. Jinxed, a vintage furniture store in Philadelphia, posts photos of its latest finds with purchase information several times a day on Instagram. Although not every item is sold, nor sold quickly, many items have been updated with a "SOLD" tag in as little as an hour after the original post.[6] Importantly, these customers are not always within the city of Philadelphia; Instagram allows the company to reach individuals an hour or more outside of the city easily, with some followers finding the store from as far away as Wisconsin. Similarly, Instagram could benefit a nonprofit organization that seeks to communicate a community's needs to its current and potential donors; for example, photographs can clearly communicate the *pathos* of a dog or cat that needs to be adopted. However, the same choice of platform does not necessarily benefit an organization that provides less visually oriented products and services. For example, the Electronic Frontier Foundation, a nonprofit focused on digital privacy and free speech, might find Instagram a challenging platform to use effectively.[7] Given its specialization, though, the organization excels on Twitter, which can encourage verbally oriented postings.

Content Creation

Once students have determined where the organization should be active on social media, they will develop guidelines for content creation. These guidelines should cover the types of content that the organization posts, how frequently the organization posts, and when the organization posts. For a retail business, as in the earlier Jinxed example, the organization might post advertisements for its products, updated information on hours (such as when the physical store needs to close early due to inclement weather), and/or requests for customer feedback. Although the general categories might look the same for businesses in the same industry, the specifics for each type of content would vary, depending on the organization's products and services, market segments, and culture. A nonprofit organization focused on animal adoption might choose to post information on available animals, requests for volunteers, and information on fundraising opportunities, among other content types. Like the retail business, the animal adoption nonprofit might share similar content types with other, similar nonprofits, but the actual content can vary due to organizational culture and goals.

Representing the frequency and timing of posts requires a keen understanding of *kairos*. On the surface, this step simply requires students to schedule a certain number of posts per week. However, scheduled posts can pose a problem when their tone conflicts with current events or regular memorials. Since 2001, September 11 has been a somber day of remembrance within the United States, but that has not stopped U.S.-based companies from offering discounts on products or, in one notable example, a request for 2,296 retweets on a post to represent each person who died in the terrorist attacks that day (Andrews, 2016). Similarly, breaking news can turn what was originally a perfectly acceptable feedback request into the potential basis for a social media crisis. Students should be prepared to indicate that at least one individual on the team will monitor important news to prevent such a crisis.

Organizations can also attempt to respond in a timely manner to current events, trending hashtags, or shared cultural touchstones, although students should be aware that such a response can backfire. In September 2014, frozen pizza company DiGiorno participated in the trending #WhyIStayed hashtag on Twitter with the following tweet: "#WhyIStayed You had pizza" (DiGiorno, 2014, cited in Griner, 2014). The social media coordinator was clearly unaware that the hashtag was intended to raise awareness of the contexts surrounding domestic violence, and the response to the company's inappropriately lighthearted tweet was swift and critical.

Guidelines for Responses to Stakeholders

Given the DiGiorno example, it's clear that students must prepare guidelines for their organization's response to criticism. To DiGiorno's credit, its social media coordinator responded to critics of the #WhyIStayed tweet with seemingly genuine, individualized apologies (Griner, 2014). Most criticism, however, does not have such immediately high stakes for an organization. Rather, most responses will be to more typical concerns about customer service, product quality, or other factors for customer experience. Moreover, these concerns are more likely to contribute to the collective memory of an organization, because they are more likely to happen for most organizations. As a result, students should develop a process for responding to both kinds of feedback within their social media strategy. Consistency in the process is key: knowing who should respond, and in which ways, ensures that the organization's voice is clearly represented and prevents dissatisfaction among stakeholders (Gallaugher & Ransbotham, 2010).

Assignment Option 2: Manage a Social Media Account

The second production-based assignment asks students to manage a social media account for their client organization. In this assignment, students are responsible for creating and posting the content on a schedule set in their client organization's social media strategy, as well as responding to low-stakes comments and concerns from stakeholders. In doing so, students should follow the social media strategy developed in the previous assignment or, if the client organization already has a social media strategy, students should use that previously developed strategy. The constraints of this assignment, instructor evaluation of the project, and students' expectations for the experience all depend on that strategy.

As part of this project, students should be encouraged to schedule their posts one day to one week ahead of time. To do this, students can use applications such as Tweetdeck or Hootsuite. These applications, or apps, allow users to schedule posts, as well as to create columns for monitoring different accounts and hashtags. These columns can be used to monitor mentions of the organization, as well, allowing students to identify and potentially prevent crises before they occur (Smith, 2015).

One note of caution: Because this is a fast-moving, public-facing project with potential effects on a client organization's organizational memory, instructors must be prepared to monitor the students' ongoing progress more closely than in assignments that permit formalized peer, instructor, and client review before publication. One strategy for review is to use Tweetdeck, Hootsuite, or another app to monitor each client's account and mentions. This strategy is more labor-intensive, though, making it less practical for instructors teaching a heavy course load. In this situation, instructors could choose to prepare these monitoring channels but review them periodically, perhaps once a week. Students could also be asked to bring challenging posts and feedback to the instructor in either option. Another monitoring strategy is to review students' scheduled posts before they are published; although this option requires the instructor to have the password for the organization's account, it allows instructors to catch potentially delicate posts before they become part of the public, collective memory for that organization.

As in the social media strategy project, this account management assignment is an excellent opportunity for collaboration. Students can each be responsible for managing a particular type of content and response or for managing the account on a particular day of the week; instructors can also encourage teams to develop their own, appropriate division of labor. In terms of timing, a graduate-level version of the assignment might be structured as a semester-long assignment. That timeframe would likely not be appropriate for undergraduates, who may need more preparatory work before they begin; thus, this project might best serve as a final or capstone project for undergraduates in business communication classes.

Like the analysis assignment, these two production-based assignments offer multiple pedagogical benefits for students. They offer students the opportunity to practice social media communication for a client organization, giving students public-facing projects to add to their portfolios. In doing so, these projects also allow students to participate in creating and maintaining the collective memory for an organization. Finally, these assignments encourage students to develop their analytical thinking ability, teamwork strategies, and written communication skills, in adherence with AACSB standards.

For more information on each assignment, please visit www.ashleypatriarca. com, where instructors will find sample assignment sheets, rubrics, and additional resources for incorporating these assignments into their own classrooms.

Notes

1 Although Twitter adapted its reply format in March 2017 to allow users to edit who received their responses, this change occurred four days after the first United incident (Reddy, 2017). Thus, every response to Watts would also have been a response to United.
2 Pass travelers, colloquially known as buddy pass travelers, are individuals who travel with airline employees or retirees (United Airlines, 2018). Their passes are purchased at reduced rates and are typically not available on full or overbooked flights.
3 The hashtag in this second tweet, #BoycottUnitedAirlines, was previously used during the 2017 crises and trended once again in 2018.
4 For an example of these responses, see the company's November 13, 2017 post and responses: https://twitter.com/PapaJohns/status/930226553681842176. The pace and volume of responses to this post seem to have influenced the company's statement about Schnatter's comments, as well as his eventual decision to leave the company.
5 Students could easily respond to a brief version of the Analysis of Organizational Memory assignment for this stage of the project.
6 This is particularly frustrating for followers now that Instagram has shifted from a linear timeline to one focused on engagement. Followers are now more likely to see popular items that have already sold than newer items that may still be available.
7 The EFF appears to have reserved an account on Instagram (@efforg), although the account has not published any posts nor followed any individuals. It's possible that this account was created by a cybersquatter, an individual who creates accounts using or mimicking brand and celebrity identities in an attempt to sell the rights to the account handle to the rightful owner (ICANN, 2018). If the account was indeed created by EFF, it was likely done in attempt to prevent such cybersquatting.

Bibliography

AACSB International. (2017). *Eligibility procedures and accreditation standards for business accreditation*. Tampa, FL: The Association to Advance Collegiate Schools of Business.
Ackerman, M. S., & Hadverson, C. A. (2000). Reexamining organizational memory. *Communications of the ACM, 43*(1), 58–64. https://doi.org/10.1145/323830.323845

Almasy, S., & Jones, S. (2018). United Airlines calls dog's death in overhead bin a "tragic accident" [WWW document]. *CNN*. Retrieved March 21, 2018 from www.cnn.com/2018/03/13/us/united-airlines-dog-dies-trnd/index.html.

Andrews, T. M. (n.d.). The practice of using 9/11 to market consumer goods backfires yet again [WWW Document]. *chicagotribune.com*. Retrieved March 21, 2018 from www.chicagotribune.com/business/ct-9-11-marketing-20160908-story.html.

Anteby, M., & Molnár, V. (2012). Collective memory meets organizational identity: Remembering to forget in a firm's rhetorical history. *Academy of Management Journal, 55*, 515–540. doi: https://doi.org/10.5465/amj.2010.0245.

Aristotle. (2009). On memory and reminiscence [WWW Document]. *The Internet Classics Archive*. Retrieved March 21, 2018 from http://classics.mit.edu/Aristotle/memory.html.

Beason, L. (1991). Strategies for establishing an effective persona: An analysis of appeals to ethos in business speeches. *The Journal of Business Communication (1973), 28*, 326–346. doi: https://doi.org/10.1177/002194369102800403.

Bird, S. (2007). Sensemaking and identity: The interconnection of storytelling and networking in a women's group of a large corporation. *International Journal of Business Communication, 44*(4), 311–339. Retrieved February 26, 2018 from http://journals.sagepub.com/doi/abs/10.1177/0021943607306135.

Bishop, J. (n.d.). United airlines accidentally sends dog on 10,000-mile trip To Japan [WWW document]. *Forbes*. Retrieved March 21, 2018 from www.forbes.com/sites/bishopjordan/2018/03/19/united-airlines-accident-sends-lost-dog-japan-kansas/.

Bourelle, A., Bourelle, T., & Jones, N. (2015). Multimodality in the technical communication classroom: Viewing classical rhetoric through a 21st century lens. *Technical Communication Quarterly, 24*, 306–327.

Carroll, B., & Landry, K. (2010). Logging on and letting out: Using online social networks to grieve and to mourn. *Bulletin of Science, Technology & Society, 30*, 341–349.

Cyphert, D. (2010). The rhetorical analysis of business speech: Unresolved questions. *The Journal of Business Communication (1973), 47*, 346–368. doi: https://doi.org/10.1177/0021943610370577.

Foser, J. (jamisonfoser). (2017, April 10). UNITED: Leggings are a breach of decorum. ALSO UNITED: We will beat you and drag you from the plane if we want your seat for our employee. Retrieved from https://twitter.com/jamisonfoser/status/851455032998350850

Foster, J. (2015). How to build a social-media strategy that works [WWW document]. *Entrepreneur*. Retrieved March 21, 2018 from www.entrepreneur.com/article/246085.

Gallaugher, J., & Ransbotham, S. (2010). Social media and customer dialog management at Starbucks. *MIS Quarterly Executive, 9*, 197–212.

Gibbs, G. (1988). *Learning by doing: A guide to teaching and learning methods*. Oxford: Oxford Polytechnic.

Griner, D. (September 9, 2014). DiGiorno is really, really sorry about its tweet accidentally making light of domestic violence [WWW document]. Retrieved March 21, 2018 from www.adweek.com/creativity/digiorno-really-really-sorry-about-its-tweet-accidentally-making-light-domestic-violence-159998/.

Hannan, M. T., & Freeman, J. (1984). Structural inertia and organizational change. *American Sociological Review, 49*(2), 149–164. https://doi.org/10.2307/2095567.

Hiltzik, M. (2017). United finds a new way to make itself look awful, and then its CEO shows how to make things worse [WWW document]. *latimes.com*. Retrieved

March 21, 2018 from www.latimes.com/business/hiltzik/la-fi-hiltzik-united-video-20170410-story.html.

Hoogervorst, P. [PHoogervorst]. (2018, March 20). *Another scandal for United Airlines after the tragic loss and mishandling of Pets during air travel. Almost one year after airport officers forcibly dragging a United passenger down an airplane aisle.* Retrieved from https://twitter.com/PHoogervorst/status/976177706311196673.

Internet Corporation for Assigned Names and Numbers. (n.d.). About cybersquatting [WWW document]. *ICANN.* Retrieved March 21, 2018 from www.icann.org/resources/pages/cybersquatting-2013-05-03-en.

Ittersum, D. V. (2009). Distributing memory: Rhetorical work in digital environments. *Technical Communication Quarterly, 18,* 259–280. doi: https://doi.org/10.1080/10572250902942026.

Johnson, D., & Sellnow, T. (1995). Deliberative rhetoric as a step in organizational crisis management: Exxon as a case study. *Communication Reports, 8,* 54–60. doi: https://doi.org/10.1080/08934219509367607.

Kallendorf, Craig, & Kallendorf, Carol. (1985). The figures of speech, ethos, and Aristotle: Notes toward a rhetoric of business communication. *Journal of Business Communication, 22,* 35–50.

Longinus. (n.d.). *On great writing* (On the Sublime). Indianapolis: Hackett.

Maza, C. (2017). Why neo-Nazis love Papa John's pizza—and other "official" alt-right companies [WWW document]. *Newsweek.* Retrieved January 5, 2018 from www.newsweek.com/white-supremacists-nazis-alt-right-pizza-papa-johns-taylor-swift-wendys-brands-708722.

Munoz, O. (2017). Statement from United Airlines CEO, Oscar Munoz, on United Express flight 3411 [WWW document]. *United Hub.* Retrieved March 21, 2018 from https://hub.united.com/united-express-3411-statement-oscar-munoz-2355968629.html.

Myers, M. (2007). The use of pathos in charity letters: Some notes toward a theory and analysis. *Journal of Technical Writing and Communication, 37,* 3–16. doi: https://doi.org/10.2190/2M77-0724-4110-1413.

Office of Aviation Enforcement and Proceedings. (2018). *Air travel consumer report.* Washington, DC: U.S. Department of Transportation.

Porter, T. (2017). Papa John's gave the middle finger to the alt-right after being proclaimed neo-Nazis' favorite pizza [WWW Document]. *Newsweek.* Retrieved January 5, 2018 from www.newsweek.com/papa-johns-just-gave-middle-finger-alt-right-after-being-proclaimed-neo-nazis-711907.

Pseudo-Cicero. (1954). *Rhetorica ad Herennium.* Cambridge, MA: Harvard University Press.

Reddy, S. (2017). Now on Twitter: 140 characters for your replies [WWW document]. Retrieved March 21, 2018 from https://blog.twitter.com/official/en_us/topics/product/2017/now-on-twitter-140-characters-for-your-replies.html.

Richardson, K., & Hessey, S. (2009). Archiving the self? Facebook as biography of social and relational memory. *Journal of Inf, Com & Eth in Society, 7,* 25–38. doi: https://doi.org/10.1108/14779960910938070.

Rovell, D. (2018, February 27). Papa John's, NFL make 'mutual decision' to end sponsorship deal [WWW Document]. *ESPN.com.* Retrieved March 20, 2018 from www.espn.com/nfl/story/_/id/22597858.

Ryan, K. J. (2004). Memory, literacy, and invention: Reimagining the canon of memory for the writing classroom. *Composition Studies, 32,* 35–47.

Smith, A. (2015). Social media monitoring. In *Share This: The Social Media Handbook for PR Professionals.* Wiley Online Books, 157–162. Retrieved from https://doi.org/10.1002/9781119207856.ch18.

Smith, A. (2018). United suspends pet cargo flights [WWW Document]. *CNNMoney*. Retrieved March 21, 2018 from http://money.cnn.com/2018/03/20/news/compa nies/united-airlines-pets/index.html.

Stack, L. (2017). After barring girls for leggings, United Airlines defends decision. *The New York Times*. Retrieved March 21, 2018 from www.nytimes.com/2017/03/26/us/ united-airlines-leggings.html.

Taylor, K. (2017a, November 1). Papa John slams NFL for "poor leadership" after player protests lead to sales slump. *Business Insider*. Retrieved January 5, 2018 from www.busi nessinsider.com/papa-john-slams-nfl-following-national-anthem-protests-2017-11.

Taylor, K. (2017b, December 21). Papa John's controversial CEO steps down after facing backlash for his criticism of NFL anthem protests [WWW document]. *Business Insider*. Retrieved January 5, 2018 from www.businessinsider.com/papa-johns-founder-steps-down-as-ceo-2017-12.

United Airlines. (n.d.). Pass travel guidelines [WWW Document]. *Pass travel*. Retrieved March 21, 2018 from https://employeerespss.coair.com/employeeres/PassRiderTerms. aspx.

Shen, L. (2017, April 11). United Airlines Stock Drops $1.4 Billion After Passenger-Removal Controversy [WWW document]. (n.d.). *Fortune*. Retrieved March 21, 2018 from http://fortune.com/2017/04/11/united-airlines-stock-drop/.

University of Minnesota. (2016). Social media strategy and best practices [WWW docu-ment]. *University Relations*. Retrieved March 21, 2018 from https://university-relations. umn.edu/resources/social-media-strategy-and-best-practices.

Van Marel, S. [saravanmarel]. (2018, March 13). How is @united airlines 1) always in some sort of scandal and 2) still in business. Always in the news for harming people and killing beloved pets. Will never fly this awful airline #BoycottUnitedAirlines. Retrieved from https://twitter.com/saravanmarel/status/973754505257979906.

Victor, D., & Stevens, M. (2017, April 10). United Airlines passenger is dragged from an over-booked flight. *The New York Times*. Retrieved from www.nytimes.com/2017/04/10/ business/united-flight-passenger-dragged.html

Walsh, J. P., & Ungson, G. R. (1991). Organizational memory. *The Academy of Management Review, 16*, 57–91. Retrieved from https://doi.org/10.2307/258607.

Wamsley, L. (2017). Library of Congress will no longer archive every tweet [WWW Document]. NPR.org. Retrieved March 21, 2018 from www.npr.org/sections/ thetwo-way/2017/12/26/573609499/library-of-congress-will-no-longer-archive-every-tweet.

Watts, S. [shannonrwatts]. (2017, March 26). 1) A @united gate agent isn't letting girls in leggings get on flight from Denver to Minneapolis because spandex is not allowed? Retrieved from https://twitter.com/shannonrwatts/status/845992819894321153?lan g=en.

INDEX

Note: Page numbers in *italics* indicate figures and page numbers in **bold** indicate tables.

removal incident 189–190; public
collective memory and 189–191; social
media and 189–191
Uptaught (Macrorie) 78

Vanhoosier-Carey, G. 104–106
Veblen, T. 55
virality 110
visual analytics 163–164, 168–170,
177–180
visual communication 161, 164
visual deliverables 92
visual rhetoric: aesthetics and 177–178;
Big Data and 169–172, 177; business
attire as 149, 154; persuasion and
148, 164; as process 171–172; social
circulation and 170

WAGR *see* writing, activity, and genre
research (WAGR)
Wall, M. A. 131
Walsh, J. P. 186–187
Wardle, E. 90
Watts, S. 189
Weber, R. 108
Welch, K. E. 123–124
Wenger, E. 91
Westlake, J. W. 69
what-would-you-do prompts 82
white papers: best practices of 135;
categories of 129; complex objectives
of 128; delivery and 122–123, 132–134,
136; development of 129; *ethos* and
122, 130; features of 129–130; genre

ecologies of 131–132, 134–135; as
marketing tools 130–132; rhetorical
moves in 129–130; "soft sell" in
130–131; use-value of 130
Whittaker, S. 126
Wickliff, G. 90
Wiens, K. 58
Willerton, R. 122, 129–135
Winsor, D. 17
Wlecke, A. 76–77
women: business schools and 14–15;
secretarial work 15–18
writing: audience addressed 71; audience
invoked 71; ecologies of 105; grammar
and style in 48; grammar knowledge in
49; imitation and 87; *inventio* (invention)
and 87–88; memory and 192; pedagogy
of 70–71; personal statement 81;
persuasive 110; practice in 86–87,
93–94, 104–105; pseudotransactional
93; reader-centered 67–68; rhetorical
theory in 104; rhetorical topics (*topoi*)
and 86; self-exploration in 67–69,
74–82; skills transfer 90; what-would-
you-do prompts 82; writer-centered 70
writing, activity, and genre research
(WAGR) 126, 129

Yates, J. 9, 12–13, 19–20

Zacharakis, A. 113
Zachry, M. 19–20, 127, 135, 188
Ziglar, Zig 133
Zuidema, L. 50